Historically Black College Leadership and Social Transformation

How Past Practices Inform the Present and Future

Historically Black College Leadership and Social Transformation

How Past Practices Inform the Present and Future

edited by

Vickie L. Suggs

The University of North Carolina at Chapel Hill

INFORMATION AGE PUBLISHING, INC.
Charlotte, NC • www.infoagepub.com

Library of Congress Cataloging-in-Publication Data

Historically Black college leadership and social transformation : how past practices inform the present and future / edited by Vickie L. Suggs.
   pages cm
 ISBN 978-1-62396-457-3 (pbk.) – ISBN 978-1-62396-458-0 (hardcover) – ISBN 978-1-62396-459-7 (ebook) 1. African American universities and colleges. 2. African American universities and colleges–Administration. 3. Educational leadership–United States. I. Suggs, Vickie L.
 LC2781.H56 2013
 378.7308996073–dc23
                                                                    2013032668

Copyright © 2014 Information Age Publishing Inc.

All rights reserved. No part of this publication may be reproduced, stored in a retrieval system, or transmitted, in any form or by any means, electronic, mechanical, photocopying, microfilming, recording or otherwise, without written permission from the publisher.

Printed in the United States of America

To my daughter, Max Grace

CONTENTS

Foreword ix
Samuel DuBois Cook

Preface xiii
Vickie L. Suggs

Acknowledgments xxix

SECTION I
BLACK COLLEGE PRESIDENTS DURING THE 1930s–1960s

1. Influences of Social Gospel: The Institutional Leadership of Benjamin Elijah Mays and Robert Maynard Hutchins 3
   Vickie L. Suggs

2. Mary McLeod Bethune: The Significance of Rhetorical Action in the Development of a Black College Leader 23
   Vickie L. Suggs

3. James Edward Shepard and North Carolina Central University: In Service to the State 43
   Vickie L. Suggs

SECTION II

CASE STUDY OF A CONTEMPORARY BLACK COLLEGE PRESIDENT

4 Black College Presidents, Institutional Leadership, and the Use of Social Media: A Case Study of Philander Smith College 61
   Vickie L. Suggs and Jennifer E. Tomon Stephens

SECTION III

BLACK COLLEGE SUSTAINABILITY

5 HBCU Pipeline to College Access: Considerations for the Twenty-First Century 91
   Torry L. Reynolds, Vickie L. Suggs, and Shayla Mitchell

6 Civic Engagement and Critical Consciousness: Culture and Traditions of Liberal Arts Education 121
   Malika Butler and Vickie L. Suggs

Conclusion 151
Vickie L. Suggs

Appendix: List of Historically Black Colleges and Universities (HBCUs) 157

About the Contributors 163

FOREWORD

Historically Black Colleges and Universities (HBCUs) are dear to my heart. I have spent over fifty years of my life devoted to helping in the development, strengthening and preservation of Black colleges and universities. I am delighted that Dr. Vickie Suggs has addressed this important study on Black college leadership and social transformation. This book will contribute to the future of Black college leadership, provide a framework of knowledge, understanding and guidance, and identify certain directions and values that illuminate the experience of Black college leadership.

From a historical perspective, there were diversified practices of Black college presidents. Some reflected a diversity of interest and perspective. Many walked the tightrope of conformity, while others followed their own individual path. The two great traditions of Booker T. Washington and W. E. B. DuBois, though different, were equally important and influential. W. E. B. DuBois, though not a college president, but certainly an intellectual leader at Atlanta University, insisted on freedom of the mind. Freedom of the mind meaning a mind without shackles and the freedom to explore all types of possibilities in the search for truth. In contrast, Booker T. Washington at Tuskegee Institute emphasized industrial education and generally following the *status quo*.

When I was a student at Morehouse College, Dr. Benjamin E. Mays stressed pursuing high ideals and noble goals of striving. He believed in rigorous, scholarly behavior and integrity. His teachings were demanding, uncompromising and fulfilling. It is no wonder that Martin Luther King, Jr. was inspired, mentored and influenced by Dr. Mays. These values that Dr. Mays championed will live through the ages.

Black college leadership is changing and the tenure of Presidents has grown shorter over the past few years and decades. College presidents no longer stay in the same position for a seemingly inordinate period of time. College Presidents are selected in various ways. Generally speaking, the Chairman of the College Board of Trustees and a small group of others no longer determine the selection of the college's President. It is not universal, but some colleges now use firms to recommend the President while others still use the Board of Trustees and selected faculty, students and alumni to choose the leaders of the institution. Fiscal affairs are no longer the primary responsibility of the President of the college or university. The President does need a keen business perspective in terms of the preservation and wise use of financial capital. The President may help to identify resources, but the fundraising is now the chief responsibility of the Office of Development. Some colleges and universities employ outside agencies and organizations to help raise funds.

In the future, colleges and universities that are serving a common purpose should increasingly share educational resources such as library facilities, faculty, seminars and student program exchanges that may strengthen the whole educational process. The consortium of the Atlanta University Center that consists of Clark Atlanta University, The Interdenominational Theological Center (ITC), Morehouse College, Morris Brown College, and Spelman College is one such example of collaboration and shared resources. Cooperation can strengthen all the institutions involved. As painful as it may seem to some college leaders, they may have to face the possibility of relinquishing their cherished autonomy and be forced to merge with other institutions in order to remain sustainable.

Black college leaders still face challenges in the twenty-first century but their primary goals should always be to offer quality education, financial aid and scholarship opportunities to students and enlist competitive faculty members. Black colleges and universities may attract outstanding students by offering access to cultural exchange programs, cutting edge science and technology programs and online learning environments. Successful Blacks should support HBCUs financially in order to ensure that they not only survive but thrive. In the end, it is important to remember the past struggles of HBCU leaders, the sacrifices they made as well as the thought and wisdom they have contributed to American life and culture.

Strong and wise leadership can inspire and mold young minds to become future leaders and transform society. Dr. Benjamin E. Mays produced many Civil Rights leaders not only on local, state and national levels, but internationally, as well. "M.L.," our nickname for Martin Luther King, Jr. during our student days at Morehouse College, is by far the most famous, influential, gifted, prophetic and luminous graduate of any HBCU. HBCUs have, over the grinding years, been successful in providing outstanding leadership in this multiracial, multiethnic, technological and highly globalized society.

—**Samuel DuBois Cook**
President Emeritus, Dillard University

PREFACE

Vickie L. Suggs

This is not yet another book about leadership as an organizational imperative, but rather a book that examines the practice of social transformation leadership from the perspective of historically Black colleges and universities (HBCUs), providing a framework to the origins and enduring presence of this institution type as part of American higher education. For HBCUs, social transformation is arguably the originating underpinning for their founding, mission, and purpose.

The quest for societal change has been instrumental in the founding and subsequent survival of the HBCU. To this end, the author maintains that social transformation leadership has been and will continue to be the practice through which Black college leaders can sustain their institution type in the midst of emerging populations, changing academic program reviews and renewals, and mandates around undergraduate recruitment and retention. Arguably, HBCUs have a mission that best correlates with changing demography, as they are not selective, elite, nor segregate based on a class system that rewards students who hail from privileged backgrounds and can afford academic access and advantages unavailable to those on the margins of society.

The framework of social transformation leadership provides a deeper understanding of the Black college historical approach to transforming communities, institutions, and nations. Their enduring role as effective agents of change can inform contemporary demands for this approach to leadership. As a means to maximize resources in a period of fiscal decline and job elimination, college and university leaders must look for innovative, yet effective ways to operate and carry out the business of higher learning (American Association for Higher Education, American College Personnel, National Association of Student Personnel Administrators, 1998).

Additionally, as HBCUs communicate and substantiate brand messaging through their mission and vision, this book is purposed to examine past practices of social transformation leadership that inform the present and will continue to inform future institutional leadership. To this end, HBCUs are urged to recognize past practices while continuing to employ and perfect its contemporary agenda within a framework of social transformation leadership.

EDUCATIONAL SIGNIFICANCE

Collectively, HBCUs are 105 federally designated post-secondary institutions founded before the Civil Rights Act of 1964 and whose primary mission was, and still is, the education of Black Americans (See Appendix A) (United Negro College Fund, 2013; White House Initiative on Historically Black Colleges and Universities, 2013; Brown, 1999; Brown & Davis, 2001; Brown Donahoo, & Bertrand, 2001; Redd, 1998). Though open to all who wish to attend, HBCUs build capacity primarily among African American matriculates. According to the National Association of Historically Black Colleges and Universities Title III Administrators, "While the 105 HBCUs represent just 3% of the nation's institutions of higher learning, they graduate nearly 20% of African Americans who earn undergraduate degrees." (About HBCUs, 2013, para. 2).

The United Negro College Fund (UNCF) punctuates this claim via its reporting on student outcomes around graduation rates, graduate school completion, and competitiveness in the job market:

1. HBCUs graduate over 50% African American professionals;
2. HBCUs graduate over 50% of African American public school teachers and 70% of African American dentists;
3. 50% of African Americans who graduate from HBCUs go on to graduate or professional schools;
4. HBCUs award more than one in three of the degrees held by African Americans in natural sciences;
5. HBCUs award one-third of the degrees held by African Americans in mathematics;

6. According to a 2004 McKinsey study, the average graduation rate at many HBCUs is higher than the average graduation rate for African Americans at majority institutions. (About HBCUs, 2013, para. 4)

The National Association of Historically Black Colleges and Universities Title III Administrators goes on to explain, "Because of their unique sensibility to the special needs of young African American minds, [HBCUs] remain the institutions that demonstrate the most effective ability to graduate African American students who are poised to be competitive in the corporate, research, academic, governmental and military arenas" (Kerr, 2001; About HBCUs, 2013, para. 3). Bettez and Suggs (2012) further punctuate this ideal by maintaining, "... these institutions serve a distinct purpose in the ecology of American higher education and the promise of college choice, given that diverse students choose a particular college curriculum, setting, culture, and mission for varied reason. Continued enrollments at HBCUs for high performing students, who prefer this particular educational environment over selective majority institutions to which they have been accepted, signal a need for this college option" (p. 304). Despite the fact HBCUs comprise only 105 institutions of higher education in the United States, proportionately; they are responsible for and contribute to—in unparalleled ways—the education of African Americans, first-generation, low income, and other underrepresented student populations. In terms of increasing diversity, Gasman (2013) maintains today, "a full quarter of HBCUs across the nation have at least a 20% non-Black student body (p. 6). Gasman goes on to argue, "Some people worry that the changing composition of HBCUs endangers the very aspect of these institutions that makes them unique; others argue that diversity makes these institutions stronger, by fostering mutual respect and an appreciation for Black culture among a broader population" (p. 6). Given the changing demography of the U.S. between now and the years 2020 and 2050 (United States Census Bureau, 2012), the increasing trends of Latino, Asian American, and White enrollments at HBCUs further enhance the institutional mission of access and inclusion for all who possess the aptitude and desire to obtain higher education.

In recent years, there has been an increase in scholarship and discussions around the importance for the higher education sector to gain a deeper understanding of the history and mission of HBCUs. In this way, the contributions of this institution type on behalf of the African American community and its roots in social transformational leadership, can inform their continued significance in a post-segregation America (Brown, 2003; Brown & Davis, 2001; Brown et al., 2001; Gasman, Baez, & Turner, 2008; Outcalt & Skewes-Cox, 2002; Saunders & Westbrook, 2001).

Educational research rarely situates text that focuses on the institutional leadership of Black college presidents, as this institution type is typically examined as monolithic and, thus, a failure to address individual institutional factors occurs (Brown, 2003; Chambers, 1972; Gasman, 2011). Gasman (2011b) further argues, "Until scholars, the media, policymakers, and the general public have a more nuanced perspective, these one-sided views, often tinged with racism, will continue to flourish in depictions of Black colleges and their leaders. They are particularly problematic when they lead to a lack of confidence in Black college leadership on the part of foundations, donors, and the public" (p. 837). To this end, an examination of the history and leadership of individual HBCU leaders can provide context from which to develop a greater understanding of distinct mission institutions and their sustainability. Namely, what historical aspects around social transformation leadership provide evidentiary support for the enduring characteristics common to Black colleges.

OVERRIDING THEME

The effects of social transformation leadership at the executive leadership level in higher education are the overriding theme supported by the work of the Higher Education Research Institute and its Social Change Model. Transformational leadership has been conceptualized as being comprised of four distinct competencies: charismatic leadership/idealized influence, inspirational motivation, intellectual stimulation, and individualized consideration (Bass, 1996).

For the purposes of this study, the author defines social transformation leadership as occurring when the Chief Academic Officer (CAO), whose likely title is president or chancellor, is a "charismatic" leader such that "followers seek to identify with the leader and emulate him or her...inspires followers with challenge and persuasion, providing both meaning and understanding...intellectually stimulating, expanding the followers' use of their abilities...individually considerate, providing the follower with support, mentoring, and coaching" (Bass & Riggio, 2005, p. 5).

Central to the overriding theme is the role of change agent, social engineer, and servant leader HBCU presidents have continually had to envision for themselves on behalf of their race. This unique perspective is linked to the context in which HBCUs were founded that has required its leaders to see beyond the day-to-day management of the college or university structure, and situate their leadership around the mission and vision of the institution in an effort to galvanize allies for whom the institution serves. These allies include, but are not limited to: the Black race and members of all races, local municipalities, state governments, the nation, and the world.

The role of the college president or CAO is prestigious, yet arduous and often times unforgiving. Nonetheless, all of the subjects of the research have proven to be effectively engaged educators, citizens, and community stakeholders, who pursue their vision and develop strategies to meet the needs of not only their respective campuses, but also the larger community and the nation. These leaders understand that to be effective, partnerships and relationship-building across institutional, administrative, and instructional boundaries must occur so that shared governance around their stated mission and vision can be fully realized. In the publication titled, *Leadership Reconsidered: Engaging Higher Education in Social Change*, the authors maintain,

> Leadership values are reflected, first and foremost, in the ends toward which any leadership effort is directed: What are we trying to change and why? What is the nature and scope of the intended change, and who will benefit? We believe that the value ends of leadership should be to enhance equity, social justice, and the quality of life; to expand access and opportunity; to encourage respect for difference and diversity; to strengthen democracy, civic life, and civic responsibility; and to promote cultural enrichment, creative expression, intellectual honesty, the advancement of knowledge, and personal freedom coupled with social responsibility. (Astin & Astin, 2000, p. 11)

Primarily, this book serves as a call-to-action for current Black college leaders to not only revisit, but also continue to perfect the practice and traditions of social transformation leadership representative of their predecessors. Second, the research seeks to engage future college and university leaders in the study of past and present Black college presidents included in this text as well as other works, because an informed account of their leadership model is vital to the narrative and critique of their own challenges and successes as social transformational leaders.

INTRODUCTION

> *Any study of the Negro college must, therefore, take into account the fact that it has, throughout its existence, been a 'have not' institution. Its responsibilities have been great and its resources meager. This does not relieve the Negro college of its obligation to the Negro people and to society. Basic to its claim for adequate support is the degree to which it has met this obligation with the resources at hand.*
> —General Education in the Negro College, 1969

The practice of social transformation leadership has remained foundational to the origins and survival of HBCUs. As race leaders respond to needs and enable the aspirations of members of their race, the author maintains social transformation leadership has remained an essential practice for institutional and student success. Arguably, Black college leadership is largely based on a *calling* or imperative to embark upon the necessary work required to overcome barriers to social, political, economic, and educational equity.

For the purposes of this publication, the author defines leadership as "not only what elected appointed public officials do, but also the critically important civic work performed by those individual citizens who are actively engaged in making a positive difference in the society" (Astin & Astin, 2000, p. 2). Specifically, Bass & Avolio (1994) define transformational leadership as occurring when leaders:

- Stimulate interest among colleagues and followers to view their work from new perspectives
- Generate awareness of the mission or vision of the team and organization
- Develop colleagues and followers to higher levels of ability and potential
- Motivate colleagues and followers to look beyond their own interests toward those that will benefit the group. (p. 2)

In this way, the role of a civically engaged social engineer is influenced by tenets of transformational leadership and remains inherent to race leaders, including Black college presidents. These individual and collective actions around collaboration result in "a series of progressively deeper and more comprehensive agreements among stakeholders" (Chrislip, 2002, p. 54).

Comparatively less has been done at predominantly White institutions (PWIs) to practically apply social transformation competencies as a leadership model in response to longstanding social, economic, political, and educational ills. Predominantly White institutions employ divergent mission statements that lean toward selectivity and fail to interrelate a collective founding and purpose, as is the case with HBCUs.

Unlike the Black college, majority institutions engage in pre-existing alliances and relationship-building which are not always inclusive of the interest of all American citizenry. To be sure, while HBCUs were founded to educate Black Americans, they have never discriminated or denied admission based on race, ethnicity, religion, and gender. Instead, HBCUs have continually cultivated social transformation in an effort to serve underrepresented populations even when funding and physical resources remain scarce.

Mainstream entities with which HBCU leaders must partner to achieve social change, do not always parallel the partnerships their PWI counterparts are able to cultivate. In this way, allies pursued by HBCU leaders are not exclusively associated with Black America, Black education, or Black life and culture. Rather, this institution type has had to engage the very systems of oppression it seeks to eradicate so that social change is realized. As a result, the Black college embodies the very role of "the modern university

[as] a 'pluralistic' institution—pluralistic in several senses: in having several purposes, not one; in having several centers of power, not one; in serving several clienteles, not one" (Kerr, 2001, p. 103). Because access to education—not selectivity—has been a central mission of the HBCU, it understands the needs of those whom society tends to disenfranchise.

In 1942, "the National Survey of Higher Education for Negroes show[ed] that, for the most part, Negro students come to college with insufficient educational preparation and poor backgrounds of family and community" (Derbigny, 1969, p. 231). The report goes on to reveal, "The Negro college, in common with American colleges generally, therefore, is called upon to deal with a wide range of aptitudes, attitudes, and interests, much of which, largely because of poor school and home backgrounds, is upon a sub-average level in relation to the national college population. This accentuates the problem of providing for individual differences" (p. 231).

Further, HBCUs have continually relied upon elements of social change including collective advancement, racial uplift, and coalition-building as they seek to assemble, brand, and sustain their distinct mission. That historical undertaking to include the educational needs of those on the margins is essential in managing contemporary challenges and considerations the Black college faces. Threats to college access and changing demography (United States Census Bureau, 2012) bring into focus the need for HBCUs as it relates to college choice. To this end, the author acknowledges notable differences in the ways in which leadership is operationalized at HBCUs and PWIs.

This publication is intended to establish an examination of social transformation leadership through the lens of higher education. Specifically, the author's intent is to focus on institutional leadership at HBCUs and provide a deeper understanding of how a collaborative approach to leadership for social change can be successfully situated to articulate and substantiate the mission of Black colleges from perspectives of the past, present, and future. Further, the application of social transformation leadership can serve as a model for HBCU leaders and even their predominantly White counterparts.

This work, a culmination of the author's education and practical experiences in student affairs, academic affairs, and educational research, reveals the importance of social transformation leadership within the field of higher education, specifically, at the executive leadership level at HBCUs. As this study brings into focus the author's research interests in Black college leadership, it also seeks to highlight the historical and contemporary effects and gains of a leadership model which strengthens capacity building and student success among HBCU matriculates.

This publication seeks to add to the body of literature an examination of single site Black college leadership through the lens of social transformation and change. This work substantiates the Higher Education Research

Institute's (1996) finding that specific values, referred to as the Seven C's, must be present in order for social change to occur:

Individual Values

1. **Consciousness of self**—Being aware of the beliefs, values, attitudes, and emotions that motivates one to take action.
2. **Congruence**—Refers to thinking, feeling, and behaving with consistency, genuineness, authenticity, and honesty towards others. Congruent persons are those whose actions are consistent with their most deeply held beliefs and convictions. Clearly, personal congruence and consciousness of self are interdependent.
3. **Commitment**—The psychic energy that motivates the individual to serve and that drives the collective effort. Commitment implies passion, intensity, and duration. It is directed towards both the group activity as well as its intended outcomes. Without commitment, knowledge of self is of little value. And without adequate knowledge of self, commitment is easily misdirected. Congruence, in turn, is most readily achieved when the person acts with commitment and knowledge of self.

Group Process Values

4. **Collaboration**—To work with others in a common effort. It constitutes the cornerstone value of the group leadership effort because it empowers self and others through trust. Collaboration multiplies group effectiveness by capitalizing on the multiple talents and perspectives of each group member and on the power of that diversity to generate creative solutions and actions. Collaboration empowers each individual best when there is a clear-cut "division of labor;"
5. **Common Purpose**—To work with shared aims and values. It facilitates the group's ability to engage in collective analysis of the issues at hand and the task to be undertaken. Common purpose is best achieved when all of the members in the group share in the vision and participate actively in articulating the purpose and goals of the leadership development activity. Recognizing the common purpose and mission of the group helps to generate the high level of trust that any successful collaboration requires.
6. **Controversy with Civility**—Recognizes two fundamental realities of any creative group effort: that differences in viewpoint are inevitable, and that such difference must be aired openly but with civility.

Civility implies respect for others, a willingness to hear each other's views, and the exercise of restraint in criticizing the views and actions of others. This is best achieved in a collaborative framework and when a common purpose has been identified. Controversy (conflict, confrontation) can often lead to new, creative solutions to problems, especially when it occurs in an atmosphere of civility, collaboration, and common purpose.

Community/Societal Values

7. **Citizenship**—The process whereby the individual and the collaborative group become responsibly connected to the community and the society through the leadership development activity. To be a good citizen is to work for positive change on behalf of others and the community. Citizenship thus acknowledges the interdependence of all who are involved in or affected by these efforts. It recognizes that the common purpose of the group must incorporate a sense of concern for the rights and welfare of all those who might be affected by the group's efforts. Good citizenship thus recognizes that effective democracy involves individual responsibility as well as individual rights.

CHANGE—Change, in other words, is the ultimate goal of the creative process of leadership to make a better world and a better society for ourselves and others. (HERI, 1996, pp. 21–23)

In many ways, Black college presidents have employed the Seven C's as they work to cultivate the art of uplifting communities by continually investing in themselves, their race, and the oft times illusive American Dream. To begin, in order for the Black college to have even been envisioned, a consciousness of self is primary. If one has an unwavering spirit in one's beliefs, values, and attitudes around social justice, it is conceivable that person will activate his or her call-to-action and assume the role as a social transformation leader.

Second, congruence in behaviors associated with one's beliefs, values, and attitudes around social justice saturates the action steps of a leader. In this way, a leader performs simply as an extension of a consciousness of self that directly informs behaviors. As the Seven C's continue scaffolding upon the other, commitment becomes foundational for the subjects of this research, who stayed the course and either founded, effectively served, or (re)visioned failing institutions into ones capable of competitively recruiting, retaining, and graduating its students.

Social transformation resides in the DNA of Black college leaders, as those in the minority have always had to negotiate not only their own world-view, but also the world-view of the majority in order to navigate and survive in a racialized society. To be sure, Black college presidents have successfully collaborated as a "means for building social capital, sustaining a democratic society, and transforming the civic culture of a community or region" (Chrislip, 2002, p. 5). As Black college leaders galvanize supporters of their vision, a common purpose is situated around the founding, mission, and vision of their institutions. This shared vision correlates the primary HBCU mission, as each institution is founded with a common purpose in mind: the education of Black Americans.

Chrislip (2002) maintains, "A collaborative process engages a disparate group of stakeholders with differing positions and, often, a long history of conflict and mutual distrust" (p. 45). As part of achieving a common purpose for the education of Black Americans, the struggle to manage differences while advocating civility in a climate of strained race relations, harassment, terrorism, and murder was not easy. Nonetheless, HBCU presidents tirelessly sought allies who recognized the inevitable differences in viewpoints, yet chose to pursue collaborative, non-violent remedies to to the problem of access to education for Blacks in America.

In seeking access to education for all, citizenship became a significant element of Black college leadership. The ideal that the Black citizenry was so blatantly discriminated against and omitted from the democratic process led Black college leaders to take action on behalf of their race—using education as their arena of activism. Ultimately, the constellation of civil discord cultivates a culture at HBCUs as sites of resistance, activism, and social change. Chrislip (2002) argues, "civic practices and governing institutions must be capable of constructively addressing the real concerns of a community or region, especially in circumstances involving diverse groups with competing values" (p. 10). Through the use of the Seven C's, the very change Black college presidents, included in this research, sought is realized in part during their tenure. Additionally, themes of collaboration and social change are continuously operationalized throughout this text, as its practice informs chapter analyses and proves instructive to the reader.

Established in 1993 by Helen and Alexander Astin, the Social Change Model was not available to the early college presidents examined. Nonetheless, the research reveals how the subjects of the research and their contemporaries are viable symbols of social transformation leadership at a time when societal change was inconceivable to many and hard-fought for those committed to the idea. The resulting acts of collaboration are often "a reactive response to difficult and challenging situations" in which "the impetus to collaborate comes more often from futility or crisis rather than from proactive, visionary leadership" (Chrislip, 2002, p. 50). In case of Black college presidents, visionary leadership was imperative in order for early race leaders to even envision a society in which equity and inclusion is available to all.

Each chapter makes meaning of how Black college leaders embody the Seven C's in an effort to bring about engaged participation, shared power, and social transformation. To this end, institutional leaders of American colleges and universities may gain a deeper understanding of the practice of social transformation leadership that partners Black colleges with unlikely allies to create pathways to college access, inclusion, retention, and graduation for emerging populations including low income, first generation, and underrepresented students. While responsive to the education of any American the education of disenfranchised Black Americans, with the aptitude and desire to learn has remained a primary focus of HBCUs since 1837.

As many institutions struggle to promote and build an institutional mission grounded in social change, HBCUs—through social transformation leadership—represent an institution type that has acted out of necessity to define and meet its stated mission. Early HBCU leaders, for example, were effective in their leadership because they understood principles and values that emulate the Social Change Model when carrying out their vision for college choice, access, and academic success for the Black race.

The author not only argues HBCU leaders performed out of necessity, but also the resulting methodologies were used to successfully navigate the procurement of necessary fiscal, physical, and human resources. Through this conscience or unconscious; intentional or unintentional work, a socially transformative campus mission already exists within the HBCU brand where customs, practices, and action steps continue to serve as an enduring blueprint for its current and future leaders. To this end, the call-to-action is for contemporary HBCU leaders to revisit or (re)vision social transformation practices using past narratives already set into motion and gifted to them by their predecessors. Though no campus leader is without missteps, the aim of the research is to highlight long-standing strategies for engaged participation and social transformation among HBCU leaders. This book pays homage to HBCU leaders who recognize the Black college as their arena of activism and emerge as leaders who wish to make certain the survival of higher education and learning for Black Americans.

OVERVIEW OF CONTENTS

Since their inception, HBCUs have long-established an archetype of community organizing, academic preparation, and leadership development resulting in social change among past and present presidents. A representative sample of their efforts and accomplishments is chronicled throughout this book.

The first section of the book provides a framework and implications for social transformation leadership and presents an overview of past Black college leaders from 1904 to 1967, including: Benjamin Elijah Mays (1940–1967), Morehouse College; Mary McLeod Bethune (1904–1942 and 1946–1947), Bethune-Cookman University; and James Edward Shepherd (1910–1947), North Carolina Central University. The second section of the book examines a single contemporary Black college president; Walter M. Kimbrough, Philander Smith College. The third section of the book explores the future of Black colleges as an institution type and implications of their competitive edge in the higher education market via curricular and co-curricular traditions, initiatives, and programs. Each of the four subjects of the book model a cross-section of the Seven C's and how the practice of social transformation leadership leads toward the "ultimate goal of the creative process of leadership—to make a better world and a better society for ourselves and others" (HERI, 1996, p. 21).

As each chapter and section of the book ends and the next begins, the author wishes to take the reader on a journey from past practices to the current and future potential of the Black college and higher education mandates relative to emerging populations, changing academic program reviews and renewals, and undergraduate recruitment and retention.

Even in the face of a grand narrative that continually questions the relevance of HBCUs in contemporary American society, there is a counter-narrative that has not been fully explored or considered. The author's intent is to emphasize the enduring acts of social transformation leadership used over time and their continued merit. To be sure, use of the Social Change Model at HBCUs is available as a point of reference that leaders representing *all* institution types may contemplate as they envision institutional and student success in an ever-changing higher education marketplace.

CONCLUSION

This book illustrates how Black college sustainability is directly linked to and deeply rooted in social transformation leadership. Collective advancement, racial uplift, and the resulting social change leadership model has remained a core competency for HBCUs and, thus, a pioneering paradigm for current and future Black college leaders. Accordingly, it is the author's assertion that institutional leadership which embodies an organizational culture toward engaged participation and shared power can more effectively articulate the purpose and mission of the Black college. Specifically, by returning to its origins (i.e., charter, mission, purpose), Black college leaders will likely identify the tools with which an institutional (re)visioning and renewal might be realized.

Regrettably, HBCU leaders find themselves in the position of validating the institutional mission and effectiveness of its high-performing institutions against the entire body of predominantly White institutions—when there exist low-performing PWIs whose outcomes are not on par with many HBCUs. In the article titled, *Truth, Generalizations, and stigmas: An Analysis of the Media's Coverage of Morris Brown College and Black Colleges Overall*, Gasman asserts,

> One of the themes receiving the most attention from the media, and perhaps the most damaging to the future of Black colleges, is that of their decline. This theme most frequently appeared in articles framed by finance and accreditation. Quite often, the media generalized the experiences at Morris Brown and applied them to Black colleges overall. (2007, p. 122)

Gasman goes on to critique the media's coverage by observing, "Of course the reporter failed to mention that many historically White institutions are struggling financially and do not offer their students the 'conveniences' provided by their wealthier counterparts" (p. 124). In what has been characterized as a post-racial society, it is this form of evaluative assumptions, coupled with an enduring narrative around HBCU inferiority that cause many uninformed detractors to conclude the Black college is no longer needed. Nonetheless, this does not mean low-performing HBCUs should not be challenged; it simply calls for HBCUs to be examined as individual sites of study and no longer as monolithic.

By examining and discussing identifiable values, characteristics, and the practical effects of social transformation leadership, it is the author's contention this institution type can position itself at the center of contemporary best practices intended to (re)vision, (re)define, and (re)purpose tomorrow's Black college and university.

REFERENCES

American Association of Higher Education, American College Personnel Association, & National Association of Student Personnel Administrators. (1998). *Powerful partnerships: A shared responsibility for learning*. Retrieved from http://www.myacpa.org/pub/documents/taskforce.pdf

Astin, A. W., & Astin, H. S. (2000). *Leadership reconsidered: Engaging higher education in social change*. Battle Creek, MI: W. K. Kellogg Foundation.

Bass, B. M. (1996). *New paradigm of leadership: An inquiry into transformational leadership*. Alexandria, VA: U.S. Army Research Institute for the Behavioral and Social Sciences.

Bass, B. M., & Riggio, R. E. (2005). *Transformational leadership*, (2nd ed). Mahwah, NJ: Lawrence Erlbaum Associates.

Bass, B. M., & Avolio, B. J. (Eds.). (1994). *Improving organizational effectiveness through transformational leadership*. Thousand Oaks, CA: Sage Publications.

Bettez, S. C., & Suggs, V. L. (Eds.) (September 2012). Centering the educational and social significance of HBCUs: A focus on the educational journeys and thoughts of African American scholars. *The Urban Review 44*(3), 303–310.

Brown, M. C. (1999). *The quest to define collegiate desegregation: Black colleges, Title VI compliance, and post-Adams litigation.* Westport, CT: Greenwood Publishing Group.

Brown, M. C., & Davis, J. E. (2001). The historically Black college as a social contract, social capital, and social equalizer. *Peabody Journal of Education 76*, 31–49.

Brown, M. C., Donahoo, S., & Bertrand, R. D. (2001). The Black college and the quest for educational opportunity. *Urban Education, 36*(5), 553–571. doi:10.1177/0042085901365002

Brown, M. C. (2003). Emics and eties of researching Black colleges: Applying facts and avoiding fallacies. In M. C. Brown & J. E. Lane (Eds.), *Studying diverse institutions: Contexts, challenges, and considerations* (pp. 27–40). New Directions in Institutional Research, no. 118. San Francisco: Jossey-Bass.

Chambers, F. (1972). Histories of Black colleges and universities. *The Journal of Negro History 57*, 270–275.

Chrislip, D. D. (2002). *The collaborative leadership fieldbook: A guide for citizens and civic leaders.* San Francisco: Jossey-Bass.

Derbigny, I. A. (1969). *General education in the Negro college.* New York, NY: Negro Universities Press.

Gasman, M. (2011a). Truth, generalizations, and stigmas: An analysis of the media's coverage of Morris Brown College and Black colleges overall. *The Review of Black Political Economy*, Summer–Fall, 111–147.

Gasman, M. (2011b). Perceptions of Black college presidents: Sorting through stereotypes and reality to gain a complex picture. *American Educational Research Journal, 48*(4), 836–870. doi:10.3102/0002831210397176

Gasman, M. (2013). *The changing face of historically Black colleges and universities.* Philadelphia: University of Pennsylvania Graduate School of Education, Center for Minority-Serving Institutions.

Gasman, M., Baez, B., & Turner, C. S. (2008). Social justice at historically Black and Hispanic-serving institutions: Mission statements and administrative voices. In M. Gasman, B. Baez, & C. S. V. Turner (Eds.), *Understanding minority-serving institutions* (pp. 203–217). Albany: State University of New York Press.

HERI (1996). *A social change model of leadership development.* Los Angeles: Higher Education Research Institute, UCLA. Retrieved at http://www.heri.ucla.edu/PDFs/pubs/ASocialChangeModelofLeadershipDevelopment.pdf

Kerr, C. (2001). *The uses of the university* (5th ed.). Cambridge, MA: Harvard University Press.

National Association of Historically Black Colleges and Universities: Title III Administrators (2013). HBCU Importance. Retrieved at http://hbcut3a.org/hbcu-lifestyle/hbcu-importance

Redd. K. E. (1998). Historically Black colleges ad universities: Making a comeback. In J. P. Merisotis & E. M. O'Brien (Eds.), *Minority serving institutions: Distinct purposes. common goals* (pp. 33–44). San Francisco: Jossey-Bass.

Outcalt, C., & Skewes-Cox, T. (2002). Involvement, interaction, and satisfaction: The human environment at HBCUs. *The Review of Higher Education, 25*(3), 331–347.

Saunders, K., & Westbrook, T. S. (2001). Historically Black colleges and universities: Lessons from the past, hope for the future. *ISPA Journal 13*(1), 2–19.

United Negro College Fund (2013). Our Member Colleges. Retrieved at http://www.uncf.org/members/aboutHBCU.asp

United States Census Bureau (2013). *U.S. Census Bureau projections show a slower growing, older, more diverse nation a half century from now.* Washington, D.C.: U.S. Department of Commerce. Retrieved from https://www.census.gov/newsroom/releases/archives/population/cb12-243.html

White House Initiative on Historically Black Colleges and Universities (2013). HBCUs and 2020 Goal. Retrieved at http://batchgeo.com/map/b5dc368cb9ba3748282d04fab97b1aec

ACKNOWLEDGMENTS

This book is a cooperative effort involving individuals, who are committed to social transformation in education and feel the need to examine, analyze, and discuss the enduring practice social transformation through the lens of Black college leadership. At this critical juncture in America higher education when attacks on the merits of HBCUs threaten college access, inclusion, and choice, the author and contributors are committed to the production of knowledge around a counter-narrative of the HBCU legacy around leadership for social justice. This legacy continues to inform the present and future context of Black colleges as centers of resistance and influence in American post-secondary education.

—**Vickie L. Suggs**
Durham, North Carolina

SECTION I

BLACK COLLEGE PRESIDENTS DURING THE 1930S–1960S

CHAPTER 1

INFLUENCES OF SOCIAL GOSPEL

The Institutional Leadership of Benjamin Elijah Mays and Robert Maynard Hutchins

Vickie L. Suggs

INTRODUCTION

While higher education comprises multiple institution types, educational researchers often frame their examination of higher education through the default lens of the four-year, traditional, majority institution. The tendency to limit the individual identity of distinct mission institutions such as HBCUs creates a challenge in comparative analyses of Black college leadership and its similarities to predominately White institutions (PWIs). Historically, Black college leadership is relegated to a universal "labeling process" (Chambers, 1972, p. 271) that rarely considers the potential likeness to mainstream college leadership. To deepen the understanding of shared institutional leadership traits among HBCUs and PWIs, this study examines the question: How did the ideals of social gospel influence Benjamin Elijah

Mays—Morehouse College and Robert Maynard Hutchins—the University of Chicago, as they each led and collaboratively developed the academic and social missions of their respective institutions? This chapter investigates the methodologies by which Benjamin Mays and Robert Hutchins infused social gospel into the leadership and curricular mission of their respective institutions.

According to Taba (1962), "Some educators interpret the social function of education chiefly as an instrument for social change, either through gradual reform by reshaping the outlook of the oncoming generation or through planned effort at reconstruction" (p. 25). Mays opts to lead through the indoctrination of civility and moral character as part of the Morehouse mission and the creation of the Morehouse Man (Carter, 1998; Jones, 1957; Rovaris, 2004). According to Rovaris (2004), "Though the creation of the 'Morehouse Man' predates the Mays administration... he is often given credit for the infusion of life into this concept" (p. 107). Thus, the Morehouse Man is the brand Mays assigns to the collective graduates of an institution that "distinguished itself singularly, if not spectacularly, in preparing Negro men for a virile, intelligent, and progressive leadership and for the effective participation in a Christian and democratic society" (Jones, 1957, p. 231). Mays attempts to accomplish the vision of its founders throughout his 27 years as president. Similarly, Hutchins understands the social usefulness of education and, thus, raises questions of whether it is possible to "achieve the social purposes one has at heart" and if it is "possible to put over a program of social reform, through the educational system" (Hutchins, 1953a, p. 49). Though the questions are raised, Hutchins does not define democracy in ways that directly deal with access and inclusion. Philosophically, democracy can be achieved through education, yet social, educational, economic, and political history clearly depicts the denial of full citizenship for Negroes. In this way, Hutchins' educational thought is largely principle-based and looks toward a larger, perhaps more abstract outcome than the more immediate need for answers Mays sought for his race. Rather, Hutchins envisions education as the forum in which democratic debate and diversity of thought can exist "for the purpose of promoting mutual comprehension" (p. 68). Hutchins' brand of education for democracy resonates throughout his 22-year leadership of the University of Chicago, as he sought to fulfill the development of moral citizens whose education "has equipped them to read and write, to think about important questions, and to discuss them intelligently" (Hutchins, 1953b, p. 70).

The subjects of this essay each identify a social and an educational sphere in which to employ the ideals of social gospel. Despite the use of the term "gospel," social gospel "coalesced more around action than belief" (White & Hopkins, 1976, p. xvi) and its leanings were toward individual consciousness as a means to social salvation. Though Mays and Hutchins share a common interest in societal transformation related to the ideals of social gospel, their individual exposure to the social gospel movement gave each a perspective that informs their educational thought and leadership persona.

A comparative analysis of the ideals of social gospel and its influence on Mays and Hutchins has not been conducted in the history of education. This chapter seeks to examine intersections that existed in the collaborative leadership of Black and predominately White institutions of higher education from the 1930s through the 1960s.

MAYS AND HUTCHINS

Benjamin Elijah Mays and Robert Maynard Hutchins are, perhaps, unlikely historical figures in which parallel leadership influences existed. Mays, president of Morehouse College, came from humble beginnings and experienced a childhood of discrimination, felt he and his family lived in "respectable poverty" (Mays, 1971, p. 20) in the South. Hutchins, president of the University of Chicago, hailed from a life of access, privilege, and the expectation to achieve a level of success similar to his forefathers. Despite such polar upbringings, each arrive at the position of college president, serve for a period of 27 and 22 years, respectively, and recognize how the ideals of social gospel could inform their professional calling and ultimately lays a rich foundation for societal change. Though they share an appreciation for the social gospel movement, Mays actualizes these ideals as an essentialist focusing on essential skills and professional practice, whereas Hutchins adopts the personal development perspective of perennialists. It is this departure that illustrates the way in which they independently reflect and put into practice, the ideals of the social gospel. As a race leader, Mays fights tirelessly for social, economic, political, and educational justice on behalf of Black Americans. As a product of a Puritan household, Hutchins believes in meaningful social uses of education and espouses the ideal that "the object of education is the improvement of society...and you have to recognize the limitations, as well as the possibilities, of education" (Hutchins, 1953a, p. 53).

Educated at Bates College (BA, 1925) and The University of Chicago (MA, 1925; PhD, 1935), Mays was also a member of Phi Beta Kappa and received numerous honorary degrees in the disciplines of Law, Divinity, Humanities, and Education (Mays, 1971). Mays says he was "'called' or driven to do something other than farming" (p. 9) and became a self-made man whose only parental encouragement for his life-long pursuit of education came from his mother, Louvenia. She fiercely believed her son was called to be a great leader of his race and always instilled in Mays the Lord would clear a pathway to the better life he envisioned for himself. In addition to his mother's unwavering support, Mays is also influenced and encouraged by the example of Negro leaders such as Booker T. Washington, Frederick Douglass, and Paul Laurence Dunbar (Mays, 1971; Rovaris, 2004). Of Dunbar's writing, Mays finds understanding:

> It is said at one time Dunbar was strongly contemplating ministry as a life's profession....[Dunbar's] qualities of God are: His social justice, His sympathy for those whose cares are heavy, His disinterest in creed, and His inclination to be moved more by actual human needs than by prayers....The idea of God is so used as to make it a vital force in man's effort to perfect some kind of social change....the idea of God and that of social welfare are inseparable. (Mays, 1969, pp. 134–135)

Mays' understanding of the interrelationship between Christianity, social change, and race leads him to believe "that in seeking a basis for the elimination of race prejudice and discrimination, we must find such a basis in something other than man. The basis for good relations is found in the Christian religion, in the proper understanding of the Christian doctrines of man, Christ, and God, and in the application of Christian insights and convictions in everyday living" (Mays, 1964, p. 10).

Despite a childhood of poverty and a quest for education that includes a 10-year pursuit of his doctorate, Mays is a committed race man who understands his moral and civic duty to lead (Mays, 1971; Rovaris, 2004; Carter, 1998). In terms of the moral precepts Mays seeks to underscore as part of his leadership, the ideals of social gospel continuously frame the institutional mission of Morehouse College. According to Samuel DuBois Cook, PhD, Morehouse graduate mentored by Mays and President Emeritus of Dillard University,

> Because of a divine restlessness implanted in his Puritan science and cultivated and cherished in the depths of his being, Bennie Mays will always be morally restless, anxious, and demanding. While understanding the foibles and moral afflictions of human nature, he is a moral perfectionist. He will not achieve moral peace; his ethical consciousness is too deep, intense, and demanding for that. The world contains too many evils and therefore challenges for the man to take a moral vacation. He is too self-demanding to have a complacent conscience. Too much remains to be done for him to become a spectator of the events, struggles, and encounters of the contemporary scene. His vision of the higher possibilities of human life is too grand; his zest for life too immense; and his concern for the lot of his fellows too vast and deep for him to have a satisfied conscience. He is moved by a vision of nobler things that will not let him go; neither will he let it go. He grips the vision and the vision him. (Mays, 1971, pp. xviii–xix)

To this end, the spiritual support of his mother may have, arguably, initiated and solidified a life-long association with social gospel theology—evidenced in Mays' dissertation, titled, "The Development of the Idea of God in Contemporary Negro Literature." To this end, Mays' faith and belief in his ability to succeed and effect change on behalf of Black Americans persists throughout his life and is reflected in his personal and professional personas. Well-respected among students and his peers, Mays sought to embody of the ideals of social gospel and mirror, in his daily life and professional practice, the principles he promotes while serving as the face of Morehouse College.

Conversely, Hutchins was a child of privilege, having been born in the Northeast to a family of educators and professionals among whom he found examples of success which informed his own educational and professional endeavors. Educated at Oberlin College (1915–1917), Yale University (BA, 1921) and Yale University Law School (LLB, 1925), Hutchins was appointed, at 28-years-old, the youngest Dean of the Yale Law School, and the youngest president of the University of Chicago at 30-years-old (Dzuback, 1991).

During his administration at Chicago, Hutchins created the Common Core in which the design of courses covers "the whole scope of human knowledge" (The Common Core, 2009, para. 1) by teaching beyond the facts and, thus, developing an intellectual curiosity and the tools of inquiry. Taba (1962) argues, "... the task of all education is to cause a maximum amount of transfer. The curriculum always must stress those things which promise most transfer, which create a mastery and understanding of matters beyond that which is taught directly" (p. 121). Accordingly, Hutchins maintains, "It must be remembered that the purpose of education is not to fill the minds of students with facts, it is not to reform them, or amuse them, or make them expert technicians in any field. It is to teach them to think if that is possible, and to think always for themselves" (Hutchins, 1936, p. 8).

Hutchins' childhood influences were most significant upon his move from Brooklyn, New York to Oberlin, Ohio at the age of eight. Life in Oberlin exposed Hutchins to the commitment its community members held toward principled citizenship. According to Dzuback (1991), Hutchins recalls Oberlin College and "the kinds of common values and ethical expectations he had known while there" (p. 65). While enrolled at Oberlin for two years, Hutchins, like Mays, becomes a member of his college debate team and uses his oratory skill to augment his graduate education and professional practice. Further, the curriculum seems to ignite Hutchins' intellectual curiosity and instinct to engage. As cited in Dzuback, Hutchins describes the course offerings and pedagogy while attending Oberlin as "the best teaching" he had "seen or experienced anywhere" (p. 16). The two years spent at Oberlin reinforced reflections later in life that "the common sense of the American people will lead them to insist, before it is too late, upon an education that will help us to be wise" (Hutchins, 1956, p. 107). This idea mirrors Taba (1962) who believes, "All decisions about education, including those about curriculum, are made within the context of a society. The values and forces of that society determine not only what manner of man exists but also to some extent what manner of man is needed" (p. 25). Indeed, the Oberlin institutional legacy of access, inclusion, educational opportunity, and principled citizenship made a lasting impression on the institutional leadership of the University of Chicago.

ORIGINS OF SOCIAL GOSPEL AND THE WISCONSIN IDEA

Social Gospel Movement

According to Ronald C. White and Charles H. Hopkins, "The social gospel never became an organized 'movement.' Rather it was a network of movements operating in different contexts. Those individuals who connected with its ideology worked through ongoing religious and secular organizations" (White & Hopkins, 1976, p. xviii). According to White and Hopkins (1976), though not an actual movement, the ideals of social gospel drew attention to and created intersections among American social, political, religious and economic interests. Thus, the social gospel "viewed itself as a crusade for justice and righteousness in all areas of the common life. The crusade recruited articulate ministers and lay persons who publicized their new points of view as pastors, educators, editors, and directors of reform organizations" (p. xii). Thus, the movement looked beyond the institutional church, developed unity through accepted religious traditions, and pursued "personal and public morality...as the foundation of a religious nation" (Hoeveler, 1983, pp. 186–187).

According to Hans A. Baer and Merrill Singer (1992), "Religious movements often emerge as forms of popular rebellion against the domination of ruling classes..." (p. 98). Thus, one could argue Mays' experiences as part of the Black church and its responsibility to "legitimize social arrangements in America [sic] society by participating in reformist political activities rather than in radical or revolutionary ones" (p. 98) are reflected in his leadership on behalf of social, political, educational, and economic justice for Black Americans. In fact, Mays is a social reformer who recognizes that, "Following the emancipation...since 1865...economic, social, and psychological factors have permeated the structure of the Negro church. Specifically, churches originated from about five causes, namely, a growing racial consciousness, the initiative of individuals and groups, splits, migrations of Negroes, and missions of other churches" (Mays, 1969, p. 14).

Similarly, one could argue Hutchins' youth in Oberlin, as well as his "parental pedagogy" in which "consistent teaching of consideration for others, personal responsibility, courtesy, community service, discerning right from wrong, and hard work" (Dzuback, 1991, p. 9) is reflected in his own affinity for the actualization of the ideals of the social gospel through higher education. Hutchins understands the "underlying paradox in American education" to be that "we believe in education for all because we believe in democracy. Belief in democracy is the belief in the capacity of the people. But we do not believe in the capacity of the people. We do not dare say that we must give up education for all because we do not dare say that we do not believe in the capacity of the people. Therefore, we continue to proclaim our devotion to education for all, but surreptitiously substituted accommodation for education" (Hutchins, 1956, pp. 98–99).

Evidenced in their commitment to lifelong learning, both men carried imprints of their broader experiences (e.g., Mays in the Black church; Hutchins while at Oberlin), and respective life lessons from childhood into adulthood. These lessons were operationalized during their service as a college and a university president.

The Wisconsin Idea

According to J. David Hoeveler (1983), the evolution of the old-time college to the new university during the late 1800s remains a noteworthy educational achievement in the United States. There are three factors which are credited with the initiation of the transformation:

> A new concern for practicality and utility in the colleges' curricular program; a democratic effort to extend the benefits of education to a wider portion of the community and to repay the public by servicing its needs; and a new academic interest in research—that is, the advancement of knowledge instead of the mere passing-on of an acquired cultural tradition. (p. 185)

Hoeveler (1976) acknowledges these three factors as contributors to the social role of the American university and how it mirrors the social context in which it exists. The "Wisconsin Idea" (p. 282) aligns with this thought, as it "pledged the University of Wisconsin to serve the state by applying its research to the solution of public problems, by training experts in the physical and social sciences and joining their academic efforts to the public, administrative functions of the state, and by extending the work of the University, through its personnel and facilities, to the boundaries of the state" (p. 185). Though the ideal of service to the state was pioneered by Governor Robert M. LaFollette, the former student of the University of Wisconsin credits its fifth president, John Bascom, as "the true originator of the Wisconsin Idea" (p. 189). According to Hoeveler, Bascom was a moral philosopher and sociologist said to be "one of the first exponents of the Social Gospel in America" (p. 189). Richard T. Ely and John R. Commons, influenced by Bascom's religious, ethical, spiritual, and moral imperative of state power, advanced the Wisconsin Idea and the relationship between "the evangelical ideals, the Social Gospel, and the new university" (p. 198). According to Hoeveler (1983), the ideals of Bascom, Ely, and Commons were largely rooted in their individual and collective efforts to define and identify a social gospel agenda for America. Conversely, Charles R. Van Hise, a student of Bascom and classmate of La Follette, interpreted the Wisconsin Idea in economic terms. In doing so, the concept "defined the state university's research activity, for new knowledge must be applied directly to the improvement of the lives of the people" (p. 201).

Though a direct or intentional articulation may not exist between the ideals of the Social Gospel Movement and the Wisconsin Idea, American institutions of higher education were called to a "new kind of gospel and a new program for social redemption" (Hoeveler, 1983, p. 202) and would likely assume a social role no matter the social context in which the institution existed. Thus, the institutional mission for colleges and universities are inextricably tied to the vision of Chief Academic Officer who must continuously acknowledge the institution's integration with public life and establish significant partnerships not only within the state, but also nationally and internationally. In this way, the ideals of the Social Gospel Movement and the Wisconsin Idea may serve simply as scaffolding upon which the social uses of higher education can be measured.

To be sure, the institutional leadership of Mays and Hutchins exemplify, in part, the principles of the Wisconsin Idea by demonstrating their concern for the comprehensive uses of the university; expanding the institutional goals of teaching, research, and service beyond its campus borders to its external communities; and fostering academic research, inquiry, and the advancement of knowledge. Further aligning with Bensimon and Neumann's (1993) call to think of leadership in a "collective form: leadership as occurring among and through a group of people who think and act together" (p. 2).

ESSENTIALISM VERSUS PERENNIALISM

Mays and Educational Essentialism

Essentialist pedagogy includes subjects such as History, Literature, Reading, Writing, Foreign Languages, Mathematics, Science, Art, and Music. William C. Bagley based essentialism on the teaching of basic subjects with few electives along with the belief educational outcomes include the development of citizenship among those who graduate. According to Bagley (1922), "School life, if it is to form an adequate training ground for adulthood, must always associate freedom and individual initiative with a rigid responsibility for results" (p. 252). Bagley goes on to posit that "courage, fortitude, initiative, efficiency, foresight,—in fact every conceivable human virtue may be given a surer footing in the individual mind through the study of history and biography..." (p. 168). Hirsch (2009) takes this idea one step further by raising the question: "Who is against educating young people so that they are able to judge the issues of the day, make a good living, raise a family, and help keep civic peace and order" (p. 65)? Hirsch argues for "common ideals and shared knowledge" (p. 66) in the spirit of Horace Mann. In this way, the common core of essentialist pedagogy resembles a content-based curriculum in which all learners cultivate respect for ones teachers, community, and fellow citizens.

As custodian of Morehouse College for 27 years, Mays commits himself to cultivating servant leaders who will perpetuate essentialist principles of a teacher-centered laboratory in which one can learn, apply knowledge, and become a life-long learner. As it relates to citizenship, Mays believes education and the acquisition of knowledge are fundamental to producing and sustaining American society. Mays also advocates educational standards to produce a mastery of skills including rhetoric (Bagley, 1922), as he was a champion debater while at Bates College and coached the debate team while also a math and algebra instructor at Morehouse College in 1921 (Rovaris, 2004; Carter, 1998).

Inspired by the writings of such race leaders as Booker T. Washington, Mays subscribed to "the things Washington desired...an opportunity for the American Negro to gain complete economic status; freedom from privileges for the Negro in proportion to the degree to which he proves himself worthy; the abolition of injustice, ignorance, poverty, and crime; and the desire to rise above any form of hatred or prejudice in his own heart" (Mays, 1969, p. 139). Mays is consistent in making the case for a triangulation between the Negro, Christianity, and democracy. In terms of race relations in America, the enduring demand on the part of the Negro that America live up to the promise of its Creed could not be ignored. Likewise, Myrdal, Sterner, and Rose (1944) examine race relations in America through the lens of morality. The Myrdal et al. argue, "From the point of view of the American Creed, the status accorded the Negro in America represents nothing more than and nothing less than a century-long lag of public morals" (p. 24). Accordingly, discrimination directed at the Negro race meant the failure to create a democratic social order and, thus, the ideals of democracy articulated by the forefathers and by those who consider themselves patriotic, is called into question. In response to the social disorder the Negro experienced during and in the wake of slavery, the Negro church became a center of influence and leadership for racial uplift. Mays advances the idea, "the Negro church is one of the greatest, perhaps the greatest, channel through which the masses of the Negro race receives adult education" (Mays, 1969, p. 58). Mays further believes,

> The opportunity found in the Negro Church to be recognized and to be 'somebody,' has stimulated the pride and preserved the self-respect of many Negroes who would have been entirely beaten by life, and possibly completely submerged. Everyone wants to receive recognition and feel that he is appreciated. The Negro church has supplied this need. (p. 281)

This assignment of value and validation as a human being is one Negro citizens and its male population, in particular, clung to in the face of blatant injustice, potential violence, and the very real threat of death. Lewison (1998) outlines the intersection of faith, morality, and intelligence where Mays finds agency and situates his educational thought as an outgrowth of a three-fold purpose designed to:

1. Train the mind to think clearly, logically and constructively
2. Train the heart to understand and sympathize with the aspirations, the sufferings and injustices of humankind
   Strengthen the will to act in the interest of the common good.
   (p. 21)

To this end, Mays sets out and achieves the creation of a pipeline to fulfilling the distinct mission Morehouse College shares with its HBCU counterparts. The relationship between Mays, educational essentialism, and the Jim Crow Era may validate the approach and deem it compatible with the narrow range of educational and vocational options available to the Negro after the Civil War. The competing methodologies of Booker T. Washington and W. E. B. Du Bois situated industrial education and classical instruction on the opposite ends of the spectrum of Negro educational capital. Further, fact-based educational thought could be argued as what Negro citizens could effectively employ as they pursued the necessary skill set to compete in a segregated America. Always at the surface and on the minds of race leaders: In what ways could the Negro navigate the social order of the South, in particular, and achieve the status and rights of full citizenship?

Mays found an enduring sense of purpose upon his return to the campus of Morehouse in 1940 as president and drew from the institutional brand during his 27 years as its leader. Ultimately, it was, according to Mays (1971), the specialness of the Morehouse spirit and the commitment of the teaching staff to instill a belief in oneself, that solidified his decision to "preserve and perpetuate" (p. 173) this legacy as president and visionary of

Hutchins and Educational Perennialism

Though he graduated summa cum laude, Hutchins experienced dissatisfaction with his undergraduate curriculum and was left with a feeling of intellectual emptiness. Hutchins (1936) laments over his educational experiences after leaving Oberlin:

> The reading periods at Harvard and Yale are ridiculous because they show how little time those universities feel should be devoted to thought. The number of hours in the classroom is the measure of the labors of both teachers and student. And the hours in the classroom are devoted to the exposition of detail. An anti-intellectual attitude toward education reduces the curriculum to the exposition of detail. (p. 37)

The significant differences in the educational experiences while at Oberlin, Yale, and Harvard had a profound effect on the way in which Hutchins viewed the role and purpose of the American university.

Like Mays, Hutchins viewed education as preparatory and foundational for life. Both were in favor of a subject-centered educational philosophy and the knowledge of a defined set of coursework. Where the two diverge is that perennialist pedagogy, according to Ryan and Cooper (2000), includes more rigor than its essentialist equivalent and argues for disciplined book learning. Perennialists endorse traditional subjects of History, Mathematics, the Arts, Science and Languages, but also place "emphasis on literature and humanities because these subjects provide the greatest insight into the human condition" (p. 272). To this end, Hutchins (1943) appeals to a national consciousness regarding the uses of the university,

> I am asking you to think, therefore, what one college and one university might do to establish for the country and the educational system the ideal of the common good as determined on the light of reason... This means understanding the great thinkers of the past and present, scientific, historical, and philosophical. It means a grasp of the disciplines of grammar, rhetoric, logic, and mathematics; reading, writing, and figuring. (pp. 59–60)

This ideal, though not explicit in its recognition of the existing discriminatory social order, is rooted in perennial educational thought and informed the service to humankind Hutchins felt called to put into practice.

According to Hutchins (1936), "The university exists only to find and to communicate the truth" (p. 5). Hutchins also believed, "Education is not a substitute for experience. It is preparation for it" (p. 127). Thus, the University of Chicago was able to evolve into a complex social structure designed to inspire inquiry, seek truth, and develop young minds to make the connection and the distinctions between education and society. During the 1930s, and in an effort to establish Chicago as the benchmark of undergraduate education, Hutchins began to employ a philosophy of educational perennialism. To this end, Hutchins' approach to the curriculum included readings of the Great Books. According to Ryan and Cooper (2000),

> The Great Books, which constitute a shelf of volumes stretching from Homer's *Iliad* to Albert Einstein's *On the Electrodynamics of Moving Bodies*, are a perennialist's ideal curriculum. For perennialists, the development of the intellect is best achieved through a teacher-directed instructional approach in the early years of schooling. Socratic dialogue is then used to help mature learners question and examine their beliefs in order to move closer to the truth. (p. 272)

Thus, the Common Core and the Socratic Method were realized and the ideals of Hutchins and Mortimer Adler captured a curricular design that introduced the Great Books as educational strategy and building blocks. According to Hutchins, "We have then for general education a course of study consisting of the greatest books of the western world and the arts of reading, writing, thinking and speaking, together with mathematics, the best exemplar of the processes of human reason. If our hope has been to frame a curriculum which educes the elements of our common human nature, this program should realize our hope" (Hutchins, 1936, p. 85). According to Dzuback (1990), though Hutchins "failed to persuade the faculty to develop a college program wholly based on the great books," (p. 65) his vision for undergraduate education and use of perennialist pedagogy continues at Chicago today.

Yale University introduced Hutchins to the liberal arts and, in turn, Hutchins (1943) advances the idea, "It must follow that if we want to educate our students for freedom, we must educate them in the liberal arts and in the great books" (p. 15). Although Hutchins did not fully make this distinction until his appointment as president of the University of Chicago, he came to understand and advocate an undergraduate curriculum that reflected his newly realized educational thought. With a familial mandate to contribute to society in meaningful ways, it is understandable and even expected that Hutchins would seek to affect change during his service as president of the University of Chicago. Like Mays, Hutchins is interested in the social uses of education and did not have to look far to find inspiration. Influences from childhood serve as a blueprint for how Hutchins

MAYS, THE DISCOURSE OF POTENTIAL, AND MOREHOUSE COLLEGE

> *There is an air of expectancy at Morehouse College. It is expected that the student who enters here will do well. It is also expected that once a man bears the insignia of a Morehouse graduate he will do exceptionally well. We expect nothing less...*
> —Benjamin Elijah Mays, *The Charge to the Graduating Class of 1961*

Like many of its HBCU counterparts, Morehouse College has experienced multiple name changes and an ever-evolving educational mission since its founding in 1867 as The Augusta Institute. Originally, the institution sought to "provide the sons of former slaves—and indeed the freed slaves themselves—with an education based on the dignity of man and the sacredness of the human personality..." (Jones, 1957, p. 231). After relocating to its present location in the Atlanta University Center, amendments to the institute's charter were secured that granted full college status and a name change to Atlanta Baptist College. In 1906, long-time faculty member John Hope would become the institution's fourth president and first Black appointed to the office. Hope was also regarded by Benjamin Mays as an enduring mentor who gave him his first teaching position at Morehouse (Carter, 1998; Mays, 1971; Rovaris, 2004). According to Giles (2006), Hope helped to solidify Morehouse College as the social and educational center of Black male leadership during his administration. Hope served until his appointment as president of Atlanta University in 1929.

In 1940, Mays left his post as the Dean of Howard University's School of Religion to accept the appointment as the sixth president of Morehouse College (Mays, 1971). The path to Morehouse College was paved with faith, preparation, and perseverance. As president of a private, liberal arts college, Mays was committed to the unique role higher education played in uplifting the race as part of the Black experience in America. Mays recognized the role the Negro liberal arts college played in training its graduates to pursue professions such as teaching, theology, business, medicine, law, and science, in spite of strained race relations in the United States. Mays (1971) reflects,

> I believe in black colleges, For twenty-seven years I was president of one where the student body was almost one hundred percent black and where the faculty and board of trustees were racially mixed. But I do not believe in a black college or university if this means that all students, all faculty and staff member, the student body, and all financial support must be black.... Nor do I

believe that the black man's educational salvation lies in weakening black colleges by draining black scholars and students away from them to attend white colleges—colleges which for the most part are not free of racism. (316–318)

Mays (1971), further articulates the student outcomes and post-graduate placement of Morehouse Men serving as agents of change and noteworthy contributors to the educational, professional, social, civic development, and growth of the their fellow countrymen. Mays believes educating the Negro and the fulfillment of its purpose are achieved through an interracial alliance. Thus, education in service to one's fellow man results in a benefit to the collective common good. Mays (1971) challenges the Negro to reject the limitations previously set before them and recognize "every able Negro mind" should have the opportunity to be "trained" (p. 222) in a college or university setting. To this end, Mays confronts the discriminatory practices of White America that assigns a "discourse of deficit" (Powell, 1997, p. 10) to the entire Negro race symbolizes how one can "deal with children as individuals coming to school with special abilities, talents and unique conceptions" (p. 222). According to Carson (1994), Mays "often used his Tuesday morning talks to the student body as occasions to express his commitment to social gospel and to challenge Morehouse students to struggle against segregation rather than to accommodate to it" (p. 163). Mays' example was far-reaching and it can be argued he affected change among virtually every Morehouse Men he cultivated.

In spite of a racialized society, Mays posits educational capital in its Black male citizens so they could compete with White America and contribute to mankind at the highest levels.

HUTCHINS, THE GREAT BOOKS, AND THE UNIVERSITY OF CHICAGO

The three worst words in education are 'character,' 'personality' and 'facts.' Facts are the core of an anti-intellectual curriculum. Personality is the qualification we look for in an anti-intellectual teacher. Character is what we expect to produce in the student by the combination of a teacher of personality and curriculum of facts.

—Robert Maynard Hutchins, *No Friendly Voice*

Upon his appointment as president of the University of Chicago, the "social crisis of the Depression led Hutchins to question the efficacy of the social sciences to solve social problems" (Dzuback, 1990, p. 58). Though the appointment of Hutchins as president of Chicago represented "a historical as well as collegial continuity for the university," the new leader faced a dilemma in deciding how to approach the institution's needs for further expansion so that the vision of William Rainey Harper might be realized (Dzuback, 1991, p. 76).

The University of Chicago was founded in 1890 by the American Baptist Education Society (ABES) and led by William Rainey Harper, a Hebrew scholar and professor at the Baptist Union Theological Seminary in Chicago who earned his PhD when he was 18 years old (Dzuback, 1991). The University of Chicago opened its doors in 1892 and the Harper administration expanded the institutional mission over the next 14 years until his death in 1906. Dzuback (1991) further notes Harper conceived leadership of a university that included an undergraduate college. This structure aligned with his new approach to undergraduate education to include a general curriculum in which students followed programs initially offered only by the College of Arts, College of Literature and Philosophy, and College of Science. Curricular revisions during the Harper years resulted in "a research culture" that "allowed faculty members who could raise money for their projects to pursue the pioneering work that built the university's departments and that gradually increased the number of courses offered to all students in the university" (p. 76).

Robert Maynard Hutchins was named the fifth president of the University of Chicago in 1929. Dzuback (1990), describes Hutchins' first years as president as representative of a "critical juncture in his life," (p. 57) as Hutchins faced significant decisions regarding the direction of the institutional mission relating to undergraduate education. According to Dzuback (1991), "Hutchins' advocacy of the great books and his disaffection with the social sciences as the central disciplines of the curriculum make sense, in light of the pressing demands he faced and his own educational and intellectual needs" (p. 107). According to Hutchins (1936),

> Clearly, the object of general education is the training of the mind....Or, to put it another way, the object of general education is to produce intelligent citizens....Facts, data, and information should be used to exemplify and enforce principles upon which intelligent action must rest....A program of general education resulting in trained minds will facilitate social change and make it more intelligent....A program of general education which is based on ideas, which leads the student to understand the nature and schemes of history, to grasp the principles of science, to comprehend the fine arts and literature, and to which philosophy contributes intelligibility at every stage, is the kind of program that we must now construct. It may seem, at first glance, remote from real life, from the facts, and from the social order. On the contrary, if we can construct it, we shall find that it may give us at last a land fit to be free. (pp. 130–131)

Hutchins had begun to set forth the curricular plan Harper once envisioned. Though he had not yet arranged the curriculum content, "his goal was to create a viable, intellectual coherent four-year liberal arts college within a university primarily devoted to research and scholarship" (Dzuback, 1991, p. 109). Mortimer Adler, an educator and philosopher with a command of the classics, helped Hutchins "construct an educational philosophy.... Adler was there when he needed him.... When Hutchins turned the college program in 1930, Adler was a faculty member serving on the curriculum committee and steering the discussion in ways the president could not" (pp. 107–108). The influence Adler had on Hutchins is noteworthy, as Hutchins came to rely on him for the creation of the general education curriculum.

Hutchins' leadership of Chicago can be described as legendary and his indelible mark on the modern American research university, unprecedented. Having succeeded in fulfilling the vision of William Rainey Harper, so too, had Hutchins fulfilled his educational and institutional creation of higher learning, clearly distinguished from his alma mater.

CONCLUSION AND IMPLICATIONS

The ideals of the social gospel movement undoubtedly influenced the institutional leadership of Benjamin Elijah Mays and Robert Maynard Hutchins. Both were thoughtful and intentional about their quest for educational excellence in service to humankind. The social objectives of higher learning, particularly as it relates to social reform, intersect with the competing interests of the institutional and instructional missions. In the modern university, this set of circumstances may impede the actualization of organizational objectives to reach beyond that of governance and pedagogy and may have an effect on the nature of social transformation leadership. Accordingly, this idea may be especially arduous for PWIs, as budget cuts, emerging populations, and mandates for the development of competencies around difference may be met with resistance from status quo assumptions and practices traditionally accepted within their organizational boundaries.

The ideals of the Social Gospel Movement and the Wisconsin Idea of 1912 complimented the educational thought of Mays and Hutchins, and their quest for the social usefulness and purpose of the college and university. Both leaders made every attempt to assemble their respective institution as a laboratory for the pursuit of knowledge, humanity, civility, personhood, and morality. Albeit, Mays' and Hutchins' respective methodologies for advancing their agendas emerged as an outgrowth of essentialist and perennialist pedagogy, they share a commitment to a just society in which all citizens subscribe to keeping their brother.

Hutchins represents a macro perspective of society in which the ideal of democracy is the end goal—justice for all in an idyllic existence, requiring the work of all men, races, ethnicities, religions, and so forth. On the other hand, Mays represents a micro, or more concentrated perspective in which the advancement of his race is priority. Although the scope of Mays' ideal differs from Hutchins', it, too, calls for an equally unprecedented social system in which all men are viewed as being equally created. One could argue the proposition of achieving their respective visions for moral and social salvation via higher education seems improbable. Perhaps there is truth to this proposition, as the ideal of democracy where there exists no equity, access, and inclusion in the American educational system, poses significant challenges. This scenario might have caused Hutchins to question his own privilege and access to education and what that means in a democratic society in which others do not enjoy the same dispensation. The scenario is equally puzzling for Mays, who desired to achieve a moral citizenry in the midst of blatant inequality and unbridled violence. Despite the obstacles faced, each left an unparalleled legacy as institutional leaders. In this way, collaborative leadership takes on a moralistic necessity to advance the lives of those following a visionary leader. Locke and Schweiger (1979) argue such an "altruism implies the sacrifice of individuality and freedom in an effort to make everyone equal" (p. 271) and Mays and Hutchins sacrificed selfish needs in exchange for the advancement of the needs of others. Ultimately, without an examination of what may [historically] be perceived as divergent institutional and curricular missions, this study reveals numerous unanticipated parallels between Mays and Hutchins and, thus, HBCUs and PWIs.

Analyses such as these can be useful in the academy's understanding of the historical, social, political, economic, and educational relevance of HBCUs. Their institutional distinction, mission, and the distinctive nature of their leaders as being collaborative are an outgrowth of their history, affiliation, characteristics, focus, governance, and geographic location (Barr, Desler, & Associates, 2000). In the case of Benjamin Mays, his institutional leadership was not only tied to the founding of Morehouse College and its mission to educate and develop Black males as leaders, but also the ideals of public service and social justice. Though little research has examined the institutional leadership of HBCUs, Morehouse College and others share similar narratives and frameworks for educational outcomes. While coursework and research in graduate programs in study of higher education focus primarily on traditional, four-year, majority institutions, developing an understanding of the purpose and collaborative leadership of Black colleges will give way to comparative analyses with their majority counterparts. Additionally, this scope of research will broaden the range of research questions, institutional leadership models, and educational influences that emerge from examinations between what has been viewed as very dissimilar institution types.

REFERENCES

Baer, H. A., & Singer, M. (1992). *African-American religion in the Twentieth Century: Varieties of protest and accommodation.* Knoxville: The University of Tennessee Press.

Bagley, W. C. (1922). *Educational values.* New York: The Macmillan Company.

Barr, M. J., Desler, M. K., & Associates. (2000). *The handbook of student affairs administration* (2nd ed.). San Francisco: Jossey-Bass.

Bensimon, E. M., & Neumann, A. (1993). *Redesigning collegiate leadership: Teams and teamwork in higher education.* Baltimore, MD: Johns Hopkins Press.

Carson, C. (1994). Martin Luther King, Jr. and the African-American social gospel. In P. E. Johnson (Ed.), *African-American Christianity: Essays in history* (pp. 159–177). Berkeley, CA: University of California Press.

Carter, L. E. (Ed.). (1998). *Walking integrity: Benjamin Elijah Mays, mentor to Martin Luther King Jr.* Georgia: Mercer University Press.

Chambers, F. (1972). Histories of Black colleges and universities. *The Journal of Negro History 57,* 270–275.

The University of Chicago (2011). *The Core.* Retrieved from https://collegeadmissions.uchicago.edu/pdfs/thecore.pdf

Dzuback, M. A. (1990). Hutchins, Adler, and the University of Chicago: A critical juncture. *The American Journal of Education 99,* 57–76.

Dzuback, M. A. (1991). *Robert M. Hutchins: Portrait of an educator.* Chicago, IL: The University of Chicago Press.

Giles, M. S. (2006). Howard Thurman: The making of a Morehouse man. 1913–1923. *The Journal of Educational Foundations 20*(1/2), 105–122.

Hirsch, E. D. (2009). *The making of Americans: Democracy and our schools.* New Haven, Connecticut: Yale University Press.

Hoeveler, J. D. Jr. (1976). The university and the social gospel: The intellectual origins of the 'Wisconsin Idea.' *The Wisconsin Magazine of History 59,* 282–298.

Hoeveler, J. D. Jr. (1983). The university and the social gospel: The intellectual origins of the 'Wisconsin Idea.' In R. M. Aderman (Ed.), *The quest for social justice: The Morris Fromkin memorial lectures 1970–1980* (pp. 185–207). Madison, WI: University of Wisconsin Press.

Hutchins, R. M. (1936). *No friendly voice.* Chicago, IL: The University of Chicago Press.

Hutchins, R. M. (1943). *Education for freedom.* Baton Rouge, LA: Louisiana State University Press.

Hutchins, R. M. (1953a). *The conflict in education in a democratic society.* New York, NY: Harper Brothers.

Hutchins, R. M. (1953b). *The university of utopia.* Chicago, IL: The University of Chicago Press.

Hutchins, R. M. (1956). *Some observations on American education.* Cambridge: The Syndics of the Cambridge University Press.

Jones, E. A. (1957). Morehouse College in business ninety years—building men. *The Phylon Quarterly 18,* 231–245.

Lewison, B. S. K. (1998). Mays's educational philosophy. In L. E. Carter (Ed.), *Walking integrity: Benjamin Elijah Mays, mentor to Martin Luther King Jr.* (pp. 215–231). Georgia: Mercer University Press.

Locke, E. A., & Schweiger, D. M. (1979). Participation in decision-making: One more look. *Research in organizational behavior, 1,* 265–339.

Mays, B. E. (1969). *A Negro's God as reflected in his literature.* New York, NY: Atheneum.

Mays, B. E. (1964). *Seeking to be a Christian in race relations.* New York, NY: Friendship Press.

Mays, B. E. (1971). *Born to rebel.* New York, NY: Charles Scribner's Sons.

Myrdal, G., Sterner, R., & Rose, A. (1944). *An American dilemma: The Negro problem and modern democracy.* New York, NY: Harper and Brothers.

Powell, L. C. (1997). The achievement (k)not: Whiteness and 'Black underachievement. In Fine, L. Weis, L. Powell, & M. L. Wong (Eds.), *Off White: Readings on race, power and society,* (pp. 3–12). New York, NY: Routledge.

Rovaris, D. J. (2004). *Mays and Morehouse: How Benjamin Elijah Mays developed Morehouse College, 1940–1967.* Maryland: Beckham House Publishers.

Ryan, K., & Cooper, J. M. (2000). *Those who can, teach.* Boston: Houghton Mifflin.

Taba, H. (1962). *Curriculum development: Theory and practice.* New York, NY: Harcourt, Brace & World, Inc.

White, R. C. Jr., & Hopkins, C. H. (1976). *The social gospel: Religion and reform in America.* Philadelphia, PA: Temple University Press.

CHAPTER 2

MARY McLEOD BETHUNE

The Significance of Rhetorical Action in the Development of a Black College Leader

Vickie L. Suggs

INTRODUCTION

The pre- to post-World War II era continued to be a period of racial consciousness and uplift for Black Americans. To this end, there were many avenues through which the acquisition of Black consciousness was achieved during the first half of the twentieth century. Much like her contemporaries, Bethune advanced educational thought rooted in four central themes: (a) demand for applied learning; (b) recognition of the importance of social standpoint and cultural identity scholarship; (c) a critical epistemology that both supported and resisted mainstream American ideals; and (d) moral existentialism grounded in a sense of communal responsibility (Evans, 2007, p. 8). In many ways, rhetoric endowed race leaders, including Black college leaders, with a venue in which to advance their agenda and reach audiences of all races. As a rhetorician, Bethune is able to make meaning of the social spaces she constructed, occupied, and within which she interacted. Goodsell (1988) references George Herbert Mead's school of thought in which "symbolic interactionism" (p. 26) results when "the individual does not act in response to inner drives alone but also in relation to the role and the place that he views himself as occupying (p. 26). One could argue Bethune had to expand the scope of her own motivations in order to make meaning of her greater role and the societal space in which she sought to occupy and purpose on behalf of her race. This ideal of finding multiple meanings for her desired brand of servant leadership informs the way in which Bethune negotiates a social space for her life's calling to remedy the broken spheres of race relations, education, economics, and social justice in the American South. The methodology employed to penetrate and affect change within these spheres—narrative language and thought or rhetoric—ultimately defines their social meaning. Of the three types of rhetoric, "judicial or forensic; deliberative; and demonstrative," (Dixon, 1971, pp. 22–23) Black college leaders such as Bethune employed deliberative oratory, as it addresses a particular popular or political policy.

In this essay, I examine the social positioning of selected speeches delivered by Bethune as well as the role her collective body of rhetoric played in the advancement of Black Americans during the early to mid-1900s. The guiding question that informs the research is:

How did the movement of deliberative rhetoric become an integral part of the public domain for race leaders during the first half of the twentieth century?

Because education was a vehicle through which collective advancement could be achieved, the mission of the Black college, in particular, was to create leaders in all fields of study who would exercise their individual agency on behalf of their race (Brown & Davis 2001; Drewry & Doermann, 2003; Du Bois; 1932, Garibaldi, 1984; Gasman, 2006; Mays, 1971; Suggs, 2009). By identifying and occupying a social space in which they could speak, Black college leaders, Bethune among them, recognized the opportunity to give voice to those whose voice had been repressed and whose social space had yet to be identified, constructed, and defined.

CONCEPTUAL FRAMEWORK

The concept of cooperative and collaborative rather than antagonistic modes of interaction and engagement is a fitting lens through which to examine the rhetorical action of Mary McLeod Bethune and her quest to identify and make meaning of a social space for herself and the Negro race during her lifetime. Arguably, Bethune embodies what it means to be a critical rhetorician, as she offers "not a detached and impersonal critique, but a critique focused on some current, local contingency" (Clark, 1996, p. 111). Bethune can further be characterized as a critical servant due to her determination to focus on the "consequences of being served" so that "... all of those persons who are touched by the institution are served and, *while being served*, they grow as persons; they become healthier, wiser, freer, more autonomous, more likely themselves to become servants" (Greenleaf, 1979, pp. 77–78).

As a critical rhetorician and servant, Bethune was tapped for roles in the administration of presidents Coolidge to Roosevelt and was instrumental in promoting a dialogue among those in political power and the Negro community (McCluskey & Smith, 1999). In this capacity she was able to affect societal transformation on behalf of the voiceless at a level no other African American had penetrated. Bethune also successfully overcame resistance in politics and public life denied Negro women for centuries. One could conclude a comparison existed between Bethune and Jane Addams, rhetorician, co-founder of Hull-House, the first American woman to receive the Nobel Peace Prize, and a charter member of the NAACP, among other accomplishments (Danisch, 2007). According to Danisch, "What makes Addams remarkable as a pragmatist and a rhetorician is her ability to develop a distinct perspective on the complexity of deliberation in a modern, large-scale democracy and her ability to practice pragmatism successfully given her own circumstances" (p. 66). Like Addams, Bethune, did not employ "agonistic rhetoric," but rather "a cooperative rhetoric that sought to bring individuals together ... to establish a 'social democracy' through which many people could participate in the articulation of a collective voice" (p. 66). Bethune's negotiation of the social space in which she occupied allowed her to view issues through a collective lens for the advancement of her race, in particular. To be sure, Bethune, like Addams, positions her speech style so that it "suggests a community-centered rhetoric tested by its consequences" (p. 66). To this end, Bethune's life experiences afford her the wisdom to distinguish intended and unintended consequences related to the ideals of democracy. Her speech-making routinely addresses misguided practices of democracy and this becomes a filter through which her rhetorical action is situated socially. As a result, Bethune finds agency in rhetorical action and relies upon speech-making as an instrument of understanding and conciliation—much like she did as a young girl attending Scotia Seminary for Negro Girls. It is during this time in her life the doctrines of Christianity crystallize and her calling as a critical servant develops. In doing so, Bethune embodies an ideology proposed by Emile Durkheim that situates civic space and religious thought as "sacred versus profane" (as cited in Goodsell, 1988, p. 27). According to Goodsell,

> Dividing the world into these two realms is *the* distinctive feature of all religious thought, said Durkheim, regardless of church doctrine or cultural setting. The two spheres are radically different both in religious belief and in ritual action, and for both realms the essential point is that the preciously sacred must be protected from the contaminated profane. Hence, sharp interdiction between the two worlds is essential. (p. 27)

Bethune's religious thought lends itself to an understanding of the sacred nature of humanity, democracy, and Christian love. It is these insightful qualities that develop Bethune's resolve in her role as educator, activist, humanitarian, and race leader. Further, it is her connection and commitment to religious doctrine that perfect Bethune's innate ability to protect what is sacred (humanity and democracy) from what is profane (discrimination, hatred, and injustice). It was upon graduation from Scotia Seminary that Bethune was introduced to the Social Gospel ideology that "human miseries resulted from systemic problems in society and not from the personal failings of the individual" (McCluskey & Smith, 1999, p. 43). In due course, an authentic commitment to social justice emerges and persists throughout her lifetime.

METHODOLOGY

In addition to rising Black consciousness, the author discusses the meaning of access through the lens of rhetorical criticism, using primary resources of two selected speech transcripts and one radio address. According to Hendrix and Polisky (1968), rhetorical criticism is the "act of rendering analytical, interpretive and evaluative judgments about specific instances of informative and persuasive discourse—spoken and written" (p. iii). Document analysis is used to investigate common themes that emerge in Bethune's speech-making. This form of inquiry allows the researcher to interpret the meaning of the text and what it is saying about "norms or rules with which the interviewee is operating, or discourses by which they are influenced, or something about how discourses are constituted, or as indicating some kind of causal mechanism in social action" (Mason, 1996, p. 109). This form of analysis brings into focus the reasons why and the conditions under which the speeches were prepared as well as their implications on education, society, politics, and culture. Additionally, the analysis allows the researcher to uncover the functionality of a social space being occupied as part of the speech setting. According to Atkinson and Coffey (2004), "... texts are constructed according to conventions that are themselves part of a documentary reality. Hence, rather than ask whether an account is true, or whether it can be used as 'valid' evidence about a setting, it is more fruitful to ask ourselves questions about the form and function of texts themselves" (p. 73).

In the case of Bethune, her rhetoric is autobiographical and, therefore, constructed as part of that "documentary reality" (Atkinson and Coffey, 2004, p. 73). This, too, is likely the case for other Black college leaders and, thus, provides insight into the origins of narrative language and thought as it relates to race relations, how the Negro constructs identity, negotiates, and operationalizes leadership roles during the early to mid-1900s. According to Hendrix and Polisky (1968), analysis of the "rhetorical setting" in which the speech or text is delivered or written will likely consider one of more of the following factors:

1. The historical milieu of the speech
2. The occasion of the speech
3. The physical setting of the speech
4. The audience of the speech. (p. 63)

Because race leaders identify and occupy a social space through which to affect change, the four factors referenced become usable resources for Bethune as she makes meaning of her own speech text, occasion, venue, and audience. These factors serve to inform the aggravating and mitigating events which lead to an act of spoken or written discourse, thus, providing a window into the circumstances that bring together Bethune and her varied audiences.

Social history is also employed as methodology for the research, as it focuses on the causes of a movement that allow the researcher to "create a dialogue between theory and their data, each informing the other" (Kaestle, 1992, p. 363). As it related to this particular study, social history informs the proliferation of rhetoric as part the development of Black college leaders during the period of examination. Biography is also used as a form of inquiry. Finkelstein (1998) argues biographical study reveals to the researcher, "... the ideological, economic, political, social and cultural crucibles within which a person develops new ways of knowing, thinking, acting, and being" (p. 47). In this way, lived experiences of Black college leaders such as Bethune bring into focus institutional significance and sustainability as well as the ways in which an individual can employ speech-making to affect educational, social, political, and cultural understanding and change.

THE BLACK COLLEGE AS A SOCIAL SPACE

In the wake of the Civil War, a concentration of more than 200 HBCUs was founded by "philanthropic associations, churches, local communities, missionaries, and private donors" in addition to state government funding (Brown & Davis, 2001, p. 33). Brown and Davis maintain,

> The first Morrill Act of 1862 provided federal support for state education, particularly in agriculture, education, and military sciences. Supplementary public support came with the passage of the Second Morrill Act of 1890 which mandated that those funds be extended to institutions that enrolled African Americans. The post-war era of reconstruction formed a unique social contract with the American citizenry.... All of these primarily government initiated, post-war activities focus on reconciling the tattered relation between America and the descendants of Africa. Without question, the historically Black college is the tangible manifestation of America's social contract with free African Americans immediately following the Civil War. (p. 34)

Despite the idea and formation of a social contract, during the period from Reconstruction to the Great Depression "black higher education in the South existed essentially through a system of private liberal arts colleges" (Anderson, 1988, p. 238). According to Anderson, this system of privately owned institutions as "sole promoters" for educating Blacks in the southern states "persisted into the late 1920s" (p. 238). Nonetheless, movement in enrollment trends did occur. Anderson cites the academic year 1926–1927 as having "13,860 black college students in American, and approximately 75%...enrolled in private colleges," (p. 238) and further notes that "by the mid-1930s ... black college students in public institutions accounted for 43% of the total black enrollment" (pp. 238–239). This shift in enrollment to include both public and private Black colleges began to solidify their collective mission and allowed Black college leaders to frame their institutional founding and educational aims in ways that included rhetorical action as a method in which to realize leadership through social change.

In the case of Bethune, it was during this period that the Daytona Educational and Industrial Training School for Negro Girls was founded and later became Bethune-Cookman College. As a Black college leader, she was remarkably strategic in her decision to focus on Florida as the location in which to provide higher education for Black women. In Bethune's estimation,

> "I think the educational situation of Florida and possibly the lower east coast is very vague. I went there because I was looking for a hard place to work.... So, I selected Daytona Beach, town where very conservative people lived and where James M. Gamble (of the Procter and Gamble Company of Cincinnati); Thomas White (of the White Sewing Machine Company of Cleveland); and other fine people [owned homes]. A fine club of women in that section formed a philanthropic group, [the] Palmetto Club, through whom I thought approaches could be made. (as cited in McCluskey & Smith, 1999, p. 47)

Accepting the challenges and potential opportunities of erecting an institution in Florida, Bethune models her visionary persona and commitment advancing the four central themes of her educational thought.

Much can be made of Bethune's influence within the educational sphere. Bethune is, indeed, industrious in her determination to secure funding for the school and uses the school as a platform to showcase the intended educational outcomes and corollary social and economic effects of educating the Negro race. Additionally, Bethune sought the counsel of Booker T. Washington, as he had become astute in appealing to White benefactors in building his school, Tuskegee Institute in Alabama (Bieze, 2008; McCluskey & Smith, 1999). Despite looking to Washington as an advisor, McClusky & Smith maintain Bethune's "domestic/science/vocational curriculum that characterized the early years of her school was modeled more on what she had experienced at Scotia than on the domestic science curriculum at Tuskegee" (p. 410). This approach reflects Bethune's independent thinking and advocacy of Black women's education which leads her to legitimate classical liberal education through tangible evidence associated with curricular design and outcomes. Bethune adopts a liberal arts curriculum and her ability to situate civic space and religious thought as sacred versus profane is also inherent to her curriculum design and philanthropic strategy for success with prospective donors. This is exampled in early letters to potential benefactors in which Bethune emphasized "the moralistic aspects of her curriculum, touting her school as a source of 'wholesome training... in the midst of ignorance and vice'" (McCluskey & Smith, 1999, p. 410). Bethune's educational thought serves as an example of how those situated on the margins of the dominant culture create a social space in which the practice of resistance to mainstream ideology emerges as an outgrowth of applied learning and knowledge of one's own cultural identity and history in order to achieve collective advancement for one's race. Throughout her lifetime, Bethune continuously embodies and articulates ideals related to social change and recognizes the education of the Negro as a form of liberation with implications for educational, societal, political, cultural, and economic transformation. She and other Black college leaders in the South like Booker T. Washington used their individual and collective agency to serve their race and bridge the racial divide that plagued the country. This relentless pursuit never wavered, despite the unsafe and, often times, deadly racial climate facing non-White American leaders whose social critique routinely called into question the very practice of American democracy.

RHETORICAL ACTION AND THE ACQUISITION OF BLACK CONSCIOUSNESS AT THE TURN OF THE TWENTIETH CENTURY

Denman (2004) chronicles, "The ancient links between rhetoric, civic life, and democracy are a part of the European heritage of rhetorical thought and practice. The history of rhetoric makes clear the teaching of rhetoric was an instrumental part of the development of that civic persona, the 'citizen-orator,' whose skills were at the service of the community" (p. 1). To be sure, at the turn of the twentieth century, Black college leaders such as Bethune, reconstituted their own access to educational, social, political, and cultural spaces so they could affect societal transformation which might then lead to the collective advancement of their race. Arguably, the commitment to the implications for their community was an integral part of agenda-setting and messaging in the development of Black college leadership. Logan (2004) advances the idea that when we look to the past for "models and uses of rhetorical education, we recognize that social change has always been partially the result of rhetorical action, oral or written arguments crafted to elicit specific responses" (p. 37). Logan further maintains, "Nineteenth-century African Americans first had to argue their entitlement to status as unenslaved human beings; thus the rhetoric of antislavery was necessary. Then blacks had to argue their rights to citizenship and to all the privileges and protections associated with it, and in response to these exigencies emerged antilynching and civil rights discourse" (p. 37). Thus, the history of slavery and denial of citizenship that entitles one to multiple social spaces, informs the aims and messaging of race leaders with respect to their mission for civil rights and equitable treatment, post-slavery. To be sure, because the origins of narrative language and thought are autobiographical, rhetoric and societal transformation have become synonymous with the Black experience in America. Accordingly, access to education, speech-making, political involvement, and scholarship related to Negro life and history help to construct and define social spaces that once were and are continuously penetrated by Black Americans in a variety of ways.

In addition to rhetorical action, the acquisition of Black consciousness through historiography is achieved in 1911 and 1915, respectively, when the Negro Society for Historical Research (NSHR) and the Association for the Study of Negro Life and History (ASNLH) were established. Founded by Arthur Alfonso Schomburg and John Edward Bruce, NSHR served as a counter-narrative to the idea that Black scholars were intellectually inferior to their White counterparts. While Schomburg is known for his personal collection of works which became known as the Schomburg Center for Research in Black Culture, New York Public Library; Bruce, a journalist and politician, "contributed to the late-nineteenth century Black history movement as a mentor, promoter[sic], bibliophile, organizer, and author of several articles and manuscripts. He ... believed that a sound understanding of African American history legitimized Black humanity, reinforced Black pride, and underpinned Black protest and civil rights struggles" (Crowder, 2004, p. 92). Similarly, Carter G. Woodson founded ASNLH as a way of recognizing the contributions and the storied history of Black Americans. The son of slaves who earned his PhD in history, Woodson "recognized the importance of slave testimony and oral history, and formulated the most fundamental perceptions about the black past" (Goggin, 1993, p. 31). Firm in her commitment to her race, Bethune held the office of president of ASNLH in addition to publishing "several important public addresses in the organization's periodical, the *Journal of Negro History*" (McCluskey & Smith, 1999, p. 6). Both organizations popularized historical analysis of the Black experience in America and served as a vehicle in the utility and professionalization in the writing of race history and cultural identity scholarship.

Miller (2005) examines a third way in which the acquisition of Black consciousness is achieved. Intervarsity debate teams were an aspect of Black education born out of the mastery of skills required in English and dramatic arts. Unlike narrative language and thought, debate represented persuasive language and thought. English teachers and drama coaches "saw their efforts as a means of subverting racial stereotypes about Negro inferiority and to counter the prevailing representations of black people in the United States" (p. 154). Ultimately, "Race leaders knew that the tactics of formal debate played into a broader civil rights strategy: the podium was the classroom for future lawyers. Prophetically, intervarsity debate was one of the first places where the color line was breached during the interwar years (p. 155).

As a cultural forum,

> Intercollegiate debate stood out from other activities.... Strictly bound by time limits and longstanding rules of argumentation and rebuttal, this brand of disquisition ultimately showcased the talents of African American collegians in terms of discipline and logic as well as oratorical skill. (p. 155)

As an educational forum, the implications of intervarsity debate on race relations during the early 1900s were many, as the opportunity to engage in interracial debates presented a welcomed proposition for Black and White debate teams. Exposure to the art of debating perpetuated a generation of Black leaders, activists, and critical rhetoricians and servants. To this end, Black college leaders were in a position to observe and evaluate the social order of the pre- to post-war era and strategize curricular and practical skills that would entrée the next generation to multiple social spaces in which they could gain access and—in turn—give voice to the voiceless of their own generation. Coupled with the art of discourse, composition, and dramatic arts, Bethune and other Black college leaders operationalize debate teams and the science of argumentation to penetrate and transform race relations in the American South.

READING, WRITING, AND RHETORICAL ACTION

The research identifies an arrangement of factors in which the acquisition of Black consciousness is achieved: Black education, the study of race history, and rhetorical action. Du Bois (1932) discusses his views of the origins and mission of Black education in his article titled, *Education and Work*, theorizing,

> The South, and more especially the Negro, needed and must have trained and educated leadership if civilization was to survive. More than most, here was land and people who needed to learn the meaning of life. They needed the preparation of gifted persons for the profession of teaching, and for other professions which would in time grow. (p. 61)

From this ideal, Suggs (2009) concludes "the purpose of education is civic in its origins and, thus, designed to create a population of skilled, trustworthy, law-abiding community members at individual, group, and institutional levels" (p. 43). This educational thought is much like the principles of rhetorical action, namely, rhetoric for social change. As such, the use of rhetoric by race leaders is essential to racial uplift. According to Logan (2004), there existed a "highly motivated first generation of black rhetorical activists" who "began the transition among African Americans from language use for self-improvement to rhetorical education for action" (p. 45).

As an example of rhetorical action on the part of the next and future generations, Black colleges established debate teams and schools of dramatic arts to groom future race leaders beyond language usage to a skillful command of argumentation and public speaking. Though the activity experienced less popularity by the late 1940s, debate proved an effective educational tool used to prepare Black youth for professions best suited to advance the race, including teaching, law, ministry, and other public service and leadership roles (Bell, 2007). According to Bell (2007), Hobart Jarrett, a member of the Wiley debate team recalls, "a time when white colleges thought that debating against a Negro institution was mental dissipation, but that view has passed forever. Negro teams have shown that they were as capable as their white opponents despite the library handicaps that limit research" (para. 27). Given the fact argumentation is the "procedure by which the speaker demonstrates the probable truth...by means of reasons and supporting materials," (Hendrix & Polisky, 1968, p. 107) preparing for a debate with little access to the proper resources makes Jarrett's claims of triumph over privileged debate teams all the more remarkable. To this end, Suggs (2009) concludes the "indoctrination of Black youth [into] the science of argumentation and deductive reasoning enabled a generation of Black leaders and activists working to change the racial status quo in America" (p. 47). Suggs goes on to describe debate as a form of "civic engagement and political discourse aligned with the rising Black consciousness present during the pre- to post-World War II era" (p. 47). Drawing from her own experiences with democracy, equity, and social justice, Bethune is able to observe, evaluate, and offer a social critique of the American South while situating higher education for the Negro as the missionary undertaking to which she was called.

CRITICAL SERVICE, SPEECH-MAKING EXCERPTS AND ANALYSIS

Through her educational thought, Bethune becomes a symbol of Black consciousness, continually seeking ways in which discourse might somehow annul discriminatory social, educational, political, cultural, and economic practices imposed upon her race. Though a primary sphere of activism for Bethune is education, rhetoric also creates a social space in which she can address enduring social inequities and serve as an intermediary on the state of race relations in American culture.

At a very early age Bethune came to understand the obstacles she had to overcome in order to enjoy privileges comparable to those extended to her White counterparts. Because her personhood and citizenship was inextricably linked to the color of her skin, Bethune set out to advocate for the societal, educational, political, cultural, and economic rights of those who were routinely disenfranchised. In this way, construction of knowledge becomes an outgrowth of rhetorical action which distinguishes the primary audience—consisting of those in support of racial equality, from the secondary audience—consisting of those opposed to this ideal. For the purposes of this study, the author suggests Black Americans represent the primary or "rhetorical audience" (Tindale, 2004, p. 182) to whom Bethune speaks, while White Americans represent the secondary or "universal audience" (p. 183) with whom she wishes to engage and persuade. The distinction between the two is that collaboration is foundational for rhetorical audience engagement while reasoning is employed when engaging a universal audience. Thus, Bethune could assume some degree of alliance as it relates to the Black Americans and their world-view as second-class citizens of a broken democracy. As the rhetorical audience, Negro citizens are invited to experience the argumentation and "can become a collaborator in it" (p. 182). The ideal of collaboration echoes the nature of and need for the Negro to galvanize around efforts to achieve racial uplift and collective advancement amid strained race relations. Further, the rhetorical audience is empowered by the validity of the discourse and, therefore, challenged to co-labor alongside the rhetorician in seeking remedies for the stated problem. Tindale (2004) finds meaning in Gorgias' speech about Helen as part of Plato's dialogues in which he argues "through the 'agency of words' the soul can experience the sufferings of others as they are relayed to it" (as cited in Tindale, 2004, p. 47). All of these ideas are seemingly at work as Bethune seeks ways to achieve collaboration by tapping into the perceived values of Black Americans and their attitude toward her as the speaker. Conversely, her approach to the secondary or universal audience of White Americans and their world-view and perceived values differs, as these types of audiences are described as "repositories of reason, sources for what is reasonable" (p. 184). Tindale (2004) maintains the importance of recognizing the worth of views that may oppose our own so that we move beyond a narrow, self-serving perspective when engaging in a particular discourse. This approach to reasoning or convincing the White audience of the stated problem is consistent with that of a dominant culture being confronted with their own privilege and how that privilege denies others, who do not belong to the dominant culture, of basic human rights (Johnson, 2006). In this way, "the principle of reason within us—which is not always activated, but arises on the occasions when this recognition operates—is what we share over and above the particularities that distinguish us" (Tindale, 2004, p. 184). To be sure, Bethune, as critical rhetorician, employs the previously mentioned idea of symbolic interactionism as a means through which to reach a level of consensus with sympathetic Whites willing to endorse the social, educational, and political advancement of Blacks via historically Black colleges and direct participation in political initiatives and agendas. The pathway to access and inclusion forged by Bethune in her personal life, parallels the journey she wishes to shepherd for her people through her professional endeavors.

Bethune's commitment to serve is an outgrowth of her religious upbringing and desire to perform any given task or interact with others in the spirit of Christian love. She finds joy in service to others and personifies critical service and its principles of selfless agency. Clark (1996) examines the critical servant as it relates to critical rhetoric and maintains,

> The agency of the critical servant is obtained by understanding the agent's subjectivity as a combination of the individual and the social. The rhetor is not merely an object, the passive slave of the demands of the community, a flatterer. Nor is the rhetor an entirely autonomous critic or subject: a discrete, self-sanctioning, detached observer who imposes a self-determined good on the community. Instead, the critic works with community givens, but also with

possibilities entailed in the history of the community. By combining community history, critical possibilities, and rhetorical performance, the critic strives to arrive at a contingent good. Simultaneously, the servant acts to open possibilities within the community by throwing the self into the conditions already set in the community's history. When the critic and servant are combined in constant interplay, the rhetor is a moral and political agent who sacrifices his or her self-interest to the community, and through this loss of self gains knowledge and power. (p. 117)

In this way, Bethune the critical servant demonstrates the servant leadership necessary to achieve the collective advancement of Black Americans while simultaneously legitimizing her own profile as a race leader. It is during this period Bethune emerges as a leading authority on societal transformation and Clark's (1996) assertion that,

> Reliance on the community means that the critic is bonded to the history of the community.... By initiating a transactional interaction between past and present, the critic calls into question the good endorsed in the present as much as the good of the past. The critic offers a judgment on the past and, as such, draws on the history of the community for the good. Simultaneously, the servant offers a judgment for the future, proposing a course of action and change for the community that the critical servant serves. (pp. 118–119)

An example of rhetorical action in response to the educational, political, economic, and social order present during the pre- to post-war era is Bethune's September 9, 1935 address delivered to the Association for the Study of Negro Life and History (ASNLH) in Chicago. This address was delivered on the occasion of the celebration of the twentieth anniversary of the Association. The following is the address in its entirety:

> This, I believe, is the supreme contribution of this Association to our day and generation—the discovery, the interpretation and the dissemination of truth in the field of Negro life—truth, scientifically arrived at, critically interpreted and universally disseminated. In the presence of this audience, I am filled with respect and intellectual humility.... I wish to observe, 'that the search for truth is not for timid souls. When we set out upon the search for truth we should not assume that we already know for certain what truth is or what the best way of life is; otherwise, why bother about a further search for truth? The search for truth may very well change our notion of what is good or best. The search for truth is a search for what is really true, not for what may be comfortable to believer, and so we dare not limit our search for truth by insisting that what we find in the search shall be something we should have thought good before we found it. The great thing is to learn to be unafraid of knowledge.'... One outcome of scientific research and investigation in the field of Negro life and history is knowledge. A vast portion of social knowledge and information is shrouded in tradition, is not recorded in books and magazines;

nevertheless, it exists, and extends far back into the hoary past.... The life struggles of Negro men and women have been chronicled by the Association, and their achievements emphasized.... The struggles and victories of these men and women under adverse circumstances have stirred us to activity in a way that the exploits of fictitious characters could never have done.... Who knows but that as Negro boys and girls have, through their study of accomplishments and achievements by Negro men and women, been pushed forward toward their destinies? This, then, it appears to me is one field in which the Association for the Study of Negro Life and History has made a distinct and constructive contribution to our modern Twentieth Century life—in the field of research and investigation, in the advancement of knowledge, in the accumulation of racial information and facts, in the discovery of truth as it relates primarily to the Negro and to Negro life.... Already we have an ample supply of investigators, but it appears to me that there is a shortage of readable and responsible interpreters, men and women who can effectively play the role of mediator between the trained investigator and the masses.... What are the meanings of the knowledge discovered? What are the implications of the facts brought to light? Whither do they lead? What is their significance? Of what value are they? What is their place in our very complex social and economic order? What use can be made of them in assisting initially, ill-adapted individuals to harmonious and beneficial adjustment? These are questions that should challenge the action and thought of our leaders. (Bethune, 1935, pp. 406–408)

Bethune sought to "influence social thought and action through public address" (Hendrix & Polisky, 1968, p. 29) and was deemed credible by her contemporaries by her life's work as an educator and activist. The rhetorical setting of the speech—which includes "the historical milieu of the speech; the occasion of the speech; the physical setting of the speech; and the audience of the speech" (p. 63)—are primary aspects examined as part of rhetorical criticism and analysis. Using the framework of scientific, critical, and universal truth-seeking, Bethune's speech addresses the significance of documenting Negro life and the Negro experience in America. She goes on to discuss the advancement, meanings, implications, significance, and value of knowledge as the outcome of scientific research and investigation as ASNLH celebrates its twentieth year of championing race history. Bethune challenges the audience to produce and identify more analysts and interpreters of the research findings so that there is a body of intermediaries situated between the trained investigators and the masses. Just as Bethune purposes herself on an individual level to give voice to the voiceless and advocate to the power structure on behalf of the common man, she implores ASNLH to do the same at the institutional level. Bethune also uses rhetoric to advance educational thought rooted in four central themes which align with the ideals proposed in her address to ASNLH: (a) demand for applied learning; (b) recognition of the importance of social standpoint and cultural identity scholarship; (c) a critical epistemology that both supported and resisted mainstream American ideals; and (d) moral existentialism grounded in a sense of communal responsibility (Evans, 2007, p. 8). Bethune's appeal to ASNLH clearly reflects the ideals of truth-seeking cultural identity scholarship, analyses, and implications. In due course, Bethune proves a lifelong defender of Negro race history and its enduring role in the efforts to acknowledge and mend the state of race relations and so that humanistic motivations overshadow rampant hatred in America.

A second example of Bethune's commitment to rhetorical action on behalf of her race as well as citizens of all races is a radio address titled, "What Does American Democracy Mean to Me?" The address aired November 23, 1939 on WNBC's, *America's Town Meeting of the Air* in New York City. The following is the address in its entirety:

> Democracy is for me, and for 12 million black Americans, a goal towards which our nation is marching. It is a dream and an ideal in whose ultimate realization we have a deep and abiding faith. For me, it is based on Christianity, in which we confidently entrust our destiny as a people. Under God's guidance in this great democracy, we are rising out of the darkness of slavery into the light of freedom. Here my race has been afforded [the] opportunity to advance from a people 80% illiterate to a people 80% literate; from abject poverty to the ownership and operation of a million farms and 750,000 homes; from total disfranchisement to participation in government; from the status of chattels to recognized contributors to the American culture. As we have been extended a measure of democracy, we have brought to the nation rich gifts. We have helped to build America with our labor, strengthened it with our faith and enriched it with our song. We have given you Paul Lawrence Dunbar, Booker T. Washington, Marian Anderson and George Washington Carver. But even these are only the first fruits of a rich harvest, which will be reaped when new and wider fields are opened to us. The democratic doors of equal opportunity have not been opened wide to Negroes. In the Deep South, Negro youth is offered only one-fifteenth of the educational opportunity of the average American child. The great masses of Negro workers are depressed and unprotected in the lowest levels of agriculture and domestic service, while the black workers in industry are barred from certain unions and generally assigned to the more laborious and poorly paid work. Their housing and living conditions are sordid and unhealthy. They live too often in terror of the lynch mob; are deprived too often of the Constitutional right of suffrage; and are humiliated too often by the denial of civil liberties. We do not believe that justice and common decency will allow these conditions to continue. Our faith in visions of fundamental change as mutual respect and understanding between our races come in the path of spiritual awakening. Certainly there have been times when we may have delayed this mutual understanding by being slow to assume a fuller share of our national responsibility because of the denial of full equality. And yet, we have always been loyal when the ideals of American democracy have been attacked. We have given

> our blood in its defense—from Crispus Attucks on Boston Commons to the battlefields of France. We have fought for the democratic principles of equality under the law, equality of opportunity, equality at the ballot box, for the guarantees of life, liberty and the pursuit of happiness. We have fought to preserve one nation, conceived in liberty and dedicated to the proposition that all men are created equal. Yes, we have fought for America with all her imperfections, not so much for what she is, but for what we know she can be. Perhaps the greatest battle is before us, the fight for a new America: fearless, free, united, morally re-armed, in which 12 million Negroes, shoulder to shoulder with their fellow Americans, will strive that this nation under God will have a new birth of freedom, and that government of the people, for the people and by the people shall not perish from the earth. This dream, this idea, this aspiration, this is what American democracy means to me. (Bethune, 1939)

According to Hendrix and Polisky (1968), speech style "has come to mean selection and manipulation of words for a desired effect.... The stylistic characteristics for which the critic should search the speech text may be generally summarized as accuracy, clarity, appropriateness, and eloquence" (p. 159). Using this criterion, Bethune demonstrates proficiency in each of these areas as she argues for the realization of a democratic nation, though the power structure of 1939 America was not ready to heed her call, entirely.

Though persuasive in nature, Bethune' speech is effective at informing listeners of the data points relevant to the Negro population, literacy, ownership of land, access to education, political participation, and equal protection during that year. Because of her use of statistical data, the listener is able to make meaning of the context in which specific information is shared. For example, the creation and purpose of ASNLH and its encouragement of scholarship in African American history serves as a measurable indication of Bethune's charge to move from the "status of chattels to recognized contributors to the American culture." Through ASNLH, NSHR, and the Black Press, race history and current events are well documented and continue to serve as a means through which awareness of the Black experience in America is raised for citizens of all races.

By and large, Bethune's argument is clear, as the listener does not encounter ambiguity in her expression of the subject. She remains direct, yet at times using symbolism and imagery of the nation "marching" toward democracy to punctuate her belief and hope that not only Black Americans care deeply about the ideals of full citizenship, but the nation as a whole. Bethune's faith in the principles of democracy is based on Christian ideology and she draws from that faith in order to envision all potential that is innate to the Negro race and can be realized. Though full access and inclusion in the American Dream had not been realized, Bethune notes a "measure of democracy" has been extended to the Negro. It is through this lens she views and aims to remedy deficits as it relates to educational, social, economic, and political equity.

In terms of appropriateness, Bethune's speech language is "appropriate to all four of the elements of the speaking situation: the speaker, the occasion, the audience, and the purpose of the subject matter of the speech itself" (Hendrix & Polisky, 1968, p. 160). As a critical rhetorician and servant, Bethune is obligated to call into question inequities that contradict the founding of this nation based on the American Creed. At the time, Bethune was not only founder of Bethune-Cookman College, she was also Vice President of the National Association for the Advancement of Colored People (NAACP). The occasion of the speech and purpose of the subject matter met the needs and requirements of discussion topics included as part of the weekly broadcast of *America's Town Meeting of the Air*, a public service project on WNBC from 1935 to 1956. Among topics discussed and debated were democracy, organized labor, the Supreme Court and the Constitution, communism, fascism, the nation's medical care system, and socialism (Dunning, 1998).

According to Hendrix and Polisky (1968), "The language of eloquence cannot be divorced from subjects that matter in the conduct of public affairs. But, given this initial vitality and significance of content, some speakers have used language which has, in and of itself, embodied unusual beauty and striking intensity" (p. 161). Bethune's speech delivery is pragmatic, controlled, deliberate, purposeful, and bold. Her voice quality not only contributes to the rhetorical effectiveness of her message, it also reveals a proud American who is sincere and committed to the ideals she consistently pronounces. Hendrix and Polisky further maintain, "Through delivery, Cicero believed, the speaker invested his ideas with meaning, significance, and power" (p. 179). Bethune embodies this persona and, it is through humanistic qualities, her speech-making positions the message not as a pointed indictment against her country, but rather a social critique to action on the part of all Americans to reverse its culture of discrimination and hate, linked directly to one's race.

CONCLUSIONS AND IMPLICATIONS

In this study, I have identified one exploratory concept in which the interrelationship between education, society, politics, and culture can be further researched: rhetorical action. Specifically, further study on Black college leaders and the significance of rhetorical action in their development can influence the way in which education, race, and institutional leadership are examined and evaluated.

The movement of deliberative rhetoric, in fact, became an integral part of the public domain for race leaders during the first half of the twentieth century, as this study examines Bethune's speech-making using the four elements of a rhetorical setting: the historical milieu of the speech; the occasion of the speech; the physical setting of the speech; and the audience of the speech (Hendrix & Polisky, 1968, p. 63). Bethune's effectiveness as a critical rhetorician and servant attributes to how each of these elements bring into focus the social, educational, political, and economic conditions during the early to mid-1900s. Suggs (2009) maintains, "Throughout history, Black leaders have used available social spaces to communicate with their masses; albeit social spaces alternative to the mainstream" (pp. 157–158). During the first half of the twentieth century, Black college leaders in the South such as Booker T. Washington, Tuskegee Institute (renamed Tuskegee University in 1985); Benjamin Elijah Mays, Morehouse College; James Edward Shepard, North Carolina College for Negroes (Renamed North Carolina Central University in 1969); and Mordecai Wyatt Johnson, Howard University were equally as committed to their race and used their position to give voice to the voiceless in an effort to uplift their race (Suggs, 2009). It is in this same tradition that contemporary Black college leaders must also identify a social space in which to occupy and speak to their masses. Social media, including blogs and other modes through which their stakeholders might be engaged, are worthy of further investigation and may prove effective strategies for a new generation of Black college leadership. Finding an arena of activism in which effective leadership can occur is an historical imperative for Black colleges—now more than ever. No matter the methodology, it is arguably a significant moment in time for Black college leaders to emerge as critical rhetoricians and collaborators so that the masses understand the continued educational consequence of historically Black colleges and universities as part of American higher education.

Though full citizenship through equality for Negroes would not be realized before her death in 1955, Bethune's appeal for increased and continued social justice on behalf of Black Americans was advanced during her lifetime, albeit in very measured amounts and at an unhurried speed. Bethune demonstrates an authentic commitment to social justice that persisted until her death. While in her 78th year of life, Bethune drafted a letter of loving anticipation and hope to her race. Bethune reflects,

> Sometimes I ask myself if I have any other legacy to leave. Truly, my worldly possessions are few. Yet, my experiences have been rich. From them, I have distilled principles and policies in which I believe firmly, for they represent the meaning of my life's work. They are the product of much sweat and sorrow. Perhaps in them there is something of value. So, as my life draws to a close, I will pass them on to Negroes everywhere in the hope that an old woman's philosophy may give them inspiration. (Bethune, 1990, p. 129)

As Bethune contemplates her life's work, one could argue she was, in fact, able to achieve all four central themes of her educational thought: demand for applied learning; relevance of cultural identity scholarship on society; a critical analysis of the acquisition and construction of knowledge; and the moral imperative civic responsibility (Evans, 2007, p. 8). Bethune's social activism and race advocacy aligned directly with these central themes—which also became common themes as part of her speech-making.

For Bethune, the agency of words provides a venue in which the collective advancement of her race could begin to be realized. Like many of her contemporaries, in the face of race prejudice throughout the American South, Bethune sought to situate herself and her message within a mainstream social space and worked tirelessly to successfully navigate the intersection between education, society, politics, and culture.

REFERENCES

Anderson, J. D. (1988). *The education of Blacks in the south, 1860–1935*. Chapel Hill, NC: The University of North Carolina Press.

Atkinson, P., & Coffey, A. (2004). Analysing documentary realities. In D. Silverman (Ed.), *Qualitative research: Theory, method and practice* (pp. 45–62). London: Sage Publications.

Bell, G. K. (2007, January). Tolson, Farmer intertwined by Wiley debate team *MarshallNewsMessenger.com*.

Bethune, M. M. (1935). The association for the study of Negro life and history: Its contribution to our modern life. *The Journal of Negro History, 20*(4), 406–10.

Bethune, M. M. (1939, November 23). What does American democracy mean to me? *America's Town Meeting of the Air*. Retrieved from http://americanradioworks.publicradio.org/features/sayitplain/mmbethune.html.

Bethune, M. M. (1990, November). My last will and testament. *Ebony Magazine, XLVI*(1) Chicago: Johnson Publishing Co.

Bieze, M. (2008). *Booker T. Washington and the art of self-representation (History of schools and schooling)*. New York: Peter Lang Publishing.

Brown, M. C., & Davis, J. E. (2001). The historically Black college as a social contract, social capital, and social equalizer. *Peabody Journal of Education, 76*, 31–49.

Clark, N. (1996). The critical servant: An isocratean contribution to critical rhetoric. *Quarterly Journal of Speech, 82*(2), 111–124.

Crowder, R. L. (2004). *John Edward Bruce: Politician, journalist, and self-trained historian of the African Diaspora*. New York, NY: New York University Press.

Danisch, R. (2007). *Pragmatism, democracy, and the necessity of rhetoric*. Columbia, SC: University of South Carolina Press.

Denman, W. N. (2004). Rhetoric, the 'citizen-orator,' and the revitalization of civic discourse in American life. In C. Glenn, M. Lyday, & W. B. Sharer (Eds.), *Rhetorical education in America* (pp. 3–17). Tuscaloosa, AL: University of Alabama Press.

Dixon, P. (1971). *Rhetoric*. London: Methuen & Co.

Drewry, H. N., & Doermann, H. (2003). *Stand and prosper: Private black colleges and their students*. New Jersey: Princeton University Press.

Du Bois, W. E. B. (1932). Education and work. *The Journal of Negro Education, 1*(1), 60–74.

Dunning, J. (1998). *On the air: The encyclopedia of old-time radio*. Oxford: Oxford University Press.

Evans, S. Y. (2007). *Black women in the ivory tower, 1850–1954: An intellectual history*. Gainesville: University Press of Florida.

Finkelstein, B. (1998). Revealing human agency: The uses of biography in the study of educational history. In C. Kridel (Ed.), *Writing educational biography: Explorations in qualitative research* (pp. 45–59). New York, NY: Garland Publishing, Inc.

Garibaldi, A. M. (1984). *Black colleges and universities: Challenges for the future*. New York, NY: Praeger.

Gasman, M. (2006). Salvaging 'academic disaster areas': The Black college response to Christopher Jencks' and David Riesman's 1967 *Harvard Educational Review* article," *Journal of Higher Education, 77*(2), 317–52.

Goodsell, C. T. (1988). *The social meaning of civic space: Studying political authority through architecture*. Lawrence, KS: University of Kansas Press.

Goggin, J. (1993). *Carter G. Woodson: A life in Black history*. Baton Rouge, LA: Louisiana State University Press.

Greenleaf, R. K. (1979). *Teacher as servant: A parable*. New York: Paulist Press.

Hendrix, J. A., & Polisky, J. B. (Eds.). (1968). *Rhetorical criticism: Methods and models*. Iowa: William. C. Brown Book Company.

Johnson, A. G. (2006). *Privilege, power, and difference* (2nd ed.). New York, NY: McGraw-Hill.

Kaestle, C. (1992). Standards of evidence in historical research: How do we know when we know? *History of Education Quarterly, 32*(3), 361–66.

Logan, S. W. (2004). 'To get an education and teach my people,' rhetoric for social change. In C. Glenn, M. Lyday, & W. B. Sharer (Eds.), *Rhetorical education in America* (pp. 36–52). Tuscaloosa, AL: University of Alabama Press.

Mason, J. (1996). *Qualitative researching*. London: SAGE Publications.

Mays, B. E. (1971). *Born to rebel: An autobiography*. New York, NY: Scribner.

McCluskey, A. T., & Smith, E. (Eds.). (1999). *Mary McLeod Bethune, Building a better world: Essays and selected documents*. Bloomington, IN: Indiana University Press.

Miller, P. B. (2005). Holding center stage: Race, pride and the extracurriculum at historically Black colleges and universities. In D. J. Libby, P. Spickard, & S. Ditto (Eds.), *Affect and power: Essays on sex, slavery, race and religion in appreciation of Winthrop D. Jordan* (pp. 141–158). Oxford, MS: University Press of Mississippi.

Suggs, V. L. (2009). *The production of political discourse: Annual radio addresses of Black college presidents during the 1930s and 1940s* (Doctoral Dissertation, Georgia State University). Retrieved from http://digitalarchive.gsu.edu/eps_diss/33/

Tindale, C. W. (2004). *Rhetorical argumentation: Principle of theory and practice*. Thousand Oaks, CA: SAGE Publications.

CHAPTER 3

JAMES EDWARD SHEPARD AND NORTH CAROLINA CENTRAL UNIVERSITY

In Service to the State

Vickie L. Suggs

INTRODUCTION

The visionary leadership of Dr. James Edward Shepard, founder and president of the National Religious Training School and Chautauqua (now North Carolina Central University-NCCU), from 1910 until his death in 1947 (NCCU, 2010a; NCCU, 2010b; Davis, 2010), is the embodiment of racial uplift and collective advancement.

A native North Carolinian, Shepard was born the eldest of 12 in Raleigh, North Carolina on November 3, 1875 to Hattie Whitted Shepard and Reverend Dr. Augustus Shepard. Shepard's parents were very active in the church and the Freedmen's Bureau (Davis, 2010; Suggs, 2009). Shepard's father, known and respected within the Durham community, graduated from Shaw University's Theological Department in 1880 and was pastor of White Rock Baptist Church located just down the road from the site where North Carolina

Historically Black College Leadership and Social Transformation, pages 43–57
Copyright © 2014 by Information Age Publishing
All rights of reproduction in any form reserved.

Central University (NCCU) would be erected in 1910 (NCCU, 2010a; NCCU, 2010b). Augustus Shepard was born in 1846 in Raleigh to Richard and Flora Shepard—both enslaved and whose owner was one-time North Carolina Governor, Charles Manly (NCCU, 2010b). Shepard was particularly close to his mother, who "received her early training at Hampton Institute in Virginia" (NCCU, 2010a, p. 4) and was a former schoolteacher who tutored him as a young boy. Mrs. Shepard shared his vision of becoming a great leader and spokesperson for his race. Mays' relationship with his mother was "one in which she maintained a strong influence on his life and education" because she was "rooted in the ministry and encouraged her son's spirituality and sense of integrity" (as cited in Suggs, 2009, p. 97). His father, who was formerly enslaved, was also instrumental in Shepard's college attendance as well as shaping his career. Shepard, like his father, was also a Baptist minister and one could make the assumption that the senior Augustus Shepard was a precursor to his son's desire to train ministers in his latter years. In many ways, Shepard followed in his father's footsteps and was skillful at positioning himself to build his own following and network of ministers—both Black and White—to help him start his training school (Davis, 2010; Suggs, 2009).

Upon graduating from Shaw University in 1894 with a Doctor of Pharmacy degree at the age of 19, he began work as a pharmacist in Danville, Virginia (Davis, 2010). Shepard married Annie Day Robinson in November 1895 after relocating to Durham to work in the "Durham Drug Company" (p. 7). He and his wife eventually welcomed the births of their daughters: Marjorie and Annie Day who graduated from Fisk University and North Carolina College, respectively. The couple relocated from North Carolina to Washington, D. C. in 1897 where Shepard worked as a Comparer of Deeds in the Office of the Recorder of Deeds with Henry P. Cheatham, who would later become United States Congressman from North Carolina. Shepard returned to North Carolina to serve as Deputy Collector of Internal Revenue in Raleigh from 1899 to1905 (Davis, 2010; NCCU, 2010b). In November 1902, Shepard was appointed as "one of two colored workers" (Executive Committee of the ISSA, 1905, p. 418) for the International Sunday School Association (ISSA) whose mission was to "promote a standardized Christian education curriculum across denominational lines" (NCCU, 2010b, p. 4). In 1905, Shepard accepted the position of Field Superintendent of Work Among Negroes for the International Sunday School Association (Davis, 2010; Suggs, 2009). In this position Shepard "traveled to several Southern states and visited many Negro ministers, churches, and Sunday-Schools.... It was at this time that he realized that if Negro ministers were to be effected [sic] spokesmen and leaders in the Negro community they must be adequately prepared both educationally and spiritually" (Davis, 2010, p. 7). He continued in this position until 1909—subsequently serving on the executive committee from 1909 to 1914 (ASALH, 1948).

Initially chartered June 28, 1909 as The National Religious Training School and Chautauqua For The Colored Race, Inc. Signatories to this enterprise were Dr. James E. Shepard, Mr. John Merrick, Mr. Charles C. Spaulding, Dr. Aaron M. Moore, Dr. Charles H. Shepard, and Mr. William G. Pearson—all of Durham, North Carolina (NCCU, 2010a). The institutional purpose stated in the charter was,

> To provide religious, industrial and literary training of the colored youth of North Carolina and other states of the United States, especially to rain men and women in the Bible and to teach practical industries such as agriculture, horticulture and domestic science and similar branches. The fundamental idea being that young men and women will be taught to work, and that religion and work go hand in hand. Also to teach any and all subjects and branches commonly taught in normal and training schools and colleges. (p. 1)

The institution has "undergone a succession of reorganizational and name changes" since its inception in 1909:

1. 1916—National Training School
2. 1923—The Durham State Normal School
3. 1925— North Carolina College for Negroes
4. 1947—North Carolina College at Durham
5. 1969—North Carolina Central University. (p. 1)

Shepard's vision for educating Blacks in the state he so loved led him to the development of an intentional pipeline through which his race could access higher education, civic engagement, and purpose around the issues relevant to their interests at the local, state, national, and international levels. This chapter examines how a Black college leader used mainstream entities to create an institution of higher education created to serve the state and race, he so loved. Shepard's commitment to improve race relations in North Carolina as well as within the entire United States informs the ways in which he built what is now North Carolina Central University. To this end, the author argues the circumstance surrounding the issue of strained race relations was optimal for social and political participation, and collaboration among all races.

PRELUDE TO EDUCATING THE NEGRO IN NORTH CAROLINA

Within the state of North Carolina 10 of its 11 historically Black colleges were founded before the turn of the century, including the oldest HBCU in the South: Shaw University:

1. Shaw University in Raleigh (1865)—private;
2. Barber Scotia College in Concord (1867)—private;
3. Fayetteville State University in Fayetteville (1867)–public, state;
4. Johnson C. Smith University in Charlotte (1867)—private;
5. St. Augustine's College in Raleigh (1867)—private;
6. Livingstone College in Salisbury (1879)—private;
7. North Carolina Agriculture & Technical State University in Greensboro (1891)—public, state;
8. Elizabeth City State University in Elizabeth City (1891)—public, state;
9. Winston-Salem State University in Winston-Salem, (1892)—public, state;
10. Bennett College in Greensboro (1893)—private. (Historically Black Colleges and Universities, 2009)

Founded after the turn of the century in 1910, today NCCU is one of 16 senior institutions within the University of North Carolina system—five of which are HBCUs (About *the* University, 2011). To this end, Shepard's desire to establish an educational, social, economic, and political space for American citizens of African descent was an enterprise he contemplated and approached with un parralleled intentionality and resolve.

Published in 1905, Shepard discusses "a brief summary of my stewardship and future needs of the field" (Shepard, 1905, p. 478) in a report filed while serving as Field Superintendent of Work for Negroes at the International Sunday School Association. Specifically, Shepard lay what can be argued as the groundwork for the formation of the National Religious Training School and Chautauqua. He asserts,

> In the Southern states, by the United States Census of 1900, are 3,077,412 children between the ages of five and fourteen. The figures show that over one third of the negro population is in childhood. The work of the International Sunday-School Association, so far as the negro is concerned, must be largely among these, to take these children and make Christian citizens of them. (p. 478)

Between 1903 and 1905, Shepard organized over 160 counties in Alabama, North Carolina, South Carolina, Tennessee, Virginia, and Georgia (Shepard, 1905, pp. 478–479). In his travels of 36,778 miles (p. 479), Shepard (1905) found,

> ...many Sunday-schools seeking to improve in method, equipment and spiritual power.... The superintendents are realizing that the boys and girls, and especially the young men, must be reached and saved, if the race is to advance. Hence they are turning to Sunday School. Better teachers are demanded, and there is a growing disposition...to supply these demands. We

have only enrolled in the Sunday-schools of the South about 798,000; where are 2,279,412 that the Sunday-school has not reached? (p. 479)

In order to better organize, Shepard called for the formation of smaller territory sizes for field workers so they could effectively manage and organize their stated territories; the appointment of the colored general secretary to direct the movements of the field force from a centralized office; the appointment of the Secretary of the People to assist with manpower and correspondence for Colored State Convention work; the appointment of the a field worker for large towns and cities; and instructional literature to assist with how to organize and maintain county organizations (pp. 479–480). It is noteworthy to mention that at the close of this published report of 1905, Professor William G. Pearson, educator, businessman, and philanthropist ("Citizens," *Pittsburgh Courier*, Section I, p. 7) who was a close, personal friend of Dr. Shepard and fellow graduate of Shaw University, was named and voted as a worker for the ISSA in Durham (p. 480). In 1907 nine "prominent African-American businessmen" (M&F Founders Celebration, 2008, p. 10) including Shepard, Pearson, John Merrick, Aaron M. Moore, Stanford L. Warren, Richard B. Fitzgerald, Jesse A. Dodson, James R. Hawkins, W. G. Stevens established Mechanics and Farmers Bank as a "state chartered commercial bank headquartered in Durham, North Carolina under the authority of a charter issued by the Legislature of the State of North Carolina" and opened for business in August 1908 (p. 10).

IN SERVICE TO THE STATE

Shepard surrounded himself with visionaries who are credited with the upbuilding of Black Durham. These race leaders included the founding charter members of what is now NCCU; a few of whom such as Mr. John Merrick and Dr. Aaron M. Moore were also paid tribute along with Professor W. G. Pearson in July 1927 for their contributions to the city of Durham and "the cause of interracial co-operation.... and their success in building up and maintaining such splendid business enterprises" ("William G. Pearson," *Pittsburgh Courier*, 1927, Section I, p. 7). One of the first druggist in North Carolina, Shepard was also a minister, politician, pharmacist, entrepreneur, world traveler, civil servant, businessman, one of the founders of NC Mutual Life Insurance Company and Mechanics and Farmers Bank of Durham, president of the Inter-Denominational Sunday School Convention (Davis, 2010).

According to Murray (1984), Shepard, elected as President of the North Carolina Teachers Association (NCTA) in 1937, "made it his goal to attack the unfair salary differential" (p. 48). Published in the *Record*, Shepard outlines his program to approach this problem:

Increase in Teacher's Salaries—Salaries of the Negro teachers of North Carolina are inadequate, and a concentrated movement should be made to raise them to the proper level. Such a movement, however, should be directed not by an outside agency which in the beginning resorts to the courts, but through the North Carolina Teachers Association. This organization, through its officers and duly appointed committee, must attempt to work out with the proper authorities a fair and adequate increase in salaries.... I believe that the North Carolina Teachers Association should stand equally for this adjustment, so that the teachers of North Carolina will be paid a salary comparable to the training, experience, and type of certificate held.... I have appointed a special committee... I am, therefore, asking the Association to endorse this plan, with the understanding that the committee will memorialize the legislature and stat school commission, seeking their wholehearted support and cooperation in this effort. (pp. 48–49)

In 1944, under the leadership of Clyde A. Erwin, state superintendent of public instruction, "the final appropriation ($507,000) for the dissemination of salary differentials" was made for the 1944–1945 term that "would equalize salaries paid by the state for white and Negro teachers" (p. 50). About Shepard, N. C. Newbold, director of the Division of Negro Education, acknowledged that "no other Negro in the South or in the whole country has spoken over radio, and to legislature committees with such freedom, frankness, and straight forwardness" (p. 50). In keeping with the tradition of Shepard's service to the state and the education and uplifting of his race, several NCCU Black faculty became president of American Teachers Association (ATA) including: William A. Robinson, ATA President 1926–1927; Alphonse Heningburg, ATA President 1937–1938; Theodore R. Speigner, ATA President 1956–1957; and Charles W. Orr, ATA President 1958–1959.

Shepard's collaborative leadership and relationship building was not limited to North Carolinians, as he invited many influential leaders to visit the campus to deliver speeches and lecture. The list of individuals whose acquaintance or friendship Shepard made includes Dr. Edwin A. Alderman, President of the University of Virginia; Dr. Herbert Aptheker, Historian and Political Activist; Louis Austin, NCCU alum and Editor of *The Carolina Times*; Governors of North Carolina: Charles B. Aycock, Thomas W. Brickett, J. Melville Broughton, Robert Gregg Cherry, Locke Craig, John C. B. Ehringhaus, Oliver Max Gardner, Robert B. Glenn, Clyde Roark Hoey, William Walton Kitchin, Angus W. McLean, ; Dr. Mary McLeod Bethune, Founder and President of Bethune Cookman University; Dr. Horace Mann Bond, President of Fort Valley State College; W. T. Bost, Editor of *The Durham Herald*; Charlotte Hawkins Brown, Founder and President of Palmer Memorial Institute; Industrialist and Benefactors: Benjamin N. Duke, Brodie L. Duke, James Duke, and Washington Duke; Dr. John Hope Franklin,

Historian and Scholar; Dr. Mordecai W. Johnson, President, Howard University; Dr. Charles S. Johnson, President, Fisk University; W. P. Stacey, Chief Justice, North Carolina Supreme Court; Dr. John C. Kilgo, President, Trinity College (now Duke University); and W. F. Warren, Superintendent, Durham City Schools (Davis, 2010, pp. 57–72). Though lengthy, this is not an exhaustive list, and only representative of the leaders and figure-heads Shepard engaged and befriended throughout his lifetime and as founder and president of his institution. He collaborated with and learned from his contemporaries as well as those with whom he may have philosophically disagreed, but was able to seek common ground around the needs of North Carolina and how his institution was exampled as one that strove to be in service to the state.

Robert La Follette, Jr., U.S. Senator from Wisconsin and founder of the Wisconsin Progressive Party (Maney, 2001) spoke November 29, 1936 on the campus in NC College for Negroes at Chapel Services in Avery Auditorium (*The Eagle*, 1936, p. 1). His "brilliant speech" outlined the causes of our own economic depression, and he gave us reason to believe that we might avoid future economic crises" (p. 1). Also known as "Fighting Bob," the Senator's speech was broadcast "over a hook-up in connection with WPTF of Raleigh" (p. 1). La Follette focused his talk on the 1929 Depression and resulting industrialization of America. Specifically, the Senator discussed the "immediate problem to be faced is that of unemployment" (p. 4). He further argued, "If government can mobilize resources and man power for the destructive purpose of war, it has the power, duty and obligation to use the same plenary powers for constructive purposes" and favored expenditures related to the New Deal over expenditures for the purpose of war (p. 4). Shepard noted the Senator's characteristic political philosophy and persona as a "Champion of the new deal and new deals" (p. 1).

His father, Robert M. La Follette, Sr. was Governor and U.S. Senator from Wisconsin and credited with the close cooperation between the University of Wisconsin and state government in the development of The "Wisconsin Idea" (Hoeveler, 1976, p. 282). As discussed in Chapter Three, like Benjamin E. Mays, Shepard, too, embodies principles of the Wisconsin Idea by demonstrating his own concern that purposed NCCU as an inextricable part of public life in the city of Durham and the state of North Carolina, in particular. To be sure, Shepard enlarged the territory of the institution so that its teaching, research, and service activities were in service to the state as part of the fulfillment of his vision of the education of Blacks in North Carolina. Mays said of Shepard in a column published in the Pittsburgh Courier, November 1, 1947:

> When President James E. Shepard of the North Carolina College at Durham died on Oct. 6, a colorful and a somewhat controversial figure passed from

the American scene. Colorful, because he was constantly in the public eye and what he said and did was often tinged with drama. Controversial, because some people criticized Doctor Shepard in his racial philosophy. But whether one did or did not agree with Jim Shepard he couldn't be ignored, was not easily dismissed, and he was heard. Many people who criticized him severely will never do as much for education and America as he did.... The growth of North Carolina College was so rapid that it almost made one dizzy to observe it. He was able to get increasingly large appropriations for the State of North Carolina. Whether Dr. Shepard's method of doing things pleased everybody is beside the point. One fact is clear. He stood on his own feet, did his work in the open, and made his approaches in a straightforward manner. He was not afraid. He could stand criticism without being embittered. What he believed, he said. He did not seek to do the popular thing. He was definitely courageous. (para. 1–2)

Mays was invited annually to the campus for nearly a decade (Mays, 1947), and became familiar with Shepard's work ethic and educational philosophy. At the time Mays was in his seventh of a 27 year tenure he would serve as Morehouse College president. About Shepard, Mays goes on to reveal, "I certainly did admire him and respected him. If I live to reach his years, I hope my work will be as permanent and enduring as I believe his will be. A great and unique figure has passed from among us. I liked Jim Shepard" (para. 6). One can certainly make the case that Mays was able to realize his hope to leave his imprint on American higher education for Blacks.

Circa 1921, Shepard published a pamphlet of the accomplishments of his institution titled, "Indisputable Facts of the Worth and Work of National Training School, Durham, N.C." (see Appendix A), which outlined 16 points of pride. To follow are excerpts from that pamphlet:

4. For the year 1922 the white people of Durham have contributed in cash and pledges for the support of this School TWO THOUSAND DOLLARS and the colored people, out of their scant earnings TWENTY-EIGHT HUNDRED DOLLARS;
5. The accounts are audited annually by Messrs. Charnley, Scott & Co. Certified Public Accountants, Charlotte, N. C.;
6. In eleven years the total property holdings of the National Training School, including plant and equipment is $185,000.00;
7. There are no mortgages, judgments or other liens against the property;
8. The student body numbers is 236, coming from eleven states, South America and Africa;
9. During eleven years of our existence 227 young men and women have been sent out in various walks and are contributing their mite to the sanity of the world;

10. The National Training School has stood squarely for a better understanding between the races in the city, state and nation;
11. The Faculty numbers twenty well-trained men and women, coming from the best Institutions of the land;
12. The annual budget is $27,000. Of this amount $14,000 must be raised by free will offering. We need our deficit and new buildings, $33,000. (Indisputable Facts of the Worth and Work of National Training School, Durham, N.C [Circa 1921])

RACE, EDUCATION, AND POLITICS IN NORTH CAROLINA

According to Gilmore (1996),

> Political repression did more than alter black men's voting rights; it began to push African American men from the interracial public sphere. As citizens and voters, African American men had represented their families in political and civic discourse. Silencing black men in public life changed their relationships with their families and their neighbors, with the Republican Party, with their churches, and with each other. Taking up the cause of disenfranchisement after the violence of 1898, whites sought to impose a civil death sentence on both black men and black women. Once successful, whites came to see black men's disenfranchisement as evidence of their unfitness for public life rather than as the cause of their exclusion from it. (p. 119)

Gilmore goes on to characterize Shepard's response to disenfranchisement campaign of 1900 when he stated, "We recognize the fact that there can be no middle ground between freedom and slavery. We cannot see that the best way to make a good man is to unman him" (p. 120). The social and political conditions during this period resulted in a the unintended consequence in which "contestation over how best to maintain civic personhood produced new leaders and marginalized old ones as black men and women tried to invent a politics that decentered polls and parties" (p. 120). Ultimately, "African American political culture survived, and black men and women began to shape strategies to meet the challenges of the new regime" (p. 120).

Shepard's vision for an educational, social, political, and economic space for his race personifies the response of Black North Carolinians who wished to (re)situate themselves as part of public life within the state. However, the approach to this dilemma, given Shepard's desire to establish a school in which to educate his race, involved political savvy that Shepard would eventually master.

By 1903, Shepard's role as Field Superintendent of Work among Negroes for the International Sunday School Movement was beginning to shape his vision for what would be the National Religious Training School and

Chautauqua. Despite his earlier criticism that political disenfranchisement left "no middle ground between freedom and slavery" (Gilmore, 1996, p. 120) he understood the importance of collaboration and relationship building in order to gain supporters for his endeavor for a school. According to Davis (2010), Shepard's school was a "combination of the philosophies of Booker T. Washington and W. E. B. DuBois. Washington's philosophy was that African Americans should have industrial and technical training. DuBois thought that African Americans should have classical education. Dr. Shepard combined both leaders' philosophies" (p. 8). Like Booker T. Washington, earlier perception of Shepard may have been characterized as one of an accomodationist; however, history has shed a much needed light on the parallel uses of politics, policy, and pragmatism that Shepard and countless race leaders had to adopt in an effort to advance the agenda of Black America. Rather than retreating or abandoning his ideology around race and education, Shepard (re)visioned his approach and promoted his vision for educating Blacks by explaining the intersection of industrial education and religion as advantageous because, "It awakens the sluggish, dormant energies of the individual and turns them into channels of usefulness; it lessens crime, reduces idleness, stops violence and teaches lessons of self-restraint, and thus builds up a better citizenship" (*Republican*, 1910, para. 1; *Times*, 1911, para. 1). Historically, Black college presidents often felt a sense of responsibility to the Negro race. Democracy and citizenry accessible to all Americans became an enduring pursuit during the 1930s and 1940s war era. To this end, Shepard produced a political discourse rooted in his own self-reflection, collaboration, power sharing, and critical thinking.

In 1943, Shepard spoke before the United States House of Representatives Ways and Means Committee, advocating on the part of the poorest-paid laborers of North Carolina:

> I do not come before you as a tax expert, but as one who had studied the justice and the fairness of taxes upon people of limited means.... Today the poorest citizen receives benefits that would cost him thousands of dollars if he had to provide then out of this own pocket... our fine public health service, both State and Federal.... In North Carolina, the average citizen receives a great deal in return for the tax dollar. His children are educated in free public schools and with free schoolbooks. Personally, I have always been in favor of the sales tax coupled with income tax. That reaches the big man with an income tax and also with sales tax for all he spends, as it does everyone. The sales tax reaches everybody in the lower brackets who pays very little income tax, or none at all. Of course, we all know that all taxes, or most of them, are borne by the consumer anyway. I think it is much better to have them all in a sales a tax and make everybody conscious of the fact that they are paying part of the cost of government and part of the cost of services the Government is rendering to the people. (Shepard, 1943, pp. 538–539)

Shepard is concerned with the least among the citizens of North Carolina. He advocates for government and taxation that proportionately considers those living on a budget and do not have dispensable income. Upon the close of his 15 minute testimony, Shepard was thanked by the Chairman of the Committee, Robert L. Doughton of North Carolina and Harold Knutson of Minnesota for his "excellent statement" (p. 541). Shepard was also praised by A. Willis Robertson of Virginia for "the fine work he is doing in Durham, N.C." and "I hope he will keep up in the future the splendid work he is rendering to his people and to the South" (p. 541).

In the Congressional Record dated Tuesday, May 6, 1947, a tribute to Dr. Shepard was given by the Honorable Clyde R. Hoey, Governor and Senator of North Carolina and the name for which the Administration Building on the campus of NCCU is named. It is noteworthy that the tribute given took place exactly five months to the day before Shepard's death. To follow is an excerpt from that tribute:

> Mr. President, I ask unanimous consent to have inserted in the Appendix to the Record an article from the Durham Morning Herald of May 4, 1947, which tells a most interesting story about a North Carolina College, one of the great institutions of North Carolina, maintained for the education of Negro boys and girls. Dr. James E. Shepard, one of the outstanding Negroes of America, and in many respects the North Carolina successor to Booker T. Washington, was the real founder of the institution, and has been its president since it was established. He has shown great wisdom in the direction of this splendid college and in his leadership and guidance of the Negro race in North Carolina and throughout the South. This article was accompanied by many pictures of this institution, its president, its large student body, and its many activities. (Congressional Record, 1947, p. A2225)

On the provision there was no objection the article titled, "North Carolina College, One of Four Institutions of Kind in United States, Stands as Monument to James E. Shepard" and written by Tom MacCaughelty, was ordered to be printed in the Record in its entirety. Indeed, Shepard fortifies an interracial alliance among citizens, educators, businessmen, and politicians within the city of Durham, the state of North Carolina, and the nation upon the realization of his vision for what is now North Carolina Central University.

THE UPBUILDING OF INTER-RACIAL ALLIANCES

By November 1, 1909 the erection of the institute began (*Norfolk Journal and Guide*, 1909, para. 3) and by 1910, Shepard opened the doors of his school and benefited from the inter-racial alliances he forged as part of his vision for the institution. Specifically, Shepard had the foresight to appoint

Judge Jeter C. Pritchard of Ashville as president of the Advisory Board. This appointment is remarkable, as Pritchard was said to have "purged black voters" and "traveled to Alabama... to extol the virtues of expelling African Americans from the [Republican] party" (Gilmore, 1996, p. 129). Among the "prominent southern white men" (Dodson, 1910, para. 3) who lent their support to the enterprise was Bishop Robert Strange of the eastern North Carolina diocese (Wilmington); Archdeacon G. W. Avent of the same theological district; The Honorable N. B. Broughton of Raleigh; the Rev. Dr. Jasper C. Massee of Chattanooga, Tenn. (Dodson, 1910). Others participating as members of the board include the Rev. C. H. Parkhusrt of New York; Rabbi Abram Simon of Washington; the Rev. Thomas H, Shannon of Newark; Gen. B. W. Green of Little Rock; Senator Lee Overman of North Carolina; D. A. Tompkins of Charlotte; and Dr. John A. Earle of Chicago (Special to the *Norfolk Journal and Guide*, October 2, 1909, para. 1). The Dodson article goes to reveal the quote Bishop Strange as expressing his support of Shepard's vision: "I am much interested in this Chautauqua for the Negro. I think highly of Dr. Shepard, and I believe this institution will be a real help to the Negro" (para. 5). In an article published by the *Georgian* August 12, 1909 and titled, "For the Practical Uplift of the Negro," the following was said about Dr. Shepard:

> Some of the foremost white citizens of Durham have become contributors to the enterprise and have also consented to serve on the advisory committee, which is made up of representative men in both sections. Gen. Julian S Carr, and ex-Confederate soldier, has accepted the treasurer-ship of the fund and Mr. B. L. Duke has donated several acres of land. The project is in every respect praiseworthy and it not only deserves but will undoubtedly receive the hearty support of the white people of the South. ("Uplift," *Georgian*, para. 8–9)

To be sure, Brodie L. Duke gifted 25 acres (*Herald*, 1909, para. 1) of land to plan for the construction of "two dormitories, costing $20,000 each, and an auditorium at a cost of $15,000. An endowment fund of $150,000 will support the faculty for the present" (para. 3). The institution was further endorsed in *The Bee* in an article dated January 9, 1909 and titled, For a Negro Chautauqua Movement Started by Dr. James E. Shepard, of Durham, N.C., and Widely Endorsed." The article points out the support of *The Charlotte Observer*, which was "the leading daily newspaper in the State of North Carolina" (para. 5). It also outlines, "No individual could have a stronger personal endorsement, no movement a warmer advocate than that afforded to Dr. Shepard and his cause by a public letter from Governor Glenn of North Carolina, to which is affixed the great seal of the State. Governor Noel of Mississippi, sees much good in the movement as presented by Dr. Shepard, and his former associates in the Sunday School Association give it hearty endorsement" (para. 5). Shepard's educational philosophy was clear:

The National Religious Training School is founded to teach that religion and work must go hand in hand. Primarily, it was formed to reach the negro minister who is ignorant and untrained. There are 30,000 negro ministers in the United States, and of this number only 10 per cent[sic] are trained, leaving the startling fact, 27,000 untrained ministers leading a comparatively ignorant mass of nearly 10,000,000 people. The negro minister exercises more than a priestly influence over his race, so he must be reached. (*Times*, 1911, para. 6)

Shepard's call for social, religious, economic, and political participation among the races is apparent throughout his lifetime. He saw a need for his race that provided the many life skills they had been denied as part of slavery and subsequent to its abolishment.

CONCLUSIONS AND IMPLICATIONS FOR COLLABORATIVE LEADERSHIP

Historically, Black college presidents often felt a sense of responsibility to the Negro race. During the post-war era principles for sustaining democracy are defined as a citizenry capable of expression through ongoing social discourse, a complex set of behaviors (i.e., self-reflection, collaboration, power sharing, and critical thinking). The visionary leadership of Dr. Shepard and the formation of the National Religious Training School and Chautauqua elucidate Shepard's methodical approach to accessing resources made available to him via North Carolinians influential in education, religion, business and commerce, and politics. These relationships situated in the mainstream afforded him a venue in which to educate and advance his race. Shepard's commitment to improve race relations in North Carolina as well as within the entire United States informs the ways in which he built what is now North Carolina Central University.

The historical conditions and obstacles surrounding Shepard and the establishing of North Carolina Central University serves to inform contemporary conditions and obstacles facing HBCU leaders that require similar leadership open to a bold vision, innovation, and risk-taking. Shepard was arguably relentless in his passion for and works on behalf of those who were disenfranchised. Further, he strove to serve the public interest and this backdrop posed a complicated dichotomy for Shepard to navigate and be understood by his race within the historical conditions and circumstances of his time. To this end, he positioned himself as a proficient collaborator who conquered territory not easily dismantled. To this end, the author concludes the circumstance surrounding the issue of strained race relations during the upbuilding of NCCU was optimal for social and political participation, and collaboration among all races.

REFERENCES

Primary Sources

Hoey, C. R. (1947, May 6). Tribute to James E. Shepard, negro educator of North Carolina. *Proceedings and Debates of the 80th Congress, First Session, 93*(85), A2225–A2226.

Mays, B. E. (1947, November). Jim Shepard. *Pittsburgh Courier,* 1.

Shepard, J. E. (1905). Work among Negroes. In *The development of the Sunday-school (1780–1905), Official Report of the Eleventh International Sunday-School Convention.* Toronto, Canada.

Shepard, J. E. (1943, October 11). Statement of Dr. James E. Shepard, President, Carolina College for Negroes, Durham, N. C. In *Hearings Before the Committee on Ways and Means, House of Representatives, Seventy-Eighth Congress, First Session on Revenue Revision of 1943.* Washington, DC: United States Government Printing Office.

Newspaper Articles

Citizens pay tribute to William G. Pearson (1927, July 3). *Pittsburgh Courier.* Pittsburgh, Pennsylvania.

Conditions of the negro characterized by one of them: Dr. James E. Shepard, of Durham, speaks to pastors. (1911, February 28). *Times.* Chattanooga, Tennessee.

Dodson, N. B. (October 13, 1910). Advisory board of national religious training school begins work.

For the practical uplift of the Negro. (1909, August 12). *Georgian,* Atlanta, GA.

Gives land for Negroes: Brodie L Duke provides site for religious training school in Durham, NC. (1909, July 11). *Herald.* New York, NY.

Noted senator speaks here. (1936, December). *Eagle, 1–2.* Durham, N. C.: North Carolina Central University.

Plan to educate Negro leaders: Dr. James E. Shepard tells of religious training school in North Carolina. (2010, February 14). *Republican.* Springfield, Massachusetts.

Will plan Dr. Shepard's new school: Board of advisors of National Religious Training School will meet. (1909, October 2). *Norfolk Journal and Guide.* Norfolk, Virginia.

Secondary Sources

Davis, L. G. (2010). *Quotations and statement of James Edward Shepard (and other information on him:) Founder of North Carolina Central University.* Winston-Salem, NC: National Black Bibliographic and Research Center.

Gilmore, G. E. (1996). *Gender and Jim Crow: Women and the politics of White supremacy in North Carolina, 1896–1920*. Chapel Hill: The University of North Carolina Press.

Hoeveler, J. D. Jr. (1976). The University and the Social Gospel: The intellectual origins of the 'Wisconsin Idea.' *The Wisconsin Magazine of History, 59*, 282–298.

M&F Founders Celebration. (February 23, 2008). Durham, NC: Mechanics and Farmers Bank.

Maney, P. (2001, Summer). Joseph McCarthy's first victim. *Virginia Quarterly Review 77*, 529–536.

Murray, P. E. (1984). *History of the North Carolina Teachers Association*. Washington, DC: National Education Association of the United States.

North Carolina Central University (2010a). *A history of units and programs from 1910 to 2010*. Durham, N.C.: North Carolina Central University.

North Carolina Central University (2010b). *Soaring on the legacy: A concise history of North Carolina Central University, 1910–2010*. Durham, N.C.: North Carolina Central University.

Suggs, V. L. (2009). *The production of political discourse: Annual radio addresses of Black college presidents during the 1930s and 1940s* (Doctoral Dissertation, Georgia State University). Retrieved from http://digitalarchive.gsu.edu/eps_diss/33/

The University of North Carolina (2011). About the University. Retrieved at http://www.northcarolina.edu/campus_profiles/index.php

SECTION II

CASE STUDY OF A CONTEMPORARY BLACK COLLEGE PRESIDENT

CHAPTER 4

BLACK COLLEGE PRESIDENTS, INSTITUTIONAL LEADERSHIP, AND THE USE OF SOCIAL MEDIA

A Case Study of Philander Smith College

Vickie L. Suggs
Jennifer E. Tomon Stephens

INTRODUCTION

Many institutions make claims via their mission statements that are inconsistent with the lived student, faculty, and staff experiences. While institutional mission statements sound promising and paint an attractive picture for prospective students and their parents, the reality may not result in the educational, social, and personal development outcomes and experiences anticipated. The research will explore institutional advancement and effectiveness related to the ideals of African American leadership. The authors will also define a set of competencies that lend itself to the achievement of this particular institutional, administrative, and instructional practice through the integrated use of social media technology.

The study employs a case analysis of Philander Smith College (PSC), a small, private, historically Black college in Little Rock, Arkansas. The guiding question that informs the research is: In what ways does institutional leadership at Philander Smith College model a parallel use of social media technologies to advance its institutional mission and, thus, the viability and sustainability of historically Black colleges and universities?

Using African-American leadership theory, brand identity/management theory, document analysis, and social media platforms as frameworks, the study will examine whether the ideals set forth by the institutional mission statement are communicated effectively via social media outlets. The authors will also discuss an historical overview of how Black college leaders such as Marquis LaFayette Harris, president of Philander Smith College (1936–1961), espoused teachings of social justice and moral education, and Benjamin Elijah Mays, president of Morehouse College (1940–1967), who shared the same educational thought, used annual radio addresses to advance his agenda for the race. Both exercised individual and institutional agency throughout the 1930s to 1960s. This overview informs an examination of the implications of the medium of that day (radio) and its audiences to contemporary social media and its audiences. Further, review of how past Black college leaders developed strategies for sustaining their institutions brings into focus contemporary uses of social media as a viable tool for institutional advancement and effectiveness.

THEORETICAL FRAMEWORK

African-American Leadership—Past and Present

African-American educators are at the front lines of advocacy for equity and access, fighting to "make education an instrument for collective liberation and uplift" (Benjamin, 2007, p. 39). African-American educators of the past, whether receiving industrial education (see Washington) or classical, liberal arts training (see DuBois), tend to fit the role of model and mentor, adhering to a mission to serve (Benjamin, 2007, pp. 39–40). Benjamin (2007) observes:

> They encouraged the philosophy of education for living; reinforced the ethos of service and racial uplift; advocated pedagogy of liberation; and stressed communal values of caring, sharing, self-reliance, hard work, and the hope for a better tomorrow. Behind the segregated walls, they taught respectability, race pride, strong spiritual and religious values, family pride and honor, strict discipline, and the need to excel, despite the racial restrictions of that era. In

short, "service before self" embodied the dominant motif for achieving common goals. (p. 40)

It is this examination of the past that informs contemporary leadership styles of Black college presidents and the aims of this study.

During the 1930s and 1940s, Black college presidents in the South, including Mordecai W. Johnson, Howard University in Washington, D.C.; James E. Shepard, North Carolina Central University in Durham; and Benjamin E. Mays, Morehouse College in Atlanta, delivered annual radio addresses broadcast on local and national stations. It is through this line of inquiry one could argue, "The method in which Black college presidents sought social equality via radio addresses incorporated vision, courage, and intentional exploitation of the rare opportunity to reach both regional and national audiences" (Suggs, 2009, p. 21). Suggs goes on to explain, "By anticipating the impact of participating in the radio program, these leaders used their agency to benefit Black America—first and foremost" (p. 21). To this end, implications for contemporary uses of media by Black college leadership to advance their mission can be made. In particular, the creation of social spaces of activism and community building in which participants are privy to institutional imperatives around process improvements, fundraising, and curriculum and instruction, for example.

Specifically, Walter M. Kimbrough, president of Philander Smith College from December 2004 to May 2012, cites Benjamin E. Mays as an institutional leader from whom he models his own leadership persona. The ways in which Kimbrough opts to lead is a testimony to Mays's enduring legacy of moral character and the branding of the "morally correct" (Rovaris, 2005) Morehouse Man while serving that institution for 27 years. Like Mays, Kimbrough assumed his presidency amidst financial and curricular challenges. Like Mays, Kimbrough is committed to the College and wants Philander Smith to compete with peer institutions and emerge as a leader in higher education. Also similar to Mays, Kimbrough makes himself readily available to students, staff, faculty, alumni and the external campus community. In 2009, Kimbrough articulates the influence of the Mays model:

> Mays provided the model for my five years as a college president. In fact, he is one of the few truly great presidents, regardless of institutional type. By reading many of his thoughts through his speeches and texts, I find three major components of a college presidency using the Mays model, a model that is desperately needed in higher education today. First, we need advocacy from presidents. In today's tough political climate, many presidents dare not risk their jobs or potential donations by taking a stand on an issue....Today, it is rare to read a passionate argument by a president. In Mays's autobiography, aptly titled *Born to Rebel*, he writes "I never ceased to raise my voice and pen

against the injustices of a society that segregated and discriminated against people because God made them black." Mays, through a number of editorials, often challenged the notions that historically black colleges should be abolished, and suggested reparations were in order. In my own way, I have sought to speak out as well, dismissing the *U.S. News* ranking system, one that rewards colleges for enrolling low numbers of poor, working, and students of color, to the ridiculous celebrations of "philanthropy" when the wealthy give to already wealthy colleges whose assets rival those of many countries. (Kimbrough, 2009, para. 4–5)

Many of today's African-American educators find themselves torn between "a collective ethos of liberation and uplift" and "an individual ethos of personal preservation as self-fulfillment" (Benjamin, 2007, pp. 40–41). Benjamin (2007) further notes, "As black college leaders move forward in the twenty-first century, their model of leadership is becoming more complex and more accountable to conflicting constituents" (p. 54). Within the increasingly prominent business-model of education, African-American educators should seek to balance the "traditional ideal of education as a moral enterprise" with the "model of education as a business enterprise" (p. 73). Kimbrough's implementation of strategic planning integrates past rituals and traditions of the Black college with futuristic innovations and organizational process improvements that shepherd the pursuit of one's infinite potential as a member of society.

Benjamin (2007) argues for a movement toward "community, culture, and consciousness" that works from the "'I' model of youth and the 'We' model of elders" (pp. 238–239). Such a movement would:

> ...extol an ideology of service to others and would embrace and build caring black communities that would confront existential issues of discrimination, poverty, peace and justice, profit, greed, and human misery. It would incorporate multiple definitions of identity, inclusive of ethnicity, class, gender and sexual orientation, age, or any affected groups. Our common group identity becomes a process in a continual state of construction. Our particular identity (gender, class, ethnicity) and our common group identity (race) interact and shape each other in a constant process of change. To build caring communities, it is crucial to understand our racial history as it connects with these other social identities. (pp. 239–240)

Informed by a variety of communication styles and social media technologies, under the leadership of Kimbrough, Philander Smith College established the building blocks that will sustain an institutional identity and brand messaging and management.

AFRICAN-AMERICAN COMMUNICATION

Communication is multifaceted and multifunctional, serving to provide information, to regulate conversation, to facilitate negotiations of identity, and to exercise social control (Hecht, Jackson, & Ribeau, 2003, p. 140). While research on the communication styles of African-Americans is varied and not without limitations, Hecht et. al (2003) have identified common themes, functional properties, and core symbols of African-American communication originating from oral traditions and performance. In order to enact culture and identity, the core symbols of *sharing, uniqueness, positivity, realism,* and *assertiveness* are expressed within a variety of communication styles.

In the case of Philander Smith College, the negotiation of identity originated in January 2005 when Kimbrough was appointed by the Board of Trustees. Upon his arrival, PSC's new leader was confronted with the very un-unique identity of the institution. In an effort to determine the state of the College, the brand-marketing firm Thoma Thoma was hired to conduct focus groups with students, staff, faculty, community members and organizations and a draft of a strategic plan was shared with the Board. One Board member raised the questions: What is the unique identity of Philander Smith College? What makes this institution different from other institutions of higher education, particularly institutions in Arkansas and minority-serving institutions (Kimbrough, 2010)? As its 12th president, it was these questions that inspired Kimbrough to conduct an historical analysis of institutional leadership at the College. A review of archival documents revealed the original, November 1866, social charter establishing Philander Smith College:

> The emancipation of four millions of slaves has opened at our doors a wide field calling, alike for mission and education work. It has devolved upon the church a fearful responsibility. The time may come when the States in the South will make some provision of the education of the colored children now growing up in utter ignorance in their midst. But thus far they have made none, nor perhaps can it soon be expected of them. Christian philanthropy must supply this lack. We cannot turn away from the appeal that comes home to our conscience and hearts. Nor can we delay. The emergency is upon us, and we must begin work now. (as cited in Kimbrough, 2010, p. 1)

The social history during the period when this charter was written, parallels the defining moment in which the United States once again finds itself in the new millennium. Understanding the historical imperative of the original social charter, the institution adopted its current mission statement in 2007. It reads:

> The mission of Philander Smith College is to graduate academically accomplished students, grounded as advocates for social justice, determined to change the world for the better.

As a historically Black college or university (HBCU), Philander Smith advocates a mission of social justice and sets out to graduate alumni who exemplify this character-based trait at the individual, group, and institutional level.

Symbols of communication valued and operationalized by PSC are *sharing, uniqueness, positivity, realism,* and *assertiveness*. According to Hecht, Jackson, and Ribeau (2003), "The core symbol of *sharing*, or *endorsing the group*, is reflective of collectivism in African American culture, which centers on "interconnectedness, interrelatedness, sharing, and interdependence" (p. 162). This collectivism is demonstrated through various forms of communication including physical touch, close physical proximity, relationship intimacy, and rituals (Hecht et. al, 2003). Accordingly, the institutional identity of social justice uses the motto, "Think Justice," to galvanize internal and external campus communities. This motto affords equal access to the academic and co-curricular aims of the College. The use of social media (i.e., Facebook, Twitter, Texting, and Blogging) as tools for institutional advancement and effectiveness equally affords access to all stakeholders who wish to acquire timely information, engage, and donate by using the medium of the day—social networking.

While *sharing* works to connect the group, *uniqueness* focuses on the individual. Because collectivism and individuality are viewed as equally important, *uniqueness* tends to be incorporated into the rituals of the *sharing* symbol through individually stylized and expressive communication patterns (e.g., the fist-bump greeting; Hecht, Jackson, & Ribeau, 2003, pp. 167–168). These communication patterns may include the use of "direct questions, public debate and argument, more active nonverbal expression..." (Hecht et al., 2003, p. 168). Kimbrough embodies this particular symbol by his personalized communication style with campus constituents. By using a blog that he authors and manages—absent of staff—Kimbrough reinforces his commitment to engaging with students, staff, faculty, alumni, and community members while signaling his own accessibility and hands-on approach to institutional leadership.

Along with a unification of collectivism and individuality, African-American communication is rooted in the spirit and vitality of African-American culture and artistic expression. Through *positivity*, or *emotionality*, the emotional content and expression of communication tends to be based on resiliency and openness of feelings (Hecht, Jackson, & Ribeau, 2003, pp. 168–169). According to Cogdell & Wilson (1980, as cited in Hecht et. al, 2003), "Expressions of positive emotionality serve the same cleansing function as religious rituals, and African American decisions often appear to be rooted in feelings and intuition rather than simple rationality" (p. 169). Strategic in risk-taking and his desire to offset the many challenges faced by the institution upon his arrival, Kimbrough employs a level of positivity that may have initially appeared to mock the former administration's tagline, "The GREAT Philander Smith College!" Kimbrough challenged the "greatness" of the institution and sets out to reverse the state of the College under the previous administration, which included the improper maintenance of proper accounting for Perkins Loans, the disbursement of Title IV aid to ineligible students who had not met nor maintained satisfactory academic progress (SAP), and censorship by the American Association of University Professors (AAUP) for not adhering to the generally recognized principles of academic freedom and tenure (Kimbrough, 2010). Despite the many hurdles the institution had to clear, Kimbrough worked diligently to build institutional, student, staff, and faculty capacity through symbols of positivity and resiliency. Of his unconventional approach to leadership and connection with his students, Kimbrough says, "To me this is a ministry" (as cited in Masterson, 2010, para, 16).

Despite a focus on being positive, the negotiation of cultural identity through African-American communication is situated within a need to "keep it real" (Hecht, Jackson, & Ribeau, 2003, p. 169). True expressions of self are represented through stylized and individualized verbal and nonverbal presentations of the difficulties of life and the toughness needed to persist toward a more positive future (Hecht et. al, 2003, pp. 169–170). Examples of this *realism* can be seen within the lyrics of blues, gospel, rap, and hip-hop music. Kimbrough's understanding of the hip-hop generation (i.e., @HipHopPrez on Twitter), Renaissance thinking, and the needs of millennial students, in general, provides navigation through the student-centered terrain he has created at PSC. The average PSC student can boast that they have his cellular number, email him directly, have been treated to lunch, or have shared their deepest secrets and life-changing events with him, as he is genuinely interested in their success as both students and future contributing members of our society. His genuine belief that all of his students can succeed is coupled with social justice-inspired programs and initiatives including a speaker series titled, "Bless the Mic;" breaking ground spring 2010 on a 60-bed, three-story, 19,770 square foot building registered to achieve LEED Certification or green building; and being awarded a $1.2 million grant from the Kresge Foundation to create a Center for Social Justice (Kimbrough, 2010; W. Kimbrough, personal communication, July 24, 2010).

Attention to realism also involves the inclusion of *assertiveness* as a communication style. Hecht, Jackson, and Ribeau (2003) have defined assertiveness as "behavior that stands up for and tries to achieve personal rights without damaging others" (p. 170). While assertiveness and aggression may be difficult to differentiate at times (with assertive communication sometimes misinterpreted as violent, like in the case of certain rap and hip-hop music, for example), the core symbol of *assertiveness* involves taking charge of one's existence in the face of oppression through communication that may be "intense, outspoken, challenging, and forward" (pp. 170–171). According to Masterson (2010):

> Early in his presidency, Mr. Kimbrough gave an indication that he wouldn't hold his tongue. When a Little Rock newspaper asked him to describe himself in one word, he chose "uncensored."...Mr. Kimbrough knows that some people consider him a controversial figure, but he doesn't see himself that way. When he brings up touchy topics, he is just trying to start a conversation, he says. He likes engaging with people who hold different opinions...Let's talk. (para. 22–23)

While the symbols of *sharing, uniqueness, positivity, realism,* and *assertiveness* may be expressed through various communication styles, Kimbrough utilizes social media to connect with constituents within and outside of the campus community. It is his awareness of the culture of today's students that enables him to effectively communicate a message of social justice.

SOCIAL MEDIA TECHNOLOGIES

Today's college students have grown up with digital media and have been utilizing social media to view and disseminate information in a personal context. Because of this, researchers suggest that these students will learn differently and demand a more engaging form of education than their earlier counterparts (Mason & Rennie, 2008, p. 8). Studies of Millennials (those born after 1982) have described these students as preferring multitasking to singletasking; learning from pictures, sound, and video over text; learning in a structured and non-linear manner; and participating in interactive and networked activities over independent study (Karpati, 2002; Oblinger & Oblinger, 2005; Raines, 2002; Veen, 2007). However, this multitasking and interactivity has also led to decreased attention spans, less reflection, poorer text literacy, and less-critical analysis of sources (Livingstone & Bober, 2005; Oblinger & Oblinger, 2005). Thus, Mason and Rennie (2008) have argued that "educators need to use the tools that are common in the social context of the day, because they are determining the way people learn" (p. 13).

Theoretically, the utilization of social media in higher education may allow users to "actively engage in the construction of their experiences, rather than passively absorbing existing content," "continually refresh" content as opposed to waiting for "expensive expert input," "develop the skills of working in teams" by supporting collaboration, and feel more motivated to learn due to the excitement of "shared community spaces and inter-group communications" (Mason & Rennie, 2008, pp. 4–5). However, shifts in the ideology and informational delivery of U.S. higher education are required to assist students in developing these increasingly important twenty-first century skills. Rudd, Sutch, and Facer (2006) have asserted that "this concept of the 'network society' calls into question what it means to be 'educated' today—what new skills, what new ways of working and learning, and what new knowledge and skills will be required to operate in and through these networks" (p. 4). Because of the characteristics of today's college students, institutions of higher education have a responsibility to use and to teach the utilization of these tools for critical inquiry and collaboration in an increasingly globalized society.

Philander Smith College and its institutional leaders have determined that the tools of social media increase institutional messaging and community development beyond traditional communication strategies. Though learning deficiencies as a result of using social media may exist, PSC believes there is ample opportunity to not only teach the skill set needed to become proficient and savvy in social media technologies, but also to train students how to use these platforms contextually as vehicles for collaboration, community outreach, and advocacy related to larger social issues. For example, coupled with the institution's Social Justice Project Advisory Board and Social Justice White Paper, one of the contributing factors that assisted in Philander Smith College's being awarded a $1.2 million Kresge Grant was the selection committee's access to the various forms of social media technologies utilized by the College. By becoming connected to the campus through its Facebook page and Twitter, the committee was able to witness its use not only as marketing tools but also as outreach to campus constituents through news and information that signal accessibility to President Kimbrough at the small, private, liberal arts HBCU. In their quest to find "bigger ways to broadcast" the institutional mission, Kimbrough and his team now have funding to create a Center for Social Justice—the very Center representative of its central mission (W. Kimbrough, S. Cole, & S. Fleming, personal communication, July 24, 2010).

According to Mason & Rennie (2008), a social network is a social structure consisting of individuals with common connections or interests and includes a variety of websites including Twitter and Facebook. In recent years, the number of Facebook users has increased to over 1 billion people (Pingdom, 2013b), with 2.7 billion "likes" recorded on Facebook every day (Pingdom, 2013a). Additionally, throughout 2012, the number of "tweets" (i.e., mini-blogs) on Twitter each day was recorded at over 175 million by more than 200 million active Twitter users (Pingdom, 2013a). Thus, these numbers demonstrate the significant need for institutions of higher education to utilize these social networking technologies, while also recognizing the difficulty in establishing relevance in such a saturated information/communication market. In the case of Philander Smith College, institutional leaders use Twitter to engage broader groups and outsiders, Facebook for current and prospective students, Texting for younger alums and current students, and Blogging for older alums and outsiders. Specific uses include Facebook for the Alumni Reunion Weekend, which targets younger alums; yet, an unintended outcome was the discovery that significant numbers of older alums were using Facebook. The event was advertised via Facebook by sending out messages and posting comments, which resulted in a more rapid response rate (W. Kimbrough & R. Hameth, personal communication, July 24, 2010).

A blog is a type of webpage that serves as an online journal, typically maintained by an individual who contributes regular entries on a specific topic or variety of topics (Mason & Rennie, 2008). For the purposes of this study, the authors focus on an educational context of the term in which a blog may be used by institutional leaders, educators, or students to extend discussion, build community, and provide updates beyond the classroom (Mason & Rennie, 2008). As of 2012, NM Incite, a Nielsen/McKinsey company, had identified over 181 million blogs, making this a popular, but potentially unchecked, form of communication (nielsenwire, 2012). Thus, at the institutional level, an effectively utilized blog consisting of text, pictures, videos, etc. may provide additional opportunities for prospective, current, and former students to connect with campus life and one another. In the case of Philander Smith College, Kimbrough began using social media technologies out of necessity because "we don't have the budget to spend $1 million each year on marketing so this is a more efficient means of getting our mission out there along with news of what is happening on campus" (W. Kimbrough, personal communication, July 24, 2010). Kimbrough further asserts, "We did look at what other presidents were doing and didn't see effective blogging... I feel my way of using technology makes it stand out" (W. Kimbrough, personal communication, July 24, 2010). Kimbrough's team echoes this ideal, crediting his youth as a generational advantage because Kimbrough pays close attention to current issues and student trends and understands the merits of social media technologies (S. Cole & S. Fleming, personal communication, July 24, 2010).

Text messaging, a final example of social media technology related to this research, refers to the exchange of brief, typed messages (approximately 160 characters or less) via fixed or portable devices over a network (NetLingo, 2009). According to TNS Global, the number of text message users as of the beginning of 2012 has increased to over 5 billion people (Ahonen, 2012). With billions of text messages sent and received each month (NetLingo, 2009), texting is a likely and increasingly used means through which college and university administrators can reach students, and for students to connect with faculty, staff, and student peers.

BRAND MEANING, MANAGEMENT, AND MESSAGING IN THE TWENTY-FIRST CENTURY

According to Batey (2008), "It is brand meaning that mediates between products and consumer motivation, thereby determining consumer behavior. A brand's meaning is determined by how the brand is perceived by the public at a conscious level and how the brand resonates with them at a semi- or subconscious level" (p. 111). In the case of Philander Smith College, its brand meaning and messaging is reinforced by the use of social media technologies that encourage access and inclusion among all campus constituents.

With this extensive use of social media, Martin (2007) has suggested that a new "renaissance" is emerging, with a shift from the fracturing of personality through endless choices to a fusion and integration caused by the construction of meaning made possible through increased Internet technologies (pp. 194–195). Through the use of open-ended processes, collaboration focused on advocacy and the advancement of the greater good, leadership that is more inclusive and less hierarchical, the recognition of cultural traditions and roots, and a preference for the authentic, institutions of higher education may utilize social media to create a structure for students through which they may develop a more integrated sense of self and community (Martin, 2007; Preston, 2001).

Kimbrough (2010) recalls:

> While browsing at a Barnes and Noble, I walked past a table of new business-related books. I came across one that stood out: *RenGen* (Renaissance Generation). The tagline of the book read, 'The rise of the cultural consumer—and what it means to your business.' I thought I'd take a chance on this book. After reading the first couple of chapters, I knew this was a wise choice. The author, Patricia Martin, defined a renaissance as a movement or period of robust creative and intellectual activity that is associated with a rebirth of civilization. Her book is about the rise of this new American renaissance generation, or RenGen, defined as 'an emerging strata of enlightened individuals who are hungry for ideas and ways to express them.' When I arrived in December of 2004, and after several months of getting to know people on campus and engaging them in discussions, I believed that Philander Smith College could enter a renaissance era. (para. 1–2)

As a historically Black college or university (HBCU), Philander Smith advocates a mission of social justice and sets out to graduate alumni who exemplify this character trait at individual, group, and institutional levels.

BACKGROUND/ORIGINS OF THE PHILANDER SMITH COLLEGE MISSION

The discussions and focus groups facilitated by Kimbrough and Thoma Thoma in 2005 and 2006 indicated a lack of unique identity. Most HBCUs utilize the same descriptors, such as "small, family atmosphere;" thus, PSC found itself at a recruitment disadvantage when compared with other peer institutions as well as predominantly White campuses with more resources and increasingly popular online education programs such as the University of Phoenix (Kimbrough, 2006; W. Kimbrough, personal communication, June 24, 2010). As a result, PSC looked for a brand message associated with the United Methodist Church due to PSC's history of affiliation with the church. Research on the tenants of the Church indicate an emphasis on social justice, and as a College that evolved from what was once Walden Seminary and Wesley Chapel United Methodist Church, PSC found a connection with a mission of social justice that dated back to the creation of PSC in 1882 (Kimbrough, 2006). Additionally, research on the current generation of young people (born between 1980 and 2000) indicates this group of college-age students is interested in the core values of "optimism, civic duty, confidence, achievement, morality, street smarts, and diversity" (Kimbrough, 2006, p. 3), which indicates an interest in issues of social justice. Coupled with research that revealed few institutions with a social justice mission (and no HBCUs), PSC identified an opportunity to create "a strong, unique identity that strengthens both [their] history as an HBCU and [their] relationship with the United Methodist Church" (Kimbrough, 2006, p. 3).

In order to ensure a "unique sustainable, and competitive advantage," as asserted by Thoma Thoma (Kimbrough, 2006, p. 3), PSC had to forge a new identity that would excite students, donors and potential donors, and community members. According to Kimbrough (2006), "Social justice is that unique identity" (p. 6). He continues:

> Students and parents today are sold a constant diet of highly ranked colleges based on how brilliant their incoming students are, their wealth, and how successful their students become after graduation. Very rarely if ever does a College indicate that it empowers young people to take up causes of the marginalized, the exploited, the disenfranchised and the disempowered. As an historically Black college affiliated with the United Methodist Church, located in Little Rock—a hub of social justice organizations and activities—Phi-

lander Smith College is uniquely positioned to graduate men and women who will be advocates for these kinds of causes. (Kimbrough, 2006, p. 6)

Kimbrough's attempts to lead Philander Smith College in defining their unique identity parallel that of Dr. Marquis LaFayette Harris when he questioned the institution's relevancy in the late 1930s. Kimbrough, seeking connection to the history of the College, found a similar focus on social justice in Harris's inaugural address from October 26, 1937 (W. Kimbrough, personal communication, June 24, 2010). In this address, Harris (1937) explains:

> The present day College must not become too satisfied with its status quo but rather constantly aware of their obligation to the community, state and society in behalf of investments in time, effort, money and good will which make possible their existence. They must sell their wares on the market of human relations. The value of which is calculated in terms of constructive service and influence for the preservation of social and spiritual values. (p. 2)

Harris goes on to discuss PSC's unique role in serving the African-American community, the responsibility to moral education through affiliation with the United Methodist Church, and the need to explore some of the fields that may be neglected by public institutions such as the Science of Human Relations and the Art of Creative Living (Harris, 1937, p. 3). Through this assertion, Harris lays out the mission of PSC to include the "First Principles of the New Educational Pattern at Philander Smith College" (Harris, 1937, p. 3). These Principles include ideals of valuing human personality, fostering community, and developing creativity. Harris describes this new curriculum as follows:

> It assumes that the purpose of the College must be defined in terms of a definite functional relation to the community and Society both directly and indirectly by projecting its departments into the community through an activity curriculum. It must disseminate such information and stimulate such activity as will incite Community development rather than community migration. It must serve indirectly through its students by directing and contributing to the most complete development of individuals and groups in such manner as will help them live life most abundantly in all its wholesome aspects. (p. 3)

Two years later, on February 2, 1939 at a dinner address delivered to the Board of Education of the Methodist Episcopal Church, Harris (1941) further defines the connection between PSC's mission, a liberal arts education, and issues of social justice:

> But by far the Church College will best serve in the strategic location of smaller colleges of Liberal Arts. Here the individual touch, personality develop-

ment, a keen sense of personal responsibility and social justice, a profound social sympathy and moral sensitiveness will take precedence over mere "fact-finding". Somehow, society must be awakened to this basic function so vital in a democracy. It is not imaginary to believe that such awakening will bring adequate support to colleges of this type. (p. 82)

With a focus on personal and social responsibility, Harris's influence on the current social justice mission of PSC is clear. To this end, through a collective, socially just process, Kimbrough strategically and humanistically uses past institutional leadership practices and identity to inform the current institutional brand.

METHODOLOGY

The institution of higher education examined in this study has unique historical and contextual factors that have influenced its approach to institutional leadership and brand management and messaging. As a small, private, historically Black college in the Midwest, Philander Smith College's institutional profile is, arguably, not viewed as being on par with many of its HBCU counterparts. Innovations in leadership styles and behaviors, brand strategy and marketing, and student recruitment have become part of an historical imperative to sustain the College. To this end, a case study; Strengths, Weaknesses, Opportunities, and Threats (SWOT) analysis; and document analysis, coupled with a semi-structured group interview examining the journey of Philander Smith College under the leadership of Kimbrough, create avenues for generalizable findings that will inform the scope of future research in terms of an institution's effective use of social media to raise its profile.

A case study is the most preferred method for this research because of the type of questions asked, because the investigators have very little control over the events, and because the focus of the study is on a contemporary phenomenon within a current context (Yin, 2003). Furthermore, the case study is a mode of inquiry that helps to understand and explain the meaning of a social phenomenon, such as the use of social media technology to connect to PSC's social justice mission, with as little disruption of the natural setting as possible. Case studies often involve observation of behaviors and the use of interviews, whether structured formally or semi-formally, such as the semi-structured group interview with PSC's President and Senior Administration. Structured formal interviews follow a rigid series of predetermined questions, whereas semi-structured interviews do not. The advantage of two practices is that it allows options of flexibility and opportunity for informal dialogue between the interviewer and interviewee and also allows the interviewer, after establishing a sense of trust with participants, to obtain information from the subjects that they might otherwise be reluctant to share (Jaeger, 1997).

In general, case studies do not claim any particular method for data collection. However, interviews and institutional documentation are the usual sources of data collection; thus, they have been utilized for this study as well (Merriam, 1998). As a result, subject observations, interviews, and documentation afford the opportunity to analyze data, and in this case, promote storytelling, discovery, and interpretation versus hypothesis testing, as well as the holistic ability to capture a concept (Merriam, 1998).

According to Yin (1984), the use of case study and its multiple data collection methods and analysis techniques provide avenues for the researchers to triangulate data in order to strengthen the research findings and conclusions. Patton (2002) elaborates on the use of triangulation by arguing, "Triangulation strengthens a study by combining methods. This can mean using several kinds of methods or data, including using both quantitative and qualitative approaches" (p. 247).

Hesse-Biber and Leavy (2004) further explain,

> What distinguishes the field of qualitative research is its diversity.... It encompasses a wide range of epistemological positions and theoretical frameworks while offering many distinct research methods....The result is that a wide range of techniques of data gathering and analysis is available to researchers. This allows for not only a wide range of researchable topics, but also a wide range of approaches to the same topic. This lends a depth to qualitative research. (pp. 5–6).

In this way, triangulation goes beyond the use of a single-method approach to validation by providing multiple methods and a deeper understanding of the researcher's findings, conclusions, and overall communication of the aims of a study.

Guba and Lincoln (1998) posit three components of the assumptions within a paradigm:

1. The ontological question
2. The epistemological question
3. The methodological question (pp. 201).

The research conducted in this study employs a paradigm or "set of basic beliefs" (p. 200) in which methodological questions "address how a researcher can ascertain the information believed to be knowable" or "what methods of inquiry will access the data a researcher is interested in" (Hesse-Biber & Leavy, 2004, p. 7)?

According to Stake (1994) "the researcher examines various interests in the phenomenon, selecting a case of some typicality, but leaning toward those cases that seem to offer the opportunity to learn....Potential for learning is a different and sometimes superior criterion to representativeness. Often it is better to learn a lot from an atypical case than a little from a magnificently typical case" (p. 243). Thus, the case study of Philander Smith College provides the researcher the opportunity to learn from an atypical social phenomenon.

Through the use of a semi-structured group interview for data collection, each participant is able to fully articulate the intended and unintended consequences of the use of social media to advance the messages delivered by the campus mission statement and "Think Justice" initiative. Further, each office is able to make meaning of what may have precipitated the "Think Justice" initiative. In this way, the strategy allows the researchers to investigate within predetermined areas of inquiry. Because the time allotted for interviews was not extensive, this systematic interview process enabled the researchers to more effectively capture the aims of the study for both the interviewers and subjects while maintaining a focused yet conversational approach to communication. Additionally, this strategy allows the researchers to determine whether or not modification to the interview approach by excluding areas of inquiry, for example, is necessary (Lofland & Lofland, 1984).

In addition to utilizing case study, completion of a SWOT analysis provided participants more time for thoughtful reflection following the semi-structured group interview. Because the purpose of SWOT analysis is to "yield strategic insights" (Valentin, 2001, p. 54), a review of the participants' SWOT analysis allowed the researchers to look more critically at the participants' self-assessment in order to develop best practices and competencies for using social media technologies. An analysis of this document submitted by participants facilitates how the reflection process more clearly defines institutional, administrative, and instructional practices. To this end, other forms of document analysis are used in this study to connect these specific practices to the language of the institutional mission.

Through document analysis of an historical mission statement during the Harris administration (1936–1961) as well as the current institutional mission statement adopted in 2007 and the Social Justice White Paper titled, *Advocates for Social Justice: A Unique Identity for Philander Smith College*, the researchers are able to more clearly define institutional, administrative, and instructional practices and competencies. By analyzing the past and current Philander Smith College mission statements, a set of competencies, or Continuum of Competencies for Using Social Media Technologies, was developed. This form of document analysis allows the researchers to view the text through the context in which it was produced while investigating common themes that emerge as part of the institutional history of Philander Smith College. Further, this form of inquiry allows researchers to make meaning of text and potential discourses—such as the ideals of social justice—that result in "some kind of causal mechanism in social action" (Mason, 1996, p. 109).

To this end, a Continuum of Competencies for Using Social Media Technologies creates the desired leadership styles and behaviors, brand strategy and marketing, and student recruitment necessary to raise the institutional profile of Philander Smith College. The Continuum is a concept involving an integrated system of competencies that serve as guiding principles for policy and praxis development and application. As part of the construction of the institutional mission statement, this Continuum allows campus administrators to revolutionize the traditional and enduring approaches to institutional messaging so that it becomes an assessment tool that provides a framework of accountability for all community members. The researchers contend that the successful and intentional delivery of academic and student services as well as an authentic sense of community can be realized using these best practices. Within the theoretical frameworks of the study, the combined results of the case study involving SWOT and document analysis, and semi-structured group interview are utilized to determine motivations and implications for institutional leadership and policy development. As a result of this study, a set of competencies around the use of social media technologies that is generalizable to peer institutions is developed.

PROCEDURE

Initial research into the use of social media by HBCUs to further a mission of social justice yielded no use of this particular practice or initiative at other institutions. However, review of the institutional mission of Philander Smith College and the social justice white paper titled, *Advocates for Social Justice: A Unique Identity for Philander Smith College*, as well as the blog of Kimbrough and the social networking sites sponsored by Philander Smith College reveals a connection between the institution's "Think Justice" initiative and their use of social media to communicate with prospective, current, and former students and other stakeholders. Thus, Kimbrough was contacted about participating (along with senior administrators from key campus offices) in a semi-structured group interview regarding their use of social media and the intentional or unintentional connection to the "Think Justice" initiative. Because of the relative infancy of this initiative, Kimbrough identifies the following campus administrators (in addition to himself) as being involved in the efforts to increase the use of social media and/or to disseminate the social justice mission on campus: Ms. Sericia Cole, Director of Public Relations; Dr. Shannon Fleming, Vice President for Institutional Advancement; and Mr. Reginald Hameth, Development Officer.

After identification of the research participants and initial contact regarding participation, the aforementioned individuals provided informed consent and received a list of the ten questions to guide the semi-structured group interview. In the spirit of the overall theme of this study, the researchers were compelled to employ a teleconferencing format for the two-hour, semi-structured group interview. The content of the interview ranged from the types of social media used by Philander Smith College to the motivations and outcomes of its use. Additionally, the participants were asked to consider the connection between the use of social media and the mission of the institution as well as to contemplate the future of social media on campus and throughout higher education. At the conclusion of the interview, the participants were asked to collectively complete a SWOT analysis, providing additional reflection on the strengths, weaknesses, opportunities, and threats related to their use of social media and their "Think Justice" initiative.

Upon receipt of the SWOT analysis, the researchers analyzed the interview responses and the participants' self-assessment for recurring themes to serve as generalizable competencies for the use of social media at peer institutions. Specifically, concepts of branding, African-American leadership, communication, and constructivism/connectivism inform the Continuum of Competencies for Using Social Media Technologies. These competencies serve as best practices for institutions who also seek to raise their profile, despite having limited resources.

While the authors did not have a preset idea of their findings, categorized data and themes consistent with critical reflection of past and existing campus community relations and mission statement text to answer the primary research question were identified. The researchers also identified specific ways in which institutional leaders can actualize the College brand via its adopted 2007 mission statement and evaluate policy and praxis implications generalizable to Philander Smith College's peer institutions. Through democratic discourse that makes meaning of the overall accountability and effectiveness of the mission, new policy and praxis can be implemented and successfully realized. As a result of this study, a more comprehensive understanding of the role institutional leadership at HBCUs can play in the use of social media can be considered.

FINDINGS

Returning to our original research question, the researchers identified ways in which institutional leadership at PSC model a parallel use of social media technologies to advance its institutional mission, thus providing some best practices for Black colleges and universities regarding the use of social media to improve viability and sustainability. The authors gleaned insight from each method of inquiry, as there were not only thoughtful responses given during the semi-structured group interview, but also a reflective component after allowing several days to complete the SWOT analysis as a group.

As it relates to enrollment trends that indicate a strengthening of PSC's academic profile, the semi-structured group interview and SWOT analysis reveal the following: From fall 2004 to fall 2009 enrollment has downtrended from 949 to 668. Nonetheless, the unconventional leadership of Kimbrough provides a reason to this rhyme. As explained by Kimbrough, in February of 2005, the institution was audited by the Student Loan Guarantee Foundation of Arkansas. One of the main findings was the college awarding Pell Grants to those who did not meet the standards set by the college or the government. As a result, Kimbrough hired a new financial aid director in June 2005 and an immediate implementation of that policy began. For two years (2006 and 2007) there was a residual drop in enrollment due to students who could not make satisfactory academic progress (SAP). By the fall of 2007, the College had purged the non-qualifying students but found it was in a position to graduate larger classes.

First-time freshmen increased from 82 in fall 2006 to 159 in fall 2009 and total new students increased from 103 in fall 2006 to 234 in fall 2009. The average high school GPA of entering freshman has increased from 2.38 in 2004 to 2.89 in 2009. A comparison of PSC and National Black Student ACT (NBACT) scores reveals an increase of average score of 15.4 (PSC)/17.1 (NBACT) in 2004 to 19 (PSC)/16.9 (NBACT) in 2009. First- to second-year retention rates increased from 51% in 2004 to 72% in 2009. Percentage of new students requiring remediation decreased from 77.2% in fall 2005 to 51.3% in fall 2009 (the fall 2009 State average was 40.4%). Across these indicators in admissions standards, a limited number of non-qualified students were admitted in an effort to more fully support their persistence to graduation; a review of curriculum was conducted; a reorganization of recruitment and admissions practices was completed; and an enrollment goal of 200–250 incoming freshmen and 50 transfer students was targeted. Kimbrough and his team have set an internal goal of 800 by 2012 and 1000 by 2016; however, the institution is on track to enroll 800 by 2011 and 1000 by 2014 (W. Kimbrough, personal communication, July 24, 2010).

Analysis of the social justice white paper reveals an intentional methodology employed by the leadership of PSC so that the institutional brand could be identified in earnest. Using institutional history as a form of inquiry, the authors identified parallels between past leadership and aims of the 1866 social charter and the social justice mission of the College adopted in 2007. These parallels are predicated on the history of PSC, the values of the United Methodist Church, and the interests of Millennials.

During the semi-structured group interview, the authors noted Kimbrough's transformational leadership style and use of a spokesperson model versus a figurehead model. This personalization of authority creates authenticity as a result of not allowing his voice to be silenced by the threat of sanctions by his Board of Trustees, instead speaking out in the best interest of all campus constituents—namely students. As a reflection of Kimbrough's commitment to social justice, his Board members are representative of racial and gender equity (34% White Males, 27% Black Males, 26% Black Females, and 13% White Females); thus, the authors argue a shared commitment to the institutional mission of social justice is not beyond the scope of the Board's capacity for building community.

Additionally, Kimbrough's educational thought around social justice, capacity building, and innovative institutional sustainability creates a "ministry" that embodies tenants of servant leadership. This sense of interconnectedness leads to a flattening of hierarchical arrangements that provide an equal opportunity for access and engagement from the cabinet level to senior administration, faculty, staff, and students to community members. Kimbrough views his role as embodying and reinforcing the values of the campus community and leading by example. He believes that he should make time to show himself as that example. As "spokesperson," he lives the values of the mission of social justice and goes beyond the rhetoric of the mission. In this way, Kimbrough has tapped into and understands the significance of sensory experience, thus connecting in very real ways with the values of those who identify with the brand meaning, messaging, and management of the PSC mission.

The authors were able to identify an interrelationship among the institutional leadership and mission and social media technologies at PSC. Unlike many other HBCUs, PSC is effectively utilizing social media to enhance their core values while seeking to offset the infiltration of online education that has successfully recruited and graduated Black students. While many online education programs lack standardized testing requirements for admission, PSC has increased their academic profile without sacrificing a commitment to access and equity. With a commitment to stay ahead of the curve with regards to emerging social media technologies, PSC has implemented a customer service and brand messaging model directly related to its mission of social justice. However, senior campus administrators emphasize such efforts could not be possible without transformational leadership that understands the nature of risk management and brand meaning, messaging, and management. As a leader, Kimbrough is in touch with the interests and needs of the students, thus allowing the campus to develop a baseline competency in the use of social media technologies for brand message delivery. Therefore, the learning curve for how to apply new technologies is minimal in comparison to campuses that have yet to embrace this strategy as a tool for raising its profile. Though the moving parts of this initiative seem to work seamlessly, ironically, Kimbrough initially viewed social media technologies separate from the "Think Justice" initiative, as he started blogging *before* the "Think Justice" motto was developed. Out of necessity, Kimbrough simply wanted to use social media as a tool to better communicate with constituents and create connections using cost-effective, innovative venues.

Philander Smith College has found a way to position itself as an HBCU that not only provides an opportunity to get a quality education but also graduate a critical mass of citizens concerned with issues of social justice. Though use of social media may not be integral to this mission, it provides a cost-effective and socially relevant tool for marketing and outreach that serves as a more efficient means of communicating the mission and campus updates.

Social media technologies have been infused with alumni giving and capital campaigns. For example, during the spring of 2009, the development office created a Facebook page for outreach to alumni; and during the spring of 2010, "Text to Give" was launched based on the success of the Haiti relief efforts and Obama campaign. Additionally, "Campaign 77," which started in November 2009 on Facebook with young alums giving $77 in honor of the 1877 founding date of the College, has resulted in increased support for the "Renaissance 100 Scholarship Campaign."

Finally, the integral part social media technologies played in the Kresge Foundation award demonstrated the ways in which a potential donor can engage and see firsthand the pre-existing commitment to social justice through institutional mission; brand meaning, messaging, and management; and campus culture. Consequently, the Kresge funded position of Director of Social Justice Initiative was realized and the position became available and filled in 2011. The Office of The Social Justice Initiative houses a Director, who sits on the President's Cabinet, a Program Coordinator, and an Administrative Assistant. Grant funding and implementation of this key administrative office with a reporting line to the president of the College, make the case to continue the PSC institutional identity regardless of future changes in executive leadership.

DISCUSSION/PROPOSED SET OF COMPETENCIES

Community Practice Model

One way that African-American leaders can move toward a "return" to a collectivist approach toward liberation is through the use of African-American community practice models. Carlton-LaNey and Burwell (1996) advocate for an understanding of the community in order to build social and political power and a focus on interdependence and group identity based on African tradition and history. In order to build this collectivism, they assert community practice should encompass "elements of advocacy, human social and economic development, social justice, and political and social action" (p. 1). This type of collective identity may be fostered through the use of several strategies: utilizing social betterment and social protest (pp. 7–26); acknowledging weaknesses but focusing on strengths (pp. 27–48); promoting education and training and organizing the local community (pp. 49–69); recognizing barriers, the need for culture-specific community awareness, and the necessity to gain community support and access to community leadership (pp. 71–90); and adapting the system to the needs of the community as opposed to expecting the individuals to adapt to the system (pp. 91–107). Recognizing the need for institutional sustainability, Philander Smith College sought a collective identity in order to galvanize its current students so that they one day become a supportive, engaged alumni base. There is clarity in Kimbrough's ultimate goals set forth by the College that echoes past Black college leadership. To this end, Kimbrough posits:

> ... [Benjamin] Mays' presidency develops real relationships with students. I was humored by an article I read about presidents with "monthly" office hours as a way to engage students. Many presidents find themselves on wild goose chases trying to raise funds, when the simplest way is to create an environment that supports and nurtures students, and those students will become giving alumni. No current president wants to do that because they are under pressure to raise money now. But for the long term viability of an institution, the only guaranteed sources of support (as our current economic crisis has shown) are not foundations or corporations, but alumni. (Kimbrough, 2009, para. 10)

The Kimbrough leadership style and educational thought have served Philander Smith College in numerous ways including increased alumni giving from 4% to nearly 16 (W. Kimbrough, personal communication, July 24, 2010). Kimbrough's example continues to secure a legacy of PSC that will one day inspire institutional leaders who also face the task of raising or sustaining the institution's profile.

LIMITATIONS OF STUDY

Two limitations of the study must be taken into consideration. First, at this early implementation stage of coordinating social media and brand message and management strategies, PSC's key leadership team has been the most engaged. To this end, there is no comprehensive use of social media technology across all campus units or sub-units; however, it is the intent of campus administration to continue to share the competitive advantages of such use and introduce to the campus community ways in which social media can enhance the stated institutional mission. Second, social media technologies was initially used out of necessity due, primarily, to budget constraints; however, since its implementation, the outcomes related to its use is now deemed vital to PSC's branding, mission, and collaborative partnerships. While, the lack of a centralized campus infrastructure such as Information Technology (IT), is a limitation, identifying a remedy to such a limitation will control for anticipated and unanticipated consequences such as capturing all students contact information to be linked on Facebook or Twitter; proactively addressing accessibility of social media technologies to those with physical and learning disabilities; and providing access via 24-hour computer lab accessibility. Addressing the two limitations above creates opportunities for cross-campus collaboration among entities such as the Office of Disability Services, Instructional Technology, and the newly hired Director for The Social Justice Initiative. Because PSC's goal is to graduate students beyond their capacity to obtain a job as well as find purpose in their immediate and global communities, collaboration among campus entities lends itself to the development of the whole student and their trajectory global citizens.

IMPLICATIONS AND CONCLUSIONS

Due to the focus on an open-ended, negotiable approach to learning that utilizes collaborative opportunities and the contextualization of learning within an emergent situation, a constructivist theory seems applicable to the utilization of social media within higher education (Mason & Rennie, 2008, p. 17). Constructivism requires an active approach to the construction of knowledge and facilitative instruction that supports this construction of knowledge (Mason & Rennie, 2008). To be sure, communications within social networking technologies and sites, blogs, wikis, etc. become means through which students may interact within communities to direct their own learning. Further, these tools of communication assist institutional leaders as they negotiate brand meaning, messaging, and management as new technologies emerge.

Because of the need for the rapid evaluation of information within this ever-changing, constantly updated information society, Siemens (2004) suggests the expansion of constructivism toward a connectivism perspective of learning that acknowledges these evolving learning tools and environments. This theory includes the idea that learning is a process of making connections and requires diverse opinions and that the capacity to "know" more is critical and requires the recognition of decision-making as a learning process (Siemens, 2004). In order to provide for these constructed and connected learning opportunities, institutions of higher education may look toward the development of online community structures to facilitate learning. However, with this decentralized communication model, colleges and universities need to help students develop evaluation, self-regulation, and collaboration skills by reconceptualizing the roles of educators from central disseminators of information to facilitators that use their expertise to guide and focus learners (Mason & Rennie, 2008). Thus, communication within social media contexts cannot replace in-person interactions, but should instead serve as another tool for increased collaboration. Because trust is essential to the effective use of social media in educational environments, institutional leaders should model the use of various forms of communication in order to gain acceptance among reluctant faculty and staff and to help students recognize the importance of critically examining the vast information available online. These ideas complement Renaissance thinking that promotes and mandates interconnectedness and community building and continues to inspire Kimbrough and his team to more closely examine the ways in which they can construct, connect, and assess institutional, administrative, and instructional competencies at Philander Smith College.

Within the Historically Black Colleges and Universities (HBCUs), social media may provide opportunities for African-Americans to become the creators of their "own destinies" through the dissemination of unified messages and positive images (Barber & Tait, 2001, pp. 260–261). However, in order for this potential to be realized, African-Americans need to be presented with the same access to social media as their European American counterparts (Barber & Tait, 2001). By utilizing social media on the campuses of HBCUs, African-American students may be provided with the access to various political, social, educational, and cultural communities available online, while also being provided with opportunities to develop the evaluative and collaborative skills necessary to effectively navigate through the wealth of information and to contribute ideas grounded in the advocacy, inclusion, cultural tradition, and authenticity desired in this new renaissance (Barber & Jones, 2001; Martin, 2007). The realization of these outcomes is, in itself, symbolic of the ways in which one can make meaning of social justice through the use of social media technologies. To be sure, the Philander Smith College brand had and will continue to have an exponential internal and external campus community benefit to its matriculates, alumni, and stakeholders while under the leadership of Dr. Kimbrough.

BEST PRACTICES AND RECOMMENDATIONS

What has been presented here is a case in which a small HBCU located in Little Rock, Arkansas improved enrollment, curriculum and fiscal resources through the everyday use of social media technologies. Philander's use of social media as a change agent for collaboration, aligns with Evans' (2010) concept that "creative collaboration [is] not just a slogan anymore....global communication that makes global collaboration and the resources emerging for social networking are resources for networked collaboration" (p. 1). The challenge for such an endeavor has been redirecting the ways in which the campus populace (faculty, staff, students and stakeholders) view collaboration. Specifically, the challenge of moving from an individual perspective to that of a collection of individuals possessing complementary skills and working in concert to execute a strategic communication plan that enhances institutional outcomes. Increased recruitment, retention, and graduation rates all benefit the masses and ensure students are opting to enroll at an institution in which they connect to and are most likely to succeed while there. Hence the following competencies, grounded in the use of social media technology that are inextricably tied to a creative collaborative leadership style of the president and overall institutional (re)visioning (Figure 4.1).

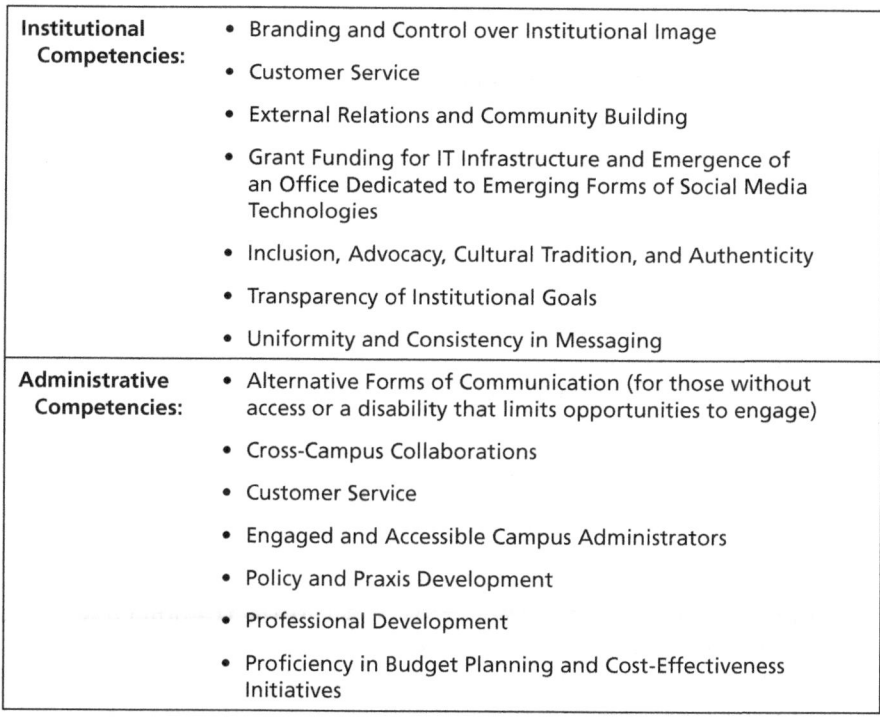

Figure 4.1 Continuum of Competencies for Using Social Media Technologies. Chart of competencies based on best practices as identified in the literature and through analysis of the practices of PSC.

(continued)

Instructional Competencies:	• Adult and Transfer Student Learning Model that Integrates Social Media as an Alternative Tool for Enrollment Management and Delivery of Customer Service
	• Alternative Instructional Technologies (with implications for Administration)
	• Faculty Moving from Disseminators of Information to Facilitators of Self-Constructed Knowledge
	• Implications for Decision-Making as a Learning Process
	• Increased Collaborations between Students and Faculty
	• Interrelationship between Social Media and Social Justice
	• Pod-casting as an Instructional Tool

Figure 4.1 (continued) Continuum of Competencies for Using Social Media Technologies. Chart of competencies based on best practices as identified in the literature and through analysis of the practices of PSC.

REFERENCES

Ahonen, T. T. (2012, May 6). Mobile services beyond messaging? Excellent TNS global survey reveals tons. *Communities dominate brands: Business and marketing challenges for the 21st century.* Retrieved from http://communities-dominate.blogs.com/brands/2012/05/mobile-services-beyond-messaging-excellent-tns-global-survey-reveals-tons.html

Barber, J. T., & Jones, S. (2001). More than you think: African Americans on the World Wide Web. In J. T. Barber & A. A. Tait (Eds.), *The information society and the Black community* (pp. 3–30). Westport, CT: Praeger.

Barber, J. T., & Tait, A. A. (2001). Is black America an information community? In J. T. Barber, & A. A. Tait (Eds.), *The information society and the black community* (pp. 259–261). Westport, CT: Praeger.

Batey, M. (2008). *Brand meaning.* New York, NY: Routledge.

Benjamin, L. (2007). *Three Black generations at the crossroads: Community, culture, and consciousness* (2nd ed.). Lanham, MD: Rowman & Littlefield.

Carlton-LaNey, I., & Burwell, N. Y. (1996). *African American community practice models: Historical and contemporary responses.* New York, NY: The Haworth Press.

Evans, S. H. (2010). *Virtual Outworlding: Arts, tech, education, how to in the virtual world.* Retrieved from http://virtualoutworlding.blogspot.com/2010/06/creative-collaboration-not-just-slogan.html

Guba. E. G., & Lincoln, Y. S. (1998). Competing paradigms in qualitative research: Theories and issues. In N. K. Denzin & Y. S. Lincoln (Eds.), *The landscape of qualitative research: Theories and issues* (pp. 193–220. Thousand Oaks, CA: Sage Pulications.

Harris, M. L. (1937, October). *Creative adjustment: A philosophy of life man's greatest need.* Inaugural speech presented at Philander Smith College, Little Rock, AR.

Harris, M. L. (1941). *The voice in the wilderness.* Boston: The Christopher Publishing House.

Hecht, M. L., Jackson, R. L., & Ribeau, S. A. (2003). *African American communication: Exploring identity and culture* (2nd ed.). Mahwah, NJ: Lawrence Erlbaum Associates.

Hesse-Biber, S. N., & Leavy, P. (Eds.). (2004). *Approaches to qualitative research.* New York: Oxford University Press.

Jaeger, R. M. (1997). Methods for research in education. (2nd ed). Washington, DC: American Educational Research Association.

Karpati, A. (2002). Net generation. *EMILE.* Retrieved from http://www.emile.eu.org/Papers1.htm

Kimbrough, W. M. (2006). *Advocates for social justice: A unique identity for Philander Smith College* [White paper]. Retrieved from http://www.philander.edu/social-justice/whitepaper.aspx

Kimbrough, W. M. (2009). *The Benjamin Mays Model.* Retrieved from http://www.insidehighered.com/advice/2009/10/30/kimbrough

Kimbrough, W. M. (2010). *The social justice initiative.* [Grant proposal by Philander Smith College to the Kresge Foundation].

Livingstone, S., & Bober, M. (2005, April). *UK children go online: Final report of key project findings.* Retrieved from http://www.york.ac.uk/res/e society/projects/1/UKCGOExecSummary.pdf

Lofland, J., & Lofland, L. H. (1984). *Analyzing social settings.* Belmont, CA: Wadsworth.

Martin, P. (2007). *RenGen: The rise of the cultural consumer—and what it means to your business.* Avon, MA: Platinum Press.

Mason, R., & Rennie, F. (2008). *E-learning and social networking handbook: Resources for higher education.* New York, NY: Routledge.

Mason, J. (1996). *Qualitative researching.* London: SAGE Publications.

Masterson, K. (2010). *'Hip Hop Prez' rejuvenates a college using a personal touch.* Retrieved from http://chronicle.com/article/Hip-Hop-Prez-Rejuvenates-a/65350

Merriam, S. B. (1998). *Qualitative research and case study application in education, revised and expanded from case study research in education.* San Francisco, CA: Jossey-Bass.

NetLingo. (2009). *Texting.* Retrieved from http://www.netlingo.com/word/texting.php

nielsenwire (2012, March 8). Buss in the blogosphere: Millions more bloggers and blog readers. Retrieved from http://blog.nielsen.com/nielsenwire/online_mobile/buzz-in-the-blogosphere-millions-more-bloggers-and-blog-readers/

Oblinger, D., & Oblinger, J. (2005). *Educating the net generation.* Boulder, CO: Educause. Retrieved from http://www.educause.edu/ir/library/pdf/pub7101.pdf

Patton, M. Q. (2002). *Qualitative evaluation and research methods* (3rd ed.). Thousand Oaks, CA: Sage Publications, Inc.

Pingdom. (2013a, January 16). Internet 2012 in numbers. Retrieved from http://royal.pingdom.com/2013/01/16/internet-2012-in-numbers/

Pingdom. (2013b, February 3). *Facebook may be the largest "country" on earth by 2016*. Retrieved from http://royal.pingdom.com/2013/02/05/facebook-2016/

Preston, P. (2001). *Reshaping communications: Technology, information, and social change*. London, UK: SAGE.

Raines, C. (2002). Managing millennials. *Generations at work*. Retrieved from http://www.generationsatwork.com/articles_millenials.php

Rovaris, D. J. (2005). *Mays and Morehouse: How Benjamin Elijah Mays developed Morehouse College, 1940–1967*. Maryland: Beckham House Publishers.

Rudd, T., Sutch, D., & Facer, K. (2006, December). Opening education: Towards new learning networks. *Futurelab*. Retrieved from http://www.futurelab.org.uk/resources/documents/opening_education/Learning_Networks_report.pdf

Siemens, G. (2004). Connectivism: A learning theory for the digital age. *elearnspace*. Retrieved from http://www.elearnspace.org/Articles/connectivism.htm

Stake, R. E. (1994). Case studies. In N. K. Denzin & Y. S. Lincoln (Eds.), *Handbook of qualitative research* (pp. 236–247). Thousand Oaks, CA: Sage Publications.

Suggs, V. L. (2009). *The production of political discourse: Annual radio addresses of black college presidents during the 1930s and 1940s* (Doctoral dissertation, Georgia State University). Retrieved from http://digitalarchive.gsu.edu/cgi/viewcontent.cgi?article=1032&context=eps_diss

Valentin, E. K. (2001). SWOT analysis from a resource-based view. *Journal of Marketing Theory and Practice, 9*(2), 54–68.

Veen, W. (2007). *Homo Zappiens and the need for new education systems*. Retrieved from http://www.oecd.org/dataoecd/0/5/38360892.pdf

Yin, R. K. (1984). *Case study research: Design and methods*. Newbury Park, CA: Sage.

Yin, R. K. (2003). *Case study research: Design and methods* (3rd Ed.). Thousand Oaks, CA: Sage Publications, Inc.

SECTION III

BLACK COLLEGE SUSTAINABILITY

CHAPTER 5

HBCU PIPELINE TO COLLEGE ACCESS

Considerations for the Twenty-First Century

Torry L. Reynolds
Vickie L. Suggs
Shayla Mitchell

INTRODUCTION

According to data from the U.S. Department of Education, African-American student enrollment at Historically Black Colleges and Universities (HBCUs) has lagged behind that of Predominately White Institutions (PWIs) since the passing of desegregation legislation in the mid-twentieth century (USDE, 2010b). Fewer than 11% of African-Americans attended HBCUs in 2009 as compared to 83% in 1961 (Hill, 1985; United States Department of Education [USDE], 2010a). With more Black college students attending PWIs than HBCUs, many Americans question the relevance of HBCUs in a post-integration society. HBCU advocates such as Brown, Freeman, Gasman, and Minor have written countless narratives and conducted numerous studies illustrating the utility of this institution type in promoting holistic student development, academic achievement and personal success for African-American students. Nonetheless, their efforts have done little to sway public opinion or increase HBCU attendance (Aud et al., 2010; Gasman & Bowman, 2011; USDE, 2010a). The question then becomes how can HBCUs reestablish relevance and successfully market themselves in a competitive higher education market? This review of the literature looks at college choice, developmental education, and collaborative leadership to inform HBCU revitalization.

HBCU FOUNDINGS

Historically Black colleges and universities are broadly defined as accredited institutions "established prior to 1964, whose principal mission was, and is, the education of Black Americans" (Higher Education Act, 1965, sec. 1061). HBCUs provided educational access and inclusion for African-Americans at a time when they were prohibited from enrolling in most existing Predominantly White post-secondary Institutions. Today, HBCUs continue to provide access and inclusion for African-Americans facing racial and economic discrimination around post-secondary educational access.

The first HBCUs appeared in the North shortly before the Civil War. Among these are Cheney University (1837) and Lincoln University (1854) both in Pennsylvania and Wilberforce University in Ohio (1856) (Brown, Donahoo, & Bertrand, 2001). Wilberforce has the notable distinction of being the first HBCU owned and operated by African-Americans. In the period following the end of the Civil War, HBCUs began to appear across the nation under the sponsorship of private religious institutions and the federally supported Freedman's Bureau (Brown, Ricard, & Donahoo, 2004; Gasman, 2008; USDE, 1985). Accordingly, a critical mass of Black colleges were situated in the American South to meet the needs of the large African-American population living there.

As the newly founded institution type began to develop, administrators were compelled to define the academic scope and purpose of HBCUs. The search for institutional direction was the catalyst in a discussion later fueled by the intellectual dialogue of W. E. B. Du Bois and Booker T. Washington (Brown et al., 2001). As prominent African-American scholars in late nineteenth century, Du Bois and Washington held the common goal of educating African-Americans. The role of education in racial uplift, however, was often a source of debate between the two. Du Bois argued Black college curricula should focus on the liberal arts, as he believed a background in the humanities would allow for the creation of the "talented tenth" who would lead the race into self-determination (Du Bois, 1903). Washington, on the other hand, believed African-Americans should focus their energies on learning trades and other forms of skilled labor. With vocational training, Washington contended, Blacks would be able to earn a living wage and pull themselves out of abject poverty. Though a pragmatist who gleaned meaning from his proposition in its practical consequences, Washington also believed in higher education for some Blacks and, accordingly, sent his own daughter to Wellesley College and later to Berlin to study music (Moore, 2003, p. 61). Similarly, Moore (2003) argues that "on the issue of education, Du Bois acknowledged that industrial education was appropriate for some blacks, and he believed that Tuskegee and Hampton were doing valuable work" (p. 61).

Although the debate between Du Bois and Washington is often distorted to highlight ideological differences, their discourse had an influential effect on the curriculum at HBCUs. Specifically, Tuskegee, Hampton, and Benedict, embraced vocational training while Fisk, Howard, Spelman, and Morehouse championed the liberal arts (Jackson, 2001). Despite their chosen curriculum, all HBCUs had to first deal with the fact that a majority of matriculating students were significantly underprepared for college level work. As a result, Black colleges worked to sustain enrollment by providing remedial instruction designed to supplement academic deficiencies (Gasman, 2008). Just as the need for HBCUs arose out of segregationist policies prohibiting Blacks from access to majority institutions, so, too, did the need for remediation in the Black college curriculum.

Taking into account African-Americans' present access to a wide range of post-secondary institution types, there are those who question the significance of HBCUs in twenty-first century. Minor (2008) traces this line of questioning to a general lack a contextual understanding concerning HBCUs, as well as the absence of a contemporary, collective HBCU statement of purpose. Minor urges HBCU administrators to capitalize on the opportunity to clearly define their role for the future, hence the implications of this particular chapter and how it might inform HBCU collaborations as part of the institutional mission. Similarly, Arroyo (2009) contends HBCUs can achieve institutional longevity and prosperity by exploiting its original mission. He provides a theoretical argument that calls for HBCUs to discontinue its attempts to compete with PWIs and, instead, align and affirm their pedagogical policies with the needs of Black students. For example, the historical HBCU approach to undergraduate admissions is to meet students where they are and help them progress to graduation (Brown, Ricard, & Donahoo, 2004). Elite PWI admissions, on the other hand, tend to focus on recruiting the academically gifted and rejecting students who cannot meet their lofty, exclusive standards (Killgore, 2009). If HBCUs were to imitate PWI practices in an attempt to gain legitimacy, they would essentially turn their backs on millions of prospective African-American college students who do not have access to quality secondary and post-secondary education. HBCUs can best meet the needs of the African-American college students by aligning admissions policies to meet students at their present academic level and reinvesting in developmental education and to assist them in degree completion.

Whether relying on the original mission or creating a new one, in today's marketplace, HBCUs would benefit from learning more about reasons why African-American students choose to enroll at this particular institution type and why others choose to attend PWIs. Doing so will inform HBCU recruitment strategies, retention initiatives, and alumni and external relations so that factors that attract students to HBCUs become measurable.

COLLEGE CHOICE AND THE HBCU LEGACY

Traditionally, there have been three popular perspectives on college choice: the economic, the sociological, and the psychological (Bergerson, 2009). Economists approach college choice as a financial investment where students carefully weigh the potential benefits of enrolling at a particular institution against the costs of doing so. The sociological models frame college choice in terms of status attainment. Here, demographic factors such as students' family income and social background figure heavily into which schools one chooses to attend and whether or not one pursues post-secondary education at all. The psychological perspective concentrates specifically on student perceptions of institutional climate. From this viewpoint, students choose to matriculate at a given college or university only if they perceive that the school's characteristics—including cost, environment, and student body—are congruent with their sense of self (Bergerson, 2009).

In 1987, Hossler and Gallagher combined elements of each of the three perspectives to form one of the most widely cited college choice models. The model describes a student's decision making process from inception to completion in terms of three distinct stages. The first stage of Hossler and Gallagher's model is predisposition. In the predisposition stage, students develop their aspirations and expectations for college based on several factors such as parental expectations, peer behavior, and teacher involvement. The next stage is the college search. Students in this stage seek out information from which they create a list of potential colleges and universities. They explore an institution's course offerings, student services, physical environment, and other amenities all in hopes of finding a school that fits their personal needs and desires. The final stage is college choice when students select an institution and later register for classes.

A major criticism of Hossler and Gallagher's (1987) model and others like it is the research focuses primarily on White students attempting to gain admission to PWIs. Scholars argue the college choice process is empirically different for racial, ethnic, and economic minorities. In the past three decades, there has been a proliferation of research that seeks to account for these differences. Kassie Freeman offers an expanded version of the Hossler and Gallagher's predisposition stage in her 2005 book *African-Americans and College Choice* that carefully considers the plight of Black students. Perna and Titus (2004) investigate the impact of state tuition increases on the college choice behavior of financially disadvantaged students. They found students from low socioeconomic backgrounds were most likely to choose a two-year college over four-year public institutions because of high perceived ("sticker price") and actual (cost after financial aid) attendance costs (pp. 503–504). Engberg and Wolniak (2009) conducted a quantitative study to determine how race related factors impact the student college choice process. The researchers found a number of areas where the general models did not address racial difference. Among the more notable of these areas are (a) high academic preparation impacted Latino student college enrollment less than other groups; (b) the academic quality of the secondary school was a better predictor of college enrollment for Blacks and Whites than other groups; and (c) White and Asian students were most likely to attend selective post-secondary institutions.

These examples are by no means an exhaustive review of the college choice research focusing on race, ethnicity, and social class. They do, however, give a glimpse into the action socially aware researchers have taken to fill large gaps in the literature.

AFRICAN-AMERICAN COLLEGE CHOICE

Virtually no literature on African-American student college choice exists before the 1970s because HBCUs were largely the only option for Black undergraduates. This coincides with the passage of the Higher Education Act of 1964 and resulting access for Blacks to enroll at PWIs. Now, there are a host of studies examining the specific case of African-American student college choice. Two of the earliest and most widely referenced studies on the topic were conducted by McDonough, Antonio, and Trent (1997) and Freeman (1999b).

McDonough et al. (1997) used quantitative analyses to test the validity of traditional college choice models when applied to African-American student populations. The results of the study called for scholars to adjust traditional models to account for cultural factors unique to African-Americans. The researchers pinpoint factors that led to Black student choice of particular institutions using data from the Cooperative Institutional Research

Program's 1993 Freshman Survey. Compared to freshman of other races, their statistical analysis found Black students:

1. Apply to more colleges (p. 19)
2. Have more difficulty getting accepted at their first choice college (p. 19)
3. Expect to take more than four years to complete their bachelor's degree (p. 16)
4. Base their decision to matriculate on the college's academic reputation and financial aid packages (pp. 18–19).

Beyond simple college choice, McDonough et al. (1997) examine the selection process of African-American students who opt to attend HBCUs. The authors identify several student characteristics that predispose students towards Black colleges. When assessing academic achievement, Black incoming freshmen who have lower high school grade point averages and SAT scores than the national average are attracted to HBCUs (pp. 18, 23). Furthermore, students who are affiliated with the Baptist church and those living in economic poverty are inclined to register at an HBCU (p. 18). One of the more astounding findings in this study is that African-Americans who rely on high school faculty and staff for college guidance are less likely to attend HBCUs than those who do not (p. 24). The authors speculate secondary school personnel do not attempt to dissuade students from HBCUs, but instead posit that guidance counselors, teachers, and other high school administrators promote PWIs because they are unfamiliar with HBCUs and the positive effect attending one has on degree completion for African-Americans. The fallout of these attitudes and behavior lingers, as Black student registration at HBCU continue to lag behind that of PWIs (Aud, et al., 2010).

To help remedy lack of competencies around minority-serving institutions (MSIs), secondary school administrators should require that all college counseling professionals be trained and knowledgeable beyond their comfort zone of PWI familiarity, and actively increase their knowledge of HBCUs and other distinct mission institutions. Doing so will enable these practitioners to maximize college choice options for all student populations who are depending on them for informed, unbiased information about all institution types included in the American higher education schema.

Freeman's (1999b) study of Black student college choice took a qualitative approach. She conducted a series of group interviews with 70 African-American high school students from various geographic locations and economic backgrounds. After questioning participants about their college decision-making process, Freeman observes three general categories that differentiated the experiences of African-American students from general college choice models. The first category, family or self influences, includes variables such as family attitudes toward post-secondary education, whether or not someone close to the student has a college degree, and students' intrinsic desire to create a better life for themselves (pp. 17–19). Like White students, African-Americans benefit from having a family member who completed college (p. 17). Nevertheless, Black students also benefit from family members who did not attend college. In the latter case, students use their family members as an example of what to avoid and develop success strategies based on the shortcoming of others (p. 18).

The second category, Freeman (1999b) uncovers is psychological or social barriers. Freemans' interviews reveal African-American students are often negatively affected by the absence of effective college advocates. Further, Black students, in comparison to their White counterparts, report the psychological barrier of feeling they were not encouraged by parents and school personnel to consider college as a viable option (pp. 19–21). Other African-American students, particularly those from predominantly Black high schools, referred to the social barrier of being/feeling racially alienated when they visited PWI campuses (pp. 20–21). The third category affecting African-American student college choice is cultural awareness. Students in Freeman's study stated increased cultural sensitivity of the curriculum, programs, and services offered at colleges would have improved their motivation to pursue post-secondary education (pp. 21–22). This issue is not discussed in most college choice literature because White students have the benefit of having their culture affirmed at PWIs.

Following the example of Freeman, McDonough and others, several researchers have investigated the African-American college choice process. Some of the literature reveals interesting caveats about how African-Americans' college search differs from students of other races. For example, Pitre (2006) studied the college aspirations of Black and White high school students. His findings show that although there was no racial difference in students' college aspirations, there is a significant relationship between race and academic achievement. Pitre ultimately concludes that, despite their desire to go to college, African-Americans in his study did not exhibit the level of academic achievement necessary for college admittance. Pitre explains that this finding is significant because,

> ...it may be an indication that these students lack information related to college admissions criteria, credentials desirable to colleges and universities, and general knowledge of the college choice process... Moreover, White and Other race/ethnicity students with higher grades may gain advantages over African-American students because they are considered by parents, teachers, and counselors to be college-bound, which could mean that they will be targeted for college choice-related information and services. (p. 570)

Pitre suggests that partnerships between K–12 systems and post-secondary institutions have the potential to bolster student success by providing students, parents and teachers with information necessary for a smooth high school to college transition.

Other studies looked at the college search of subpopulations within the race. Muhammad's (2008) research illustrates gender differences among Black men and women. Specifically, her data shows African-American males receive less support from school counselors in their college search in comparison to Black females. Likewise, Smith and Fleming's (2006) study of gender gaps in college enrollment finds that African-American mothers tend to encourage their daughters to aspire to attend college more than their sons (2006). Strayhorn, Blakewood, and DeVita (2008) looked at the identity interaction or race and sexual orientation in their study of African-American gay men. The seven participants in their study assert they consciously restricted their college search to PWIs where they felt they could openly acknowledge their sexuality. The participants chose not to apply to HBCUs because felt they African-American communities hold negative perceptions of gay men. This study stands in contrast to others that identity HBCUs as a safe cultural space for African-American students. One can challenge the participants' perceptions of disapproval of gay students at HBCUs as well actual acceptance of Black LGBTQ students at PWIs given other research stating that the difficulty of coming out on college campuses is similar across all cultural backgrounds (Tyre, 2009).

Another segment of African-American college choice literature explicitly examines African-American students' decision to attend HBCUs after desegregation. Astin and Cross (1981) wrote one of the first articles on the topic. They found many Black students in the 1970s chose to go to HBCUs under the compelling influence of family friends and high school teachers. Astin and Cross also discovered these students were drawn to the cultural experience and the strong academic reputation associated with HBCUs. Similarly, decades later, Freeman (1999a) identified three major determinants prompting African-American students to select an HBCU: (a) knowing someone who attended an HBCU; (b) seeking his or her racial/ethnic roots; and (c) lacking of cultural awareness at PWIs. Van Camp, Barden, and Sloan (2010) honed in on race-specific reasons African-Americans attend HBCUs. The authors reveal students were more likely to attend an HBCU if race is central to their personal identity or they have limited contact with other Black people. Additional findings of the research include the fact that more students from California are choosing HBCUs in the wake of Proposition 209 (Tobolowsky, Outcalt, & McDonough, 2005). This finding correlates to the West Coast being a region devoid of HBCUs. Further, these findings run counter to claims that diminishing enrollments at HBCUs after the passage of the Higher Education Act of 1965 somehow bear witness to the irrelevance of HBCUs in terms of college choice and mass access to higher education.

While there is a good amount of research on African-American students' selection of HBCUs, there is a shortage of research examining factors that dissuade students from choosing HBCUs. Palmer, Maramba, and Lee (2010) recently conducted a study which focused on this exact topic. The authors interviewed Black undergraduates asking reasons they excluded HBCUs from their college choice process. Student participants cited several practical reasons for not attending an HBCU including location, availability of finaincial aid, and unfamiliarity with HBCUs. More distrubuingly, many students failed to consider HBCU in their college searches as a result of misconceptions and blatant sterotypes about the institutions. Students in the study reported they believed HBCUs are less diverse, less academically vigorous, and more party-oriented than PWIs. The authors note that students embraced these aversive views without having any empirical evidence to substansiate their claims. HBCU stakeholders will have to rely on collabrative means of debunking these stereotypes because the task is much too overwhelming for a single institutional leaders to tackle alone. Leaders might elicit an acurrate portrayal of HBCUs through partnerships with K–12 adminstrators in the form of college counselor training and HBCU campus visits, distribution of HBCU marketing materials, and on-site secondary school college fairs.

CURRENT AFRICAN-AMERICAN STUDENT ENROLLMENTS

If students are not attending HBCUs, the question becomes, "Where are they attending?" National statistics show a significant number of African-American students (34%) are currently enrolled in two-year colleges (Aud et al., 2010). Researchers find Black students are drawn to junior and community colleges because of: (a) low cost relative to other post-secondary options; (b) convenience in terms of location and ability to enroll part-time; and (c) open accessibility (Sissoko & Shiau, 2005). Another 15% of African-American students are attending for-profit institutions. Matriculation at proprietary institutions often comes as a result of open admission, reduced time commitment for degree completion, and the availability of online courses (U.S. Department of Education, 1999).

The reality that both two-year colleges and for-profits draw nearly one half of the Black student population is significant for future HBCU recruitment strategies and considerations. Rather than competing directly with the PWI college market, HBCUs would be best served by recognizing the academic practices at these institutions and adapting them to fit HBCU needs. For instance, the common thread between two-year colleges and for-profits is that there is open admission and an element of convenience. Many Black students are not in the position to attend school full-time and benefit from the option of part-time status or taking courses online. Further, because these schools admit students regardless of their previous academic performance, they attract thousands of Black students from low quality high schools and those who did not perform well on standardized tests. The distinction here is HBCUs do not simply accept low performing students, but rather accept students with the potential to complete college coursework despite an academic background and social economic status preferred by predominantly White institutions. Because of the long-standing Black college mission around educating those who have the aptitude to learn and the desire to do so, it is conceivable the HBCU is best equipped to compete with PWIs to develop the academic needs of underrepresented populations—regardless of race.

LIMITATIONS OF THE LITERATURE

While the literature includes several descriptions of HBCUs and the African-American college choice process, it is Arroyo's (2009) research that is the only one to situate its study using an organizational perspective. The origins of HBCUs are distinctly unique from other institution types based on their founding mission of mass access and student development. Despite this core mission, Arroyo's research suggests HBCUs have largely adopted the structure and policies of PWIs to the point they have relinquished much of their uniqueness. This assertion is critical to the future of HBCUs because from the standpoint of sustainability, for example, this institution type must maintain their unique and unparalleled niche in the academic market. Arroyo's hypothesis is compelling, but has not been explored empirically. Accordingly, future research on HBCUs and Black students' college choice activity may benefit from the application organizational theory.

INFLUENCES OF AMERICAN K–12 SYSTEM

The American educational system has as its aim graduating well prepared students. The question is: for what are they prepared? Over the years schools have prepared students for several outcomes: work, college, to compete in a global society, etc. Two goals of American education have never changed: preparation for work and preparation for college. To prepare students, elementary and secondary schools have followed a fairly set curriculum. The K–12 curriculum undergoes minor changes almost yearly in every state; however, the basic structure has remained the same. Students take courses in English, history, social studies, mathematics, and science. This curriculum began to take shape as early as 1893 with the National Education Association's (NEA) Committee of Ten report. Education administrators, philosophers and academics contributed to the creation of this, more narrow, curriculum. The curriculum supported by the Committee of Ten did not offer much curricular choice and aimed to prepare all students in the same way, regardless of aspiration. Twenty-five years later a paper called the Cardinal Principles of Secondary Education argued that schools should offer a broad curriculum that differentiated among students who aspired to college and those who aspired to work (NEA, 1918). This curriculum was considered "differentiated" and was to offer a vocational, general and academic track (Lee & Ready, 2009; Kliebard, 1987). The result was an academic track which looked very close to the suggestions of the Committee of Ten and general and vocational tracks with pared down versions of the narrow curriculum, the addition of civics and health, and elective courses in vocational subjects. With the launching of Sputnik in 1957 the American curriculum began to focus more on math and science in order to better compete with the Russians in the Space Race (Kliebard, 1987). While most educators would argue students are prepared for the world of work, there are very few true vocational courses in K–12 schools today. Most of the curriculum is designed to help students who are interested in entering college. As kindergarten prepares for elementary school, elementary prepares for middle school and middle school prepares students for high school; the high school curriculum has increasingly attempted to ready students for life in college.

Wilensky (2007) contends the U.S. K–12 educational system feels pressure to produce students prepared to pass traditional college entrance requirements such as the Scholastic Aptitude Test (SAT) and American College Test (ACT). In an article on high school teaching and college expectations in college English courses, Patterson and Duer (2006) discuss what high school English teachers and college English professors think are the important skills and concepts for incoming college students. They rely on a series of surveys to gauge attitudes and identify inconsistencies with the curriculum noting, "The survey results also suggest that curriculum differentiation, or tracking, continues to influence the kind of instruction some students receive" (Patterson & Duer, 2006, p. 81) In this situation students continue to learn the basic subjects, but some students learn more or at a faster pace than others. Wilensky (2007) furthers this line of thinking, arguing, "it is the hyper-academic focus of college entrance requirements that leads to the success of only a few, the outright failure of others and the low achievement of many in our K–12 system" (p. 249). Wilensky believes schools prepare the top students, while the other students are left with "academic failure—or at least educational mediocrity" (p. 250). With this, Wilensky blames the achievement gap on the curriculum. The ongoing goal of preparing students for the best colleges has left many students to miss out on an education fit for or specific to them. Wilensky holds that this has led to tracking and sorting of students so that those who are most obviously able are given the best education and those who may struggle academically are left with the basics. Stephanie Southworth and Roslyn Arlin Mickelson (2007) found that tracking in Charlotte, North Carolina was influenced by gender, race and the school's racial composition (p. 515). Southworth and Mickelson (2007) contend,

> If the tracking process were largely meritocratic, net of family background, peer orientation and prior achievement, students' race and gender would not affect their track placement... These ascriptive correlates of track placement undermine claims that tracking allocates opportunities to learn primarily in ways that are commensurate with students' abilities. (p. 515)

Southworth and Mickelson (2007) conclude these schools continue to "reflect enduring patterns of social inequality" (p. 516), as tracking is a mainstay in contemporary American schools and may be a contributing factor to gaps in student achievement and they provide evidence that gaps may be based on race and gender.

The curriculum is one factor influencing the gap in student achievement, yet there are several others: funding gaps for poor students of color, health gaps between poor students and wealthy students (Ladson-Billings, 2007) and class size (Chubb & Loveless, 2002). Another important contributor to the achievement gap is negative attitudes about poor and minority students. Gloria Ladson-Billings (2007) highlights attitudes stemming from cultural deficit theories that could lead educators to believe poor and minority students cannot achieve; she believes negative beliefs about these students and their families places the blame on "students, their families and in some cases individual teachers" (p. 321). She continues, "It constructs students as defective and lacking. It admonishes them that they need to catch up" (p. 321).

Given the factors influencing student achievement in K–12 schools, those seeking to enter college as first time freshmen may need remediation to help them gain the skills needed to complete college. Attewell, Lavin, Domina, and Levey (2006) note, "About 40% of traditional undergraduates take at least one such course, and remediation is even more common among older nontraditional students" (p. 886). Remediation may grant access to college for students who have had less opportunity than others; however, remediation is not only for students who are disadvantaged or minorities. Attewell, et al. (2006) found students from suburban, rural, and high SES families took remedial courses in large numbers (p. 914). This wide swath of students needing remedial help may be linked to Wilensky's

(2007) argument that the "hyper-academic" secondary curriculum is not adequately preparing a number of students for either work or college. Considering this information, developmental education may provide a needed form of academic assistance and access for many students capable of degree completion.

DEVELOPMENTAL EDUCATION IN AMERICAN HIGHER EDUCATION

Developmental education at American colleges and universities arose to address the incongruence between K–12 curricula and the admission requirements of colleges and universities. Its roots can be traced back as far as the seventeenth century in the form of tutoring. Now, the field has evolved into a vast array of exercises aimed at enhancing student growth and learning. While developmental education has long been a critical component of higher education, it is frequently overlooked in the literature or regarded as a mark of academic inferiority (Arendale, 2002a; Stahl, 2001). However, if educators take a thorough look at the practice, they would find that developmental education has had a tremendous impact on higher education.

For the purposes of this chapter, it is necessary to define developmental education as there is often times much confusion about its meaning within the Academy. Developmental education is an umbrella category for a series of services that support the intellectual and personal growth of underprepared college students (National Association for Developmental Education [NADE], 2011). The term, adopted from student affairs rhetoric, appeared in 1970s (Arendale, 2005). NADE (2011) defines developmental education formally as "a field of practice and research within higher education with a theoretical foundation in developmental psychology and learning theory... [that] promotes the cognitive and affective growth of all post-secondary learners" (para. 2). Developmental education can take many forms including personal, academic, and career counseling, tutoring, supplemental instruction, academic advising, mentoring, college preparatory programs, freshman seminars, basic reading, writing, and math courses and life skills instruction (Arendale, 2005; NADE, 2011).

One problem scholars encounter in the discussion of developmental education is its perceived link to remediation. The terms are often used interchangeably, signifying that they are one in the same. Not only is equating developmental education and remediation erroneous, but it also fails to acknowledge the breadth and scope of developmental practices. Much of the confusion stems from the fact remediation was the primary term used by educators from the 1860s through the early 1960s (Arendale, 2005). Remedial education generally focuses on identifying cognitive skill deficits and using coursework to correct for presenting inadequacies (Parker, Bustillos, & Behringer, 2010). This objective is only one component of developmental education which seeks to address students' academic, interpersonal, and psychological needs (Casazza, 1999).

Somewhat similar to the HBCU mission to educate those who wanted to and were capable of learning, early American colleges were generally open to any White male who could afford to attend. As colleges and universities began to develop admissions requirements, however, the need for developmental education became apparent because the Colonies developed post-secondary education before secondary education was fully developed and perfected (Thelin, 2004). Harvard initiated the trend of selective admissions in 1642 by requiring its freshman class to read, write, and speak Latin and Greek (Arendale, 2002b). Yale soon adopted this requirement and later added that students pass exams rating skills in math (Arendale, 2002b). Several other colleges followed suit and required students meet certain expected proficiencies before gaining admittance to the institution. Arendale argues the newly established admissions requirements posed a significant problem since most prospective students were grossly underprepared. He identified two prevailing reasons for the academic shortcomings. The first of these was the absence of a comprehensive public education—the paucity of public schools meant that only the wealthy and privileged had access to basic education. The second reason was that Americans were not well versed in classical languages.

Faced with the prospect of losing a significant number of enrollees, colleges turned to tutoring to supplement student learning. Arrangements were made for undergraduates to study under the tutelage of faculty or clergy affiliated with the institution until they were deemed adequately prepared to pass the admissions requirements (Arendale, 2002b). Even after being successfully admitted to college, many students found it difficult to meet the academic rigor of the Latin-based classroom. The schools responded by assigning tutors to assist struggling students with language acquisition (Boylan & White, 1987).

Tutoring remained the predominant form of developmental education until the mid-nineteenth century. The next stage of developmental education, remediation, spawned from passing of the Morrill Acts and the subsequent birth of new colleges and universities. The Morrill Act of 1862 and 1990 authorized state acquisition of federal land for the purpose of establishing colleges. This legislation sparked an unprecedented expansion of higher education across the nation. The newly founded institutions granted college access to previously excluded segments of the American population (Casazza, 1999). Students at these schools, like the more privileged undergraduates before them, exhibited a great need for learning assistance because they had inadequate secondary schooling.

It soon became apparent that colleges and universities would have to move from tutoring to a more intentional approach of accommodating marginal students. Widespread student under-preparedness ushered in a wave of courses in fundamental content areas such as writing, math and spelling. Along with the introduction of remedial courses came the emergence of full academic departments dedicated to teaching basic skills. The Department of Preparatory Studies at the University of Wisconsin in 1849 is oft cited as the first systematic delivery of developmental education (Brier, 1984). Other schools followed the University of Wisconsin's lead and adopted similar programs at their own institutions. By 1889, approximately 80% of the post-secondary schools in America had some form of college preparatory program (Boylan & White, 1987). Boylan and White (1987) note that preparatory programs were especially prevalent at women's colleges and HBCUs during this time period when discriminatory practices largely prohibited women and African-Americans' access to quality secondary education.

College preparatory programs offering remediation remained the most popular form of developmental education until the mid-twentieth century when America took another vested interested in educational access. An important factor weighing on the delivery of developmental education during this period was the creation of the community college. The advent of the community college offered an alternative to college preparatory programs by allowing students to complete remedial course outside of the baccalaureate institution (Markus & Zeitlin, 1993). Four-year colleges and universities subsequently reduced their commitment to college preparatory programs in favor of more selective admissions standards. While relegating developmental education to community college may have benefitted four-year college academic rankings, it has had detrimental effects on retention for developmental students. For example, Moore, Jensen & Hatch (2002) found retention for all developmental students was much higher for students attending four-year schools that those attending two-year schools.

Between the late 1970s and early 1990s more contemporary developmental education services emerged. Among these are counseling services, learning communities and supplemental instruction. These services differed from their predecessors because they did not only target underprepared students. Instead, they were open and available to the entire student population regardless of achievement level. It is also around this time that we begin to see developmental education in the form of learning centers and college access initiatives such as Federal TRIO programs, Gear Up, and others (Parker, Bustillos, & Behringer, 2010). The federal government played a key role in the creation for these programs by providing financial support for higher education. The new practices represented a shift in developmental education to address students holistically. They also signified a concerted effort to reduce the stigma of receiving learning assistance at the college level.

Despite the advancement in the delivery of developmental education, the field became the subject of heated debate in the early 1990s. Opponents of developmental education, including state government officials, called for a drastic reduction of developmental services. The crux of their argument rested upon the idea that developmental education forced the public to pay for secondary education twice (Ignash, 1997). A second source of contention in the debate involved which schools should provide developmental education. Several scholars and legislators petitioned for the confinement of developmental education to technical or community colleges.

Developmental educators responded to these issues with research findings in support of the field. First they issued a decree calling for developmental education to remain at all institutions of higher learning. In this statement, developmental educators argued that moving developmental education to two-year colleges would inflict undue restraints upon the economically disadvantaged and adult students (National Association for Developmental Education [NADE], 1998) due to their restricted resources and financial obligations. Next, developmental educators argued secondary schools generally only prepare the top students, while other students are left with "academic failure—or at least educational mediocrity" (Wilensky 2007, p. 250). So, the public was not paying twice for pre-college courses because fewer than 40% of high schools students had access to college preparatory courses in the first place (Saxon & Boylan, 2001). They then produced studies verifying the efficacy and impact of developmental education in promoting equity and access and they documented the fact that remediation spent less than 1% of post-secondary expenditures and that (Moore, Jensen, & Hatch, 2002; Bettinger & Long, 2009).

In spite of the evidence in support of developmental education, many colleges and universities decreased their commitment to developmental education programs. As of 2007, twenty-two U.S. higher education systems reduced or eliminated remedial courses and ten states prevented or discouraged public four-year institutions from offering remedial courses (Russell, 2008). The effect of this particular legislation has had a detrimental impact on the education of all student populations in need of these services to augment their college experience. Turning students away from a four-year institution has permanently limited countless students from the opportunity to earn a Bachelor's degree, effectively widening the already substantial earnings gap in the United States. Such is the case of the City University of New York (CUNY) system. CUNY adopted a policy to limit developmental education to community colleges in 2000. During the three years following this policy change at least 5,000 students were "de-admitted" from CUNY four-year colleges and did not enroll elsewhere (Russell, 2008). To this end, the dissolution of development education has been shown to directly relate to enduring issues of college readiness that impairs the educational and professional future of those seeking access to higher education at a four-year institution.

DEVELOPMENTAL EDUCATION AND THE MISSION OF HBCUS

The distinction between the aims of remediation and developmental education is especially salient when reflecting upon the historical mission of HBCUs. HBCUs were created not only to provide higher education, but to advance self-actualization for African-Americans. HBCUs therefore tailor their policy and practice to engage students intellectually while simultaneously supporting students' spiritual, social, and emotional growth.

The very function and mission of HBCUs prior to and immediately following the Civil War can be defined as developmental in nature. HBCUs were charged with the responsibility of educating a populace that, for the most part, had been denied access to education in its most rudimentary of forms. HBCUs responded by designing their curriculum to supplement student knowledge and provide the psycho-social development necessary for African-Americans to thrive as citizens. Boylan and White (1987) maintain HBCUs did an exceptional job of developing their undergraduates both intellectually and personally and even go so far as to say "some of the most amazing feats of developmental education were accomplished at historically Black institutions in the United States" (p. 6). HBCUs can remain true to their historical mission by admitting students based on their desire to learn in spite of inequality in educational access and, in turn, engage in collaboration to furnish the resources necessary for academic achievement.

As developmental practices at HBCUs have evolved much in the same pattern as they have among other institution types, HBCUs now successfully offer freshman seminars, learning centers, supplemental instruction, Federal TRIO programs, and the like. Unfortunately, Black colleges have also shied away from offering basic skills courses over time due to the availability of community colleges, limited resources, and public dissent. Basic skills courses remain essential, nonetheless, because the social order in America continues to create structures that disproportionately provide access for many African-Americans to educational resources required for college success. Given the successful legacy of developmental education at HBCUs and the continued disparity of educational access and opportunity for African-American students, it is only natural and befitting that this institution type continues to offer comprehensive developmental education programs. In this way, HBCUs can reinvest in developmental education via basic skills courses and collaborating externally (i.e., articulation agreements) with other entities that do offer such courses, such as local community colleges.

LIMITATIONS OF THE LITERATURE

The literature shows developmental education has always played a role in higher education. It also confirms the notion that developmental education will remain an essential component of higher education as long as high school requirements and college admission standards remain disparate. Nevertheless the literature suffers from certain limitations.

A major limitation is most of the research focuses on developmental education at community colleges. Future studies should work to compel the public to reinvest in developmental education, particularly at Bachelor degree-granting institutions. The following passage from Boylan, Bonham, & White (1999) echoes this sentiment:

> Four-year institutions of moderate to low selectivity serve a critical function in higher education. They make the opportunity for a baccalaureate degree and its social and economic benefits available to students who do not qualify for more prestigious institutions.... If such institutions are to fill their niche in our higher education system, they must admit some poorly prepared students and must provide some means of supporting these students. (p. 96)

Future research might explore ways in which four-year schools incorporate developmental education into their curriculum. Studies of developmental programs at four-year HBCUs will prove particularly informative since developmental education has been an integral part of their mission since inception.

The case for developmental education at four-year institutions can be further advanced by demonstrating diminished student success when developmental services are restricted to two-year schools. Several existing studies find students who attend community college are less likely to complete a bachelor's degree than those who begin the college experience at a four-year school. Others assert the effects are even more substantial for students from underrepresented backgrounds. For example, Moore Jensen & Hatch (2002) reveal a retention rate of 32.9% for African-Americans with developmental needs at four-year colleges compared to a mere 17.4% for those attending a two-year institution. These statistics show all the more need for the reinvestment of HBCUs in developmental education, as mass access to education remains under the guise of standardized tests, de facto discrimination, and efforts to relegate those first-generation, low income, and underrepresented students to a higher education "tracking system." Proponents of developmental education, as well as HBCU leaders, are encouraged to capitalize on these findings and use them to advance their own agenda with prospective and current students as well as internal and external collaborators.

A second limitation of developmental education literature: the research is primarily centered on PWIs. There are very few studies on developmental education at HBCUs and other minority-serving institutions, despite the fact scholars acknowledge superior implementation of developmental strategies at these institution types (Arendale, 2002a; Boylan & White, 1987). The lack of research on the developmental practices of HBCUs is indicative of persistent hegemonic beliefs that HBCUs are academically inferior and students of color are inherently low quality and lacking potential as learners. The only exception to this narrative trend is an historical article written about HBCUs and their use of developmental education (Jones & Richards-Smith, 1987). Nonetheless, the article, though informative, is very general and does not provide specific examples of developmental practice at single site institutions. Additionally, the article was written 25 years ago and, therefore, excludes any recent strategies or policy changes around the issue since that time. Future research might concentrate on the empirical study of developmental education at HBCUs and the positive impact it has on student outcomes. To this end, it is imperative that HBCUs be recognized for their contributions to the field. The Black college commitment to developing students of all academic levels has spanned the history of higher education and stands firmly as an exemplary model from which administrators can establish more effective developmental education policies and practices at all American colleges and universities.

COLLABORATIVE LEADERSHIP AND IMPLICATIONS FOR HBCUS

It can be well argued HBCUs have done more to advance the higher education of African-Americans than any other group or entity. The current challenge for HBCU leaders is to promote the relevance and uniqueness of Black colleges within the spectrum of American higher education. When considering the amount of financial, material, and human resources it will take to accomplish this task, it is clear that HBCU leadership must continue to seek effective and innovative collaborative partnerships with internal and external stakeholders. Collaboration can inform revitalization efforts by indicating ways in which HBCUs have and will continue to re-establish their proven legacy and distinguish themselves as a unique brand of higher education and college choice. As no other institution type specializes in the education of African-Americans, first-generation, low-income, and the underrepresented, HBCUs must continue to tailor their institutional mission and purpose to the needs of this student populace. The primary ways in which HBCUs can accomplish this mandate is to intentionally forge internal and external collaborations around developmental education and college choice.

This chapter demonstrates how HBCUs have emerged as models of collaborative and social transformation leadership since inception. Whether unintentional or out of shear necessity, HBCUs remained faithful to their mission by maintaining mutually beneficial alliances. One area of profound collaboration is found in the relationship between HBCUs and religious organizations. Several HBCUs were created and sustained through direct collaboration with churches. For instance, the American Missionary Society and African Methodist Episcopal Church provided the capital, manpower, and physical structures needed to erect HBCUs including Fisk University, Howard University, Paul Quinn College, and Wilberforce University. Another example of collaborative leadership at HBCUs involves the many ways in which faculty and staff work together to ensure student achievement. Black college leadership implements internal collaboration in the form of student support services and community resources such as libraries and K–12 schools to produce comprehensive developmental education programs. To be sure, these programs were and continue to remain essential to the achievement of students who needed support in meeting their educational goals.

Considering their noteworthy success over time, HBCU leadership is encouraged to revisit and recommit to the core principles of collaborative leadership in the market of contemporary higher education. Waning enrollment and a diminished public image many HBCUs face require decisive modifications in institutional policies, procedures, and practices. The authors argue collaboration is the most efficient and effective means of addressing these issues. The task of executing the institutional mission while recruiting, retaining, and graduating increased numbers of African-American college students, requires the collective efforts of several entities.

HBCUs are well served when they continue to pursue innovative, productive partnerships beyond their campus borders. College choice models discussed as part of this research reveal several ways HBCUs can use external partnerships to attract prospective students and increase enrollment numbers. HBCUs leaders could use external collaborations to modify existing outreach efforts and concentrate efforts on revamping their public image by highlighting institutional effectiveness around developmental education and college choice. To this end, research confirms African-American students are at a disadvantage when it comes to receiving encouragement to attend college. Keeping this finding in mind, PWIs can afford to focus their admissions efforts during the latter stages of high school, while HBCUs must start much earlier. Thus, HBCU recruiters should, therefore, reach out to prospective students when they are in middle school (i.e., seventh, eighth, and ninth grades) to promote post-secondary education, in general, and the institution type of HBCUs, specifically. The research also shows students are more likely to attend an HBCU if they have a friend or family member encourage enrollment (Freeman, 1999b; Freeman, 2005; McDonough, Antonio, & Trent, 1997). HBCU leadership should capitalize on this finding by distributing to their alumni, age -appropriate college materials to disperse to middle and high school students in their communities. Additionally, leadership could create training videos using social media such as YouTube and Facebook groups to train alumni to engage students through direct marketing for their alma mater.

A second external collaborative recruitment strategy is to engage K–12 system administrators. As mentioned previously, the research indicates that secondary school personnel are not actively endorsing HBCUs (McDonough, Antonio, & Trent, 1997). HBCU recruiters could drastically improve HBCU referral rates by building interactive relationships with college counselors and providing information sessions, training, and factual information about institutional histories and features. Recruiters might begin with mutually beneficial activities such as inviting counselors to the HBCU campus for a continuing education for-credit workshop, Black college staff might volunteer to sponsor student financial aid workshops at designated feeder high schools, or engage in co-planning college fairs. These relationships could later be expanded to meet the specific needs of both parties. Ultimately, K–12 college counselors would benefit professionally and personally by obtaining accurate knowledge about HBCUs and college choice so that students will receive usable information about HBCUs as an option.

When it comes to improving the HBCU image, the college choice literature provides several collaborative recommendations. The literature encourages HBCUs to counter negative stereotypes by highlighting their academic profiles (as academic reputation is one of the most salient factors in African-American students' college choice process), and showcasing their student body diversity (Palmer, Maramba, & Lee, 2010). HBCU leaders can address both academic reputation and demographic concerns through collaboration. For example, HBCUs, civil organizations, and media outlets can work together to develop a marketing campaign that features examples of academic excellence and student diversity at HBCUs. These three entities could publish documents and videos profiling successful HBCU graduates and the fact that HBCUs are diverse with more than 15% of public HBCU non-Black student enrollment (Allen & Jewell, 2002).

A final recommendation on how HBCUs can use collaboration to improve their image stems from research about the academic needs of many African-American students and the historical practice of developmental education. The literature shows that African-American students often aspire to go to college, but are not fully equipped to do so. Many Black students also face restrictive circumstances that prevent full-time college registration. The continued need for developmental education presents a unique opportunity for HBCUs to improve their recruitment and retention strategies and initiatives. If HBCU leadership were to call for a comprehensive reinvestment in developmental education programs at their institutions, they could potentially increase enrollment while retaining high academic standards. Developmental education also presents a means of preserving HBCUs' historical mission for equity and inclusion among its learners. In this way, HBCU leaders would need to skillfully coordinate the cross-campus collaboration of faculty and staff in order to provide the full spectrum of developmental services such as tutoring, counseling, basic skills courses, and freshman seminars. External partnerships and articulation agreements with K–12 schools systems and community colleges are needed as well because they facilitate access to prospective students and demonstrate a willingness to accommodate students' academic needs.

The preceding suggestions are only a sample of how collaborative leadership can further address the challenges HBCUs face. Table 5.1 provides a more extensive list of circumstances where collaboration promotes the historical mission and future sustainability of HBCUs. The information in the table is informed by college choice literature and the principles of developmental education (see Table 5.1).

CONCLUSION

In a time of changing demographics and concerns about recruitment and graduation rates, it is the contention of this chapter that HBCU stakeholders must reinvest in their historical origins and commitment to collaborative leadership. HBCUs have thrived in unsupportive environments and with meager resources only because of their ability to maintain productive partnership both within and outside of the institution (Allen & Jewell, 2002, Brown, Donahoo, & Bertrand, 2001). The authors of this chapter, therefore, conclude the use of old alliances and the generation of new relationships will be the best refuge for HBCUs in the twenty-first century and beyond. Finally, the information included in this chapter suggests that now is the time for PWIs to imitate the longstanding collaborative and societal change practices of HBCUs, as they can glean a great deal from their HBCU counterparts in this instance. Specifically, HBCUs can serve as a model of social transformation leadership for PWIs who are navigating changing demographics and an increase in the underrepresented student populace during the current and projected economic downturn. To be sure, HBCU student-centered practices, exampled by the adoption of developmental education, could also well inform PWIs' attempts to increase

TABLE 5.1 Addressing Factors that Lead African-American Students to Choose PWIs over HBCUs

Factors	Underlying Issue	Collaborative Solutions
Economic		
Location	Students choose PWIs in close proximity to their home to save money—this issue is particularly salient in states where there are no HBCUs	• Pursue agreements with other states to match in-state tuition rates • Provide incentives for out-of-state students and demonstrate that HBCU out-of-state tuition in many southern states is less than in-state tuition at many colleges in the North • Establish articulation agreements, consortium agreements, and student exchange programs with PWIs
Financial Aid	Students choose PWIs because they provide better financial aid packages including athletic scholarships	• Work with Black churches and civic groups to actively assist prospective student completing federal and state financial aid applications to maximize eligibility • Adjust course offerings to maximize the number of full-time students—thus increasing financial aid eligibility • Work with athletic associations to increase scholarship opportunities • Use social media and web space to publicize available public and private scholarships, then assist student in completing the applications
Sociological Factors (SES, school system and family resources)		
Counselor Recommendations	Many African-American students do not have access to college choice resources and subsequently choose PWIs based on the recommendation of high school faculty and staff	• Create opportunities to increase dialogue and interaction with high school staff (i.e., guidance counselor campus visits, college nights at local high schools and websites dedicated to college counselor information) • Provide high school staff with marketing material and college applications • Coordinate marketing events/informational sessions with professional organizations such as state and regional chapters of the American school Counselor Association
Sticker Price	Student enroll at PWIs because they do not fully understand the financial aid process	• Work with guidance counselors and financial aid agencies to help students understand the difference between "sticker price" and the actual cost of attendance

(continued)

TABLE 5.1 Addressing Factors that Lead African-American Students to Choose PWIs over HBCUs (continued)

Factors	Underlying Issue	Collaborative Solutions
Community College Enrollment	Students choose to attend community colleges for cost effectiveness and program offerings	• Create partnerships and articulation agreements with local community colleges • Encourage currently enrolled HBCU students to create relationship with prospective students at community colleges • Hold transfer student recruitment and registration events on community college campuses
Academic Needs	Underprepared students choose PWIs that offer developmental education or are denied admission to their first-choice institution	• Work with K-12 systems to develop admissions practices that consider a prospective student's access to quality college prep courses and resources • Return to original access mission which included comprehensive developmental education programs
Enrollment Flexibility	Students choose to attend PWIs based on their ability to enroll part-time or take courses online	• Collaborate with other institutions to provide a variety of course delivery formats including accelerated courses, classes held on weekends, online and hybrid courses
Psychological factor (Person-institutional fit)		
Personal development	Students enroll at PWIs because they offer programs and services for underrepresented groups	• Partner with social justice organizations to provide culturally relevant programing to services to address the needs of underrepresented groups such as GLBTQ students and religious minorities
Institutional climate	Students enroll at PWIs because they perceive them to be more diverse	• Use social media and campus resources to highlight existing diversity • Work with international institutions to promote study aboard opportunities
Program offerings	Student choose PWIs because they offer academic programs that are not available at	• Develop student exchange programs or consortium agreements that allow students to take courses outside of their home institution
Academic reputation	Student choose to attend PWIs because they believe HBCUs lack academic vigor	• Highlight academic programs in marketing materials and social media outlets (i.e., Facebook, YouTube, etc.)

(continued)

TABLE 5.1 Addressing Factors that Lead African-American Students to Choose PWIs over HBCUs (continued)

Factors	Underlying Issue	Collaborative Solutions
		• Collaborate with other HBCUs and predominantly Black colleges to produce and publish African-American student centered information sources including data from FactBooks, Common Data Sets and placement statistics rankings)
		• Pursue accreditation from well-respected agencies or membership with esteemed organizations
		• Encourage students to review ranking systems that specifically address the needs of African-American students instead of those that do not (i.e., lists produced by *Black Enterprise* or *U.S. News & World Report*'s HBCU rankings
		• Establish working relationships with external media outlets to publicize HBCU academic accolades

Source: Freeman, K. (1999a). HBCUs or PWIs? African American high school students' consideration of higher education institution types. *Review of Higher Education, 23*(1), 91–106. doi:10.1353/rhe.1999.0022; Freeman, K. (1999b). The race factor in African Americans' college choice. *Urban Education, 34*(4), 4-25. doi:10.1177/0042085999341002; Hossler, D. & Gallagher, K. S. (1987). Studying student college choice: A three-phase model and the implications for policymakers. College and University, 62(3), 207-21.; McDonough, P. M., Antonio, A., & Trent, J. W. (1997). Black students, Black colleges: An African American college choice model. *Journal for a Just and Caring Education, 3*(1), 9-36; Muhammad, C. (2008). African American students and college choice: A consideration of the role of school counselors. *NASSP Bulletin, 92*(2), 81-94. doi:10.1177/0192636508320989; Palmer, R. T., Maramba, D. C., & Lee, J. (2010). Investigating Black students' disinclination to consider and attend historically Black colleges and universities (HBCUs). *National Association of Student Affairs Professionals Journal, 13*(1), 23-45.

retention and persistence among the aforementioned student populations. Additionally, PWIs could glean from HBCUs, strategies for working with diverse learners to build competencies around race, class, and culture in view of U.S. Census predictions for increased Black and Brown populations through 2050 (U.S. Census, 2008). The tradition of HBCU collaboration as an outgrowth of the Seven C's, stands as a prudent call for every American college and university to invest their time and resources into future success of all students.

REFERENCES

Allen, W. R., & Jewell, J. O. (2002). A backward glance forward: Past, present, and future perspectives on historically black colleges and universities. *Review of Higher Education, 25*(3), 241–261. doi:10.1353/rhe.2002.0007

Arendale, D. R. (2002a). A memory sometimes ignored: The history of developmental education. *Learning Assistance Review, 7*(1), 5–13.

Arendale. D. R. (2002b). Then and now: The early years of developmental education. *Research and Teaching in Developmental Education, 18*(2), 5–23.

Arendale, D. R. (2005). Terms of endearment: Words that define and guide developmental education. *Journal of College Reading and Learning, 35*(2), 66–82.

Arroyo, A. T. (2009). Orienting public historically Black colleges and universities for the future: Aligning their historic mission with appropriate pedagogical policy. *Journal of Race & Policy, 5*(1), 67–78.

Astin, H. S., & Cross, P. H. (1981). Black students in Black and White institutions. In G. E. Thomas (Ed.), *Black students in higher education: Conditions and experiences in the 1970s* (pp. 11–17). Westport, CT: Greenwood Press.

Attewell, P., Lavin, D., Domina, T., & Levey, T. (2006). New evidence on college remediation. *The Journal of Higher Education, 77*(5), 886–924.

Bergerson, A. A. (2009). College choice as a comprehensive process. *ASHE Higher Education Report, 35*(4), 21–46. doi:10.1002/aehe.3504

Bettinger, E. P., & Long, B. (2009). Addressing the needs of underprepared students in higher education: Does college remediation work? *Journal of Human Resources, 44*(3), 736–771.

Boylan, H. (1988). Historical roots of developmental education. *Review of Research in Developmental Education, 4*(4), 1–4.

Boylan, H. R., Bonham, B. S., & White, S. R. (1999). Developmental and remedial education in postsecondary education. *New Directions for Higher Education, 108,* 87–101.

Boylan, H. R., & White, W. G. (1987). Educating all the nation's people: The historical roots of developmental education. *Review of Research in Developmental Education, 5*(3), 1–4.

Brier, E. (1984). Bridging the academic preparation gap: An historical view. *Journal of Developmental & Remedial Education, 8*(1), 2–5.

Brown, M. C., Donahoo, S., & Bertrand, R. D. (2001). The Black college and the quest for educational opportunity. *Urban Education, 36*(5), 553–571. doi:10.1177/0042085901365002

Brown, M. C., Ricard, R. B., & Donahoo, S. (2004). The changing role of historically Black colleges and universities: Vistas on dual missions, desegregation, and diversity. In M. C. Brown & K. Freeman (Eds.), *Black colleges: New perspectives on policy and practice* (pp. 3–28). Westport, CT: Praeger.

Brown v. Board of Education of Topeka, 347 U.S. 483 (1954).

Casazza, M. E. (1999). Who are we and where did we come from? *Journal of Developmental Education, 23*(1), 2–6.

Chubb, J. E., Loveless, T. (2002). Bridging the achievement gap. In J. E. Chubb & T. Loveless (Eds.), *Bridging the achievement gap* (pp.1–10). Washington, DC: Brookings Institution.

Civil Rights Act of 1964, 42 U.S.C. § 2000d (1964).

Du Bois, W. E. B. (1903). The talented tenth. In B. T. Washington (Ed.), *The Negro problem: A series of articles by representative American negroes of today.* (pp. 31–75). New York, NY: James Pott & Company.

Engberg, M., & Wolniak, G. (2009). Navigating disparate pathways to college: Examining the conditional effects of race on enrollment decisions. *Teachers College Record, 111*(9), 2255–2279.

Freeman, K. (1999a). HBCUs or PWIs? African-American high school students' consideration of higher education institution types. *Review of Higher Education, 23*(1), 91–106. doi:10.1353/rhe.1999.0022

Freeman, K. (1999b). The race factor in African-Americans' college choice. *Urban Education, 34*(4), 4–25. doi:10.1177/0042085999341002

Freeman, K. (2005). *African-Americans and college choice: The influence of family and school.* Albany, NY: SUNY Press.

Gasman, M. (2008). Minority-serving institutions: An historical backdrop. In M. Gasman, B. Baez, & C. S. Turner (Eds.), *Understanding minority-serving institutions* (pp. 18–27). Albany, NY: SUNY Press.

Gasman, M., & Bowman, N. (2011). How to paint a better portrait of HBCUs. *Academe, 97*(3). Retrieved from: http://www.aaup.org/AAUP/pubsres/academe/2011/MJ/Feat/gasm.htm

Higher Education Act, Pub. L. No. 89-329. 20 U.S.C. §1061 (1965).

Hossler, D., & Gallagher, K. S. (1987). Studying student college choice: A three-phase model and the implications for policymakers. *College and University, 62*(3), 207–221.

Ignash, J. M. (1997). Who should provide post-secondary remedial/developmental education? *New Directions for Community Colleges,* 100, 5–20. doi:10.1002/cc.10001

Jackson, C. L. (2001). *African-American education: A reference handbook.* Santa Barbara, CA: ABC-CLIO.

Jewell, J. O. (2002, January). To set an example: The tradition of diversity at historically Black colleges and universities. *Urban Education, 37*(1), 7–21. doi:10.1177/0042085902371002

Jones, H., & Richards-Smith, H. (1987). Historically Black colleges and universities: A force in developmental education. *Review of Research in Developmental Education, 4*(5), 1–3.

Killgore, L. (2009). Merit and competition in selective college admissions. *Review of Higher Education, 32*(4), 469–488. doi:10.1353/rhe.0.0083

Ladson-Billings, G. (2007). Past the achievement gap: An essay on the language of deficit. *The Journal of Negro Education, 76*(3), 316–323.

Lee, V. E., & Ready, D. D. (2009). U.S. High school curriculum: Three phases of contemporary research and reform. *The Future of Children, 19*(1), 135–156.

Markus, T., & Zeitlin, A. (1993). Remediation in American higher education: A "new" phenomenon? *Community Review, 13*(1), 13–23.

McDonough, P. M., Antonio, A., & Trent, J. W. (1997). Black students, Black colleges: An African-American college choice model. *Journal for a Just and Caring Education, 3*(1), 9–36.

Minor, J. (2008). A contemporary perspective on the role of public HBCUs: Perspicacity from Mississippi. *Journal of Negro Education, 77*(4), 323–335.

Moore, J. M. (2003). *Booker T. Washington, W. E. B. Du Bois, and the struggle for racial uplift.* Wilmington, Delaware: Scholarly Resources, Inc.

Moore, R., Jensen, M., & Hatch, J. (2002). The retention of developmental students at four-year and two-year institutions. *Research and Teaching in Developmental Education, 19*(1), 5–13.

Muhammad, C. (2008). African-American students and college choice: A consideration of the role of school counselors. *NASSP Bulletin, 92*(2), 81–94. doi:10.1177/0192636508320989

National Association of Developmental Education. (1998). *Need for developmental education at four-year institutions.* Retrieved from: http://www.umkc.edu/cad/nade/nadedocs/psde4y98.htm

National Association of Developmental Education. (2011). *Developmental education* [Definition]. Retrieved from http://www.nade.net/AboutDevEd.html#Definition

National Education Association. (1894). *Report of the committee of ten on secondary school studies with the reports of the conferences arranged by the committee.* New York, NY: American Book Company.

National Education Association. (1918). *Cardinal principles of secondary education* (NEA 1918–035). Washington, DC: Government Printing Office. Retrieved from http://ia600309.us.archive.org/25/items/cardinalprincipl00natiuoft/cardinalprincipl00natiuoft.pdf

Palmer, R. T., Maramba, D. C., & Lee, J. (2010). Investigating Black students' disinclination to consider and attend historically Black colleges and universities (HBCUs). *National Association of Student Affairs Professionals Journal, 13*(1), 23–45.

Parker, S. (2011). *Driving integrated marketing strategies with collaborative leadership.* Retrieved from http://www.business2community.com/strategy/driving-integrated-marketing-strategies-with-collaborative-leadership

Parker, T. L., Bustillos, L. T., & Behringer, L. B. (2010). Remedial and developmental policy at a crossroads. Retrieved from: www.gettingpastgo.org/docs/Literature-Review-GPG.pdf

Patterson, J. P., & Duer, D. (2006). High school teaching and college expectations in writing and reading. *The English Journal, 95*(3), 81–87.

Perna, L. W., & Titus, M. A. (2004). Understanding differences in the choice of college attended: The role of state public policies. *The Review of Higher Education, 27*(4), 501–525. doi:10.1353/rhe.2004.0020

Pitre, P. E. (2006). College choice: A study of African-American and White student aspirations and perceptions related to college attendance. *College Student Journal, 40*(3), 562–574.

Russell, A. (2008). *Enhancing college student success through developmental education.* Washington, DC: American Association of State Colleges and Universities.

Saxon, D. P., & Boylan, H. R. (2001). The cost of remedial education in higher education. *Journal of Developmental Education, 25*(2), 2–8.

Sissoko, M., & Shiau, L. R. (2005). Minority enrollment demand for higher education at historically Black colleges and universities from 1976 to 1998: An empirical analysis. *Journal of Higher Education, 76*(2), 181–208. doi:10.1353/jhe.2005.0015

Smith, M. J., & Fleming, M. K. (2006). African-American parents in the search stage of college choice: Unintentional contributions to the female to male college enrollment gap. *Urban Education, 41*(1), 71–100. doi:10.1177/0042085905282255

Southworth, S., & Mickelson, R. A. (2007). The interactive effects of race, gender and school composition on college track placement. *Social Forces, 86*(2), 497–523.

Stahl, N. (2001). Historical perspectives: With hindsight we gain foresight. In D. B. Lundale & J. L. Higbee (Eds.), *Histories of developmental education* (pp. 10–13). Minneapolis, MN: Center for Research on Developmental Education and Urban Literacy, University of Minnesota.

Strayhorn, T. L., Blakewood, A. M., & DeVita, J. M. (2008). Factors affecting the college choice of African-American gay male undergraduates: Implications for retention. *National Association of Student Affairs Professionals Journal, 11*(1), 88–108.

Thelin, J. R. (2004). *A history of American higher education.* Baltimore, MD: The Johns Hopkins University Press.

Tobolowsky, B., Outcalt, C., & McDonough, P. (2005). The role of HBCUs in the college choice process of African-Americans in California. *Journal of Negro Education, 74*(1), 63–75.

Tyre, Y. S. (2009). *Understanding African-American lesbian and gay identity development within a historically black college environment* (Doctoral dissertation, Auburn University). Retrieved from http://etd.auburn.edu/etd/bitstream/handle/10415/1729/TyreFinalCopy.pdf?sequence=4

United States Census. (2008). *Population projections.* [Data file]. Retrieved from http://www.census.gov/population/www/projections/summarytables.html

U.S. Department of Education. (1985). *The traditionally Black institutions of higher education 1860 to 1982* (NCES). Retrieved from http://nces.ed.gov/pubs84/84308.pdf.

U.S. Department of Education. (1999). *Students at private, for-profit institutions* (NCES 1999-178). Retrieved from http://nces.ed.gov/pubs2000/2000175.pdf

U.S. Department of Education. (2004). *Historically Black colleges and universities, 1976 to 2001* (NCES 2004–062). Retrieved from http://nces.ed.gov/pubs2004/2004062.pdf

U.S. Department of Education. (2010a). *Fall Enrollment Survey* (IPEDS-EF:90). Washington, DC: U.S. Government Printing Office. Retrieved from http://nces.ed.gov/programs/digest/2010menu_tables.asp

U.S. Department of Education. (2010b). *The condition of education 2010* (NCES 2010–028). Retrieved from http://nces.ed.gov/pubs2010/2010028.pdf.

Wilensky, R. (2007). High schools have got it bad for higher education—and that ain't good. *Phi Delta Kappen, 89*(4), 248–256, 258–259.

Van Camp, D., Barden, J., & Sloan, L. (2010). Predictors of Black students' race-related reasons for choosing an HBCU and intentions to engage in racial identity-relevant behaviors. *The Journal of Black Psychology, 36*(2), 226–250. doi:10.1177/0095798409344082

CHAPTER 6

CIVIC ENGAGEMENT AND CRITICAL CONSCIOUSNESS

Culture and Traditions of Liberal Arts Education

Malika Butler
Vickie L. Suggs

> *Active and collaborative learning take on additional meaning when students—as part of their academic requirements—apply what they are learning to the community and in some cases improve the quality of life of residents in a nearby community.*
> —Kuh, Kinzi, Schuh, & Whitt (2005, p. 200)

INTRODUCTION

The rich and storied history of historically Black colleges and universities (HBCUs) is a testament to their past and contemporary relevance in American higher education. Amid relentless discriminatory practices around access and equitable funding to higher education for Blacks, HBCUs have remained steadfast in their mission to educate and develop a continual cohort of influential leaders in the arenas of education, science, medicine, law, and politics.

The list of the Black intelligentsia, who promote racial uplift and collective advancement is seemingly endless. Arguably, the feats among HBCUs are remarkable. Nonetheless, critics of this institution type have constructed a narrative that describes them as "academic disaster areas" with a subpar education and second-rate faculty (Jencks & Riesman, 1967, p. 19).

Arguments such as inadequate facilities, scarce resources, and the omission of strong HBCUs representation among popular college rankings polls have been used as even more fuel to question the validity of these institutions, as well as their contemporary presence in American higher education. The enduring scrutiny and attacks HBCUs have had to defend are largely over-generalizations and misinformation appropriated by individuals, who lack understanding of the historical and contemporary issues faced by these institutions.

When discussing HBCUs it is important to realize while these institutions are not perfect, they have overcome countless obstacles, yet continue to maintain a legacy that proportionally demonstrates the uses of this institution type as it relates to maintaining a model for mass educational access and choice for those willing and capable of learning.

Although HBCUs comprise only 3% of all colleges and universities (Kelderman, 2010), 70% of all Black doctors and dentists, 50% of all Black engineers and school teachers, and 35% of all Black attorneys have received their baccalaureate degrees from HBCUs (Avery, 2009). The advancements of HBCUs demonstrate the exceptional curricular and co-curricular education that prepares students for graduate education and civic engagement upon degree completion.

These student outcomes run counter to the largely unexamined metanarrative critics posit and the general public has come to believe. The distinct mission of HBCUs extends beyond the walls of the classroom, thus developing the efficacy of students who attend remains a complement to academic achievement. This co-curricular aim is highlighted by the positive student outcomes which include positive relationships with faculty, higher academic achievement and more affirmative psychological outcomes (Allen, 1992; Price, Spriggs, & Swinton, 2011).

Further, the environment in which these relationships are cultivated is one of support with a special emphasis on providing a holistic student development. Administrators and faculty expect students to use their talents to give back as stewards of the institution or support the cohort that enrolls after them as a way of creating a critical community of learners and those who support their journey to obtain knowledge.

These pedagogical practices are noteworthy and should not be viewed simply as phenomenon negates—this approach negates the unique culture of HBCUs as centers of purpose that cultivate the value of racial uplift and collective advancement within all, who choose to attend. Instead, HBCUs behaviors around student development are intentionally and suited to develop those talents possessed by students, who may otherwise be overlooked and undervalued.

This study will interpret how the specialized mission of HBCUs and implementation of a liberal arts curriculum develop a critical consciousness within students, which cultivates outcome around civic engagement and social activism. The chapter will also examine retention rates at HBCUs and the collaborative ways in which civic engagement and social activism can be used as components or indicators in the facilitation of greater retention rates among HBCUs.

THEORETICAL FRAMEWORK

Massive and strategic attempts were made to use educational structures to destroy "critical consciousness," to alienate Africans from tradition and from each other, to teach African inferiority and European superiority.
—Asa Hilliard (2001, p. 25)

Critical Consciousness

Critical consciousness is a term coined by sociologist, Paulo Freire, who suggests there should be an emphasis placed on an understanding of social, political, and economic oppression. In order to fully acquaint one with these social constructs, it is imperative for an individual to interpret how these constructs affect them, In order to do this, one must be able to have an understanding of one's own identity and how this identity may be subject to forms of oppression.

Freire's (1973) theory of critical consciousness discusses how the transformation of society is due to the transitioning between "historical epochs," (p. 5). These epochs manifest change, but in this change becomes a divide between the ways in which people react to them. Radicals and sectarians are the groups that are a result of this manifested change. Freire identifies radicalization as, "... predominately critical, loving, humble and communicative, and therefore a positive stance. The man who has made a radical option does not deny another man's right to choose.... He tries to convince and convert, not to crush his opponent. The radical does, however, have the duty.... to react against the violence of those who try to silence him—of those who, in the name of freedom, kill his freedom and their own." (Freire, 1973, p.10). The radicalization of an individual allows them to reach a level of critical transitivity that allows, "depth in the interpretation of problems...refusing to transfer responsibility...rejecting passive positions" (Freire, 1973, p. 18).

Education and advocacy are two major components of critical consciousness. Education builds upon advocacy because the tools used as part of the learning experience help students to navigate systems of oppression, which is a component of advocacy. These tools can be found when looking at components of Strayhorn and Hirt's (2008) construction of a social justice framework, which focuses on the construction of civic engagement of students that attend HBCUs and Hispanic-Serving Institutions (HSIs).

The researchers also discuss the use of tools such as the empowerment of the dis-empowered by providing a voice for those without one, in addition to cultural maintenance and critique, which includes promoting racial pride and identity, democracy, and citizenship. This arrangement of competencies around critical consciousness parallels the mission of HBCUs and the use of liberal education in creating engaged citizens and servant leaders.

THE HBCU MISSION & LIBERAL ARTS EDUCATION

Civic engagement at HBCUs is fostered through a triangular continuum (see Figure 6.1). At the center of this continuum seats the purpose of HBCUs, which is defined as the mission of the institution. The HBCU purpose is situated at the center of the continuum because, as the focal point and foundation, it constructs the ways in which all of the moving parts will work as a collective to develop civic engagement among students.

The peak of the triangular continuum is collaborative leadership (president's vision), which directs and informs critical consciousness and the liberal arts curriculum. The president uses the mission of the institution to direct his vision. Noting the president's vision can alter the institutional environment, the placement of vision is at the top of the triangle, as the president's vision will delineate how effectively the curriculum (liberal arts) is realized as part of the institution's intended student outcomes (critical consciousness and civic engagement).

The liberal arts curriculum is used as the vehicle to develop critical consciousness. Through the use of engagement, student-centered learning, and teaching a broad number of disciplines that provide a worldview perspective, the liberal arts curriculum is a mechanism that helps students to articulate, identity, and develop essential tools that bring about ecology of critical consciousness.

This toolbox, created as an outgrowth of the liberal arts curriculum, manifests in students a critical consciousness that allows them to navigate then galvanize the campus and global communities through social activism

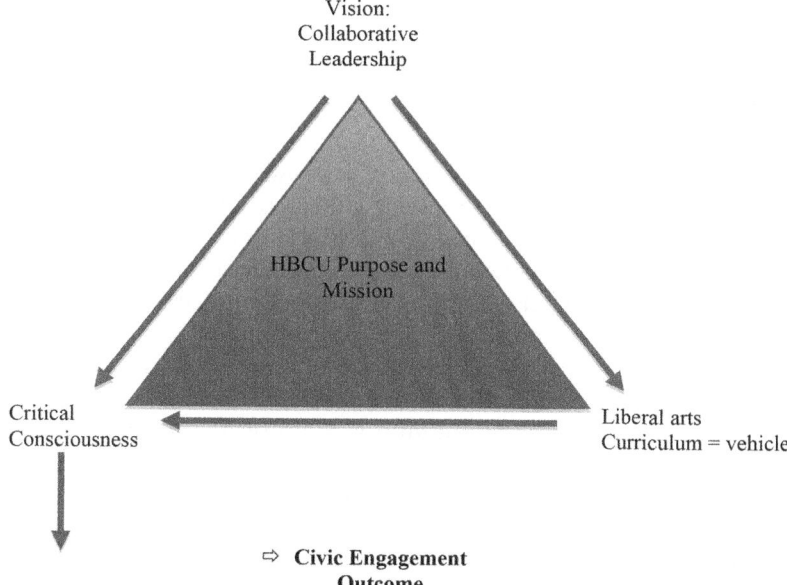

Figure 6.1 Development of civic engagement through liberal arts and critical consciousness.

and civic engagement. This outcome is achieved because students begin to deconstruct social constructs such as racism, sexism, and classism.

The capacity of students to negotiate societal behaviors and norms that promote difference as threatening is gleaned from their own enlightenment or enrichment as stewards of the liberal arts curriculum. Kuh suggests students who are immersed in a liberal arts curriculum "tend to gain more in intellectual and personal development..." (2007, p. 122). This assertion can be referenced in concluding why and how students develop this particular set of competencies.

Students are educated in ways that help them discern the effects of these "isms" as well as ways to counter them; in other words, as HBCU students' critical consciousness manifests into a privilege that allows the successful maneuvering and dismantling of a social system created to marginalize them.

To be sure, HBCU students are equipped with the tools to counter White privilege and racism in ways that students attending other institutions are less able because they are not able to fully identify systems of oppression and the ways in which they can deconstruct social norms that discount those populations that are not considered belonging to the majority.

The liberal arts curriculum, critical consciousness, and civic engagement are interwoven into a continuum that ignites a sense of urgency and responsibility within students who attend HBCUs. The focus of liberal arts education is the arts and sciences, ranging from History to Political Science. Since this curriculum has been standard at many HBCUs, the institution type has used this classification as an instrument to require courses focusing on the Diaspora (Jean-Marie, 2006).

Through these courses, students are taught of the hardships and inequities of marginalized populations, specifically Black Americans, who were descendants of slaves. Because the Black college teaches matriculates about the prevalence of inequities around such issues as race and class, it is fitting that Paulo Freire's (1973) critical consciousness theory can frame the foundational principles that HBCUs have employed to instill in their students the importance of social activism. Arguably, the liberal arts foundation of the HBCU mission directly impacts the development of critical consciousness, which, in turn, creates an intrinsic sense of civic engagement in the development of graduates and alumni, who go on to serve as local, state, national, and global leaders.

The authors posit that HBCUs develop a critical consciousness, which leads to civic engagement among matriculates. Thus, understanding the importance of the HBCU purpose is rooted in their mission because this institutional statement is often times synonymous with the institutional purpose.

Recognizing the link between the mission and purpose leads one to a deeper understanding of how the institutional purpose is central to the development of critical consciousness. According to Scott (2000) "The experience of historically Black colleges and universities in preparing students for civic engagement is inextricably bound to the missions of the institutions" (p. 264). Jean-Marie (2006) further argues the mission of HBCUs is directed by three principles which are three-fold,

> First they provided education to newly freed slaves that was rich in Black history and tradition. Second they delivered educational experiences that were consistent with the experiences and values of many Black families. Thirdly, they provided a service to the Black community and the country by aiding in the development of leadership, racial pride, and return services to the community. (p. 87)

In assessing each of the principles of the HBCU institutional mission, there is an articulation between each principle and the implications they have on the development of critical consciousness. Accordingly, the first principle explains the importance of providing an education rich in Black history with the standpoint that those attending HBCUs comprise marginalized groups.

While those marginalized groups included newly freed slaves during the inception of HBCUs (Jean-Marie, 2006), they now include: minority, low income, and first generation students (Kelderman, 2010). Representative of this idea, archival research reveals the Bennett College curriculum mandated all students to take a Negro History class during their freshman or sophomore year, this mandate could be seen in the Bennett Bulletins that were reviewed (*Bulletin of Bennett College for Women*, vol. 1, no. 3, 1927–1928).

The Negro History course provided a synopsis of the experience of African-Americans from 1865 to the present as well as surveying the current experiences of African-Americans (*Bulletin of Bennett College for Women*, vol. 1, no. 3,1927–1928). While North Carolina Central University (NCCU) and North Carolina Agricultural &Technical State University (NC A&T) did not make the Negro History course a requirement, these institutions still offered classes that taught the history of African-Americans (*Annual Catalogue North Carolina College for Negroes*, 1927–1928. North Carolina Central University Archives, Durham, NC & *Bulletin of A&T College*, Greensboro NC, 1933.)

The use of Black history within the curriculum, whether it be optional or mandatory, is explicative of Freire's (1973) ideals around critical consciousness, which suggest students be educated and provided with tools used to attack the oppression they and others face. By learning about cultural identity via Black history coursework, students become equipped with extensive knowledge of how oppression marginalizes people and communities. Thus, they are able to use this production of knowledge to best navigate and challenge systematic racism and discrimination.

The second principle depicts how HBCUs try to provide students with experiences aligned with Black family values (Jean-Marie, 2006). Similar to the Black community, the cornerstone of HBCUs has been Christianity. To this end, NCCU was initially founded as an institution for the training of ministers; Bennett College was organized by the Methodist church; and NC A&T established a religious doctrine within their institutional culture (*Bulletin of A&T College* Greensboro, NC, 1925; *Bulletin of Bennett College for Women*, 1927–1928; & Seay, *A History of the North Carolina College for Negroes*, 1941. North Carolina Central University Archives, Durham, NC).

For HBCUs, using religious doctrine became a means through which students could become active community organizers and race leaders. Informed by the influences of Christianity, administrators and faculty of these institutions were able to instill in students a purpose-driven life and the tools for which to live a life of service. To be sure, the values of the church enabled HBCUs to cultivate students as servant leaders, who were compelled to work on behalf of their community because of the interrelationship between service and the Christian faith.

The third principle describes HBCUs as providing a service by developing leaders with racial pride who will be of service to their community (Jean-Marie, 2006). This final principle combines all aspects of critical consciousness, whereas HBCU students form identity as part of the institutions goal to develop them as active community members and servant leaders.

Specifically, the institutional mission is to groom students to fight against social, economic, political, and educational injustices. The mission is so pronounced, scholars have noted, "Among institutions of higher learning, HBCUs seek to bridge the gap between the haves and the have-nots. To bridge the gap, transformative leaders are needed at HBCUs to be the voice of social change..." (Jean-Marie, p. 88, 2006).

Given the ideals of the third principle, in particular, HBCUs ensure students are provided with adequate tools to fight against instances that create disparate treatment for their race and others belonging to populations that are not viewed as normative. In the book, *Understanding Minority-Serving Institutions*, Strayhorn and Hirt (2008) suggest part of the social justice framework includes "empowerment of the disempowered," which states that, "Justice of this sort aims to analyze systemic oppression, thwart repression, and empower" (p. 209).

The development of individuals, who can serve in this type of leadership capacity, promotes a critical consciousness, as engaging in this way allows one to fight the status quo and fight for a system of change and equality. This ideal parallels the HBCU mission around racial uplift and why its purpose is situated at the center of the triangular continuum.

THE LIBERAL ARTS CURRICULUM AS A CONDUIT FOR STUDENT SUCCESS

While the purpose of HBCUs is the underpinning for generating critical consciousness and civic engagement, the liberal arts curriculum provides the vehicle through which student outcomes are successfully delivered. Kuh (2007) examine tenets that comprise the liberal arts curriculum including:

1. A primary focus on teaching
2. Actively engaging students in learning
3. Developing students holistically and creating community.

Reviewing the tenets of the liberal arts curriculum it can be noted how these ideals are similar to those of service learning, which state the presence of a, "teaching and learning strategy that integrates meaningful community service with instruction and reflection to enrich the learning experience, teach civic responsibility, and strengthen communities" (National Service Learning Clearinghouse, 2011, para. 1).

The building of community and civic engagement is still persistent at Black colleges today. Examples of this include students at Howard University Medical School and Meharry Medical College providing medical care including physical examinations not only for African-Americans but other races as well (Scott, 2000). Mbajekwe (2006) notes this during his interview with the president of Spelman College, Dr. Beverly Tatum, who describes the services the young women participate in by stating, "... like for example Spelman students majoring in Spanish are working as translators in the local hospital and Spelman students who are taking a sociology course on survey research methods are using these methods in the local community to do these assessments for a local health center" (p. 47).

To this end, the building of community by actively engaging students in learning—which is at the center of liberal arts and service learning—is at work in and out of the classroom setting. These practices also develop a capacity within students to understand the purpose of giving back because they themselves have realized their individual purpose and identity around service to their community.

Aside from the tenets used to describe the pedagogy of the curriculum, a liberal arts education can also be characterized with a broad focus in the arts and sciences, including courses within the foreign languages, history, English, mathematics, social sciences, and applied sciences. Providing individuals with the opportunity to explore a variety of disciplines allows one to develop a broader, more informed worldview, which, in turn, develops a critical consciousness. This worldview allows one to interpret issues in a variety of ways while seeking solutions to confront and remedy the marginalization of those belonging to targeted groups.

Kuh (2007) reports that National Survey for Student Engagement (NSSE) data shows, "Seniors at liberal arts colleges are more likely to have done community service or volunteer work" (p.128). This should not be a surprising factor since Sullivan (2000) posits one of the tenets of liberal arts education is to "... bring the humane and civic arts to bear upon the problems and concerns of the present" (p. 20).

This statement elucidates how a liberal arts education is heralded as a vehicle that supplies students with the tools to attack societal ills and find solutions. While HBCUs incorporate the liberal arts curriculum within their pedagogy, majority institutions are also informed by this curriculum.

What makes the instruction of the liberal arts curriculum different at HBCUs is the specialized mission of this institution type. Using the curriculum to inform student outcomes around civic engagement, and the mission and purpose of HBCU as the foundation, the development of critical consciousness becomes representative of the distinct difference between the use of a liberal arts curriculum at HBCUs and predominantly White institutions (PWIs).

While noting the distinctions between the uses of a liberal arts curriculum at HBCUs in comparison to PWIs, it is also important to recognize how the vision of college presidents complements the aims of the curriculum as well as other aspects of campus life and culture. In this way, leadership conveys a vision for inspiring the populace.

METHODOLOGY

This chapter focuses on archival research, document analysis, and retention data to examine indicators associated with liberal arts curriculum and its effects on the development of critical consciousness and civic engagement within students attending the sites of the study located in North Carolina:

1. Bennett College, a private liberal arts, women's college founded as a co-educational institution in 1873 and located in Greensboro
2. North Carolina Central University (NCCU), the nation's first public liberal arts college founded in 1910 for African-Americans and located in Durham
3. North Carolina Agricultural & Technical State University (NC A&T), a public, land-grant, doctoral-granting research university founded in 1891 and located in Greensboro.

The primary research question of the study is how the tradition of a liberal arts curriculum at HBCUs informs contemporary higher education practices around civic engagement and critical consciousness among its matriculates.

Archival research is described as, "any research in which a public record is the unit of analysis" and "...involves attempting to answer questions about people by investigating a portion of the seemingly infinite amount of recorded information they generate" (Dane, 1990, p. 169). In this way, a review of archival documents allows the researchers to examine the academic and social vision for student development grounded in the leadership style of Black college presidents at three institutions in the South, spanning a 45-year period.

From an analysis of the course offerings, policies, and retention data, the researchers can further connect the traditions of liberal education in a contemporary context and make meaning of not only how institutional leaders used liberal education to uplift the race, but also why this curriculum is unique to HBCUs and sets them apart from their predominantly White institutional counterparts when examining student outcomes around critical consciousness and civic engagement.

The use of course bulletins ranging from 1910 to 1955 at Bennett, NCCU, and NC A&T State University is used to discern the types of curriculum employed as well as co-curricular activities that fostered student outcomes associated with the liberal arts tradition. The study is situated in the American South because of its critical mass of HBCUs as well as the state of North Carolina having the largest number of historically Black colleges and universities. Further, the examination period selected was in direct correlation with specific institutional presidents, who embodied visionary leadership over an extended tenure of service that resulted in institutional growth in the areas of curriculum development and design, enrollment, and physical resources, for example.

Additional to the use of course bulletins, school newspapers, the city newspapers discussing student protests during the Civil Rights movement, and booklets documenting the respective university histories, all were used to assess what type of civic engagement and social activism were modeled by matriculates. To this end, the use of archival documents assists the researcher in recognizing the social climate of the past, in particular.

Singleton (1988) maintains, "Outside the discipline of history, however, historical analysis moves beyond description to the use of historical events and evidence to develop a generalized understanding of the social world" (p. 364). To be sure, understanding the social atmosphere of the HBCU campus culture provides a deeper understanding of how the institutional culture becomes an agent of change in the cultivation of critical consciousness among students. The development of critical consciousness, in turn, equips students to deconstruct societal ills around race and class, for example.

Historical inquiry is important to this particular study, as Sherman and Webb (1988) maintain the process, "...seeks to interpret and explain the significance of past experiences, not merely document them. As historical facts do not speak for themselves, the past becomes relevant to the present only through interpretation and evaluation" (p. 36).

In this way, upon review of the HBCU environment between the years 1910 and 1955, the authors are able to interpret the influence of the liberal arts curriculum on social activism displayed by students during this period. This interpretation may, subsequently, provide implications for contemporary student learning and engagement outcomes.

Content analysis is used to review all other documents found in the archives. Content analysis is described as a research technique that "provides new insights, increases a researcher's understanding of particular phenomena, or informs practical action." (Krippendorf, p. 18, 2004) and "....used to make objective and systematic inferences about theoretically relevant messages." (Dane, 1990, p. 170).

Dane (1990) and Krippendorf (2004) imply the use of content analysis could help direct future teaching and professional practices to improve student engagement. They also propose that interpreting this information in new ways can help understand the student standpoint as well as the position of campus administrators to provide answers to the how's and why's around student development.

To this end, content analysis assists the researcher in identifying themes found within the study. The book, *Approaches to Social Research* explains, ".... content analysts truly engages in analysis by relating content categories to one another or by relating the characteristics of the content to some other variable." (Singleton, 1988, p. 376). In applying this method, themes around student activism within the Civil Rights Movement, and student protests against administrative rules, are explored and examined.

Aside from focusing on themes, content analysis also urges the importance of context. Krippendorf (2004) suggests, "...texts acquire significance in the contexts of their use.... A context is always someone's construction, the conceptual environment of a text, the situation in which it plays a role." (p. 27).

Krippendorf advocates further for context by maintaining, "Texts have meaning relative to particular contexts, discourses, or purposes. Every content analysis requires a context within which the texts make sense and can answer the analyst's research questions." (p. 24). For the purposes of the study, context informs the ways in which a liberal arts curriculum fosters critical consciousness that leads one to become a champion of social activism and civic engagement.

Finally, comparative analysis is used to review how retention at HBCUs is related to student outcomes around critical consciousness and civic engagement. Using data from the UNC System database titled, *Retention, Graduation, and Persistence Rates of First-Time Full-Time Freshmen*, assessments will be made in the effectiveness of retention at HBCUs in comparison to PWIs over a 20-year period.

The decision to use the UNC System to examine and compare retention at HBCUs and PWIs is because North Carolina is home to the largest number of HBCUs that grant baccalaureate degrees (Minor, 2008). There are currently 11 HBCUs in the state of North Carolina. Five of these institutions are included in the UNC-system: Elizabeth City State University, Fayetteville State University, North Carolina A&T State University, North Carolina Central University, and Winston Salem State University.

Another benefit to accessing data from the UNC System is the ability to examine a number of institution types that share the same "academic core missions" (Academic Affairs, The University of North Carolina, para. 1). The development of the UNC system began in 1931 with three predominantly White institutions: The University of North Carolina at Chapel Hill, North Carolina State College (now North Carolina State University) and Women's College (now The University of North Carolina at Greensboro).

By 1969, three additional campuses were introduced into the System and in 1971 legislation was passed to bring in the state's 10 remaining public institutions—which was the completion of the System (History & Mission, The University of North Carolina, n.d.). Because the system did not include

HBCUs, until the 1970s, there is no data on retention, graduation, and persistence that precede this decade, thus the data set used is comprised of the years 1990–2010 (Daphne Dow, personal communication, July 11, 2011).

COLLABORATIVE LEADERSHIP: SHEPARD AND BLUFORD

The origins and maintenance of Black education can be attributed to the use of collaborative leadership. Preceding the work of Black college presidents, newly freed African-Americans incorporated agencies of collaborative leadership to advocate for not only Black education, but universal education.

For example, there is the case of the state of Mississippi. In *Cultural Capital and Black Education,*" the collective contributions of the community effectively working with state agencies helped the African-Americans in Mississippi to push for more educational opportunities for Black children, as well as poor white children of Mississippi, and also adults (Span, 2004).

Schoolhouses were formed on former plantations and many Black organizations such as the Mason, church organizations, and the people in the community donated money as well as time (Span, 2004). The use of collaborative leadership afforded educational opportunities in Mississippi because of the advocacy of the newly freed slaves and the internal and external relationships they developed in the community (Span, 2004).

While Black higher education was not the primary focus in the advocacy for universal education, the collaborative efforts of African-Americans in Mississippi can be attributed to the cultivation of these institutions, as the communities were foundational pieces of collaborative leadership, later used to help support and sustain HBCUs.

Establishing the case for social transformation and collaborative leadership, the authors briefly discuss two HBCU presidents: James E. Shepard, NCCU and Ferdinand D. Bluford, NC A&T State University. Their transformative visions and collaborative leadership styles helped the growth of their institutions physically, academically, and financially; ultimately, increasing student satisfaction and an enhanced liberal arts curriculum.

While internal collaboration, through the efforts of faculty, staff, and administrators are essential to the implementation of these outcomes, during Shepard's and Bluford's era, external collaborations were especially necessary due to the racial discrimination and resulting strained race relations throughout the country. Thus, this chapter will focus on collaboration external to the university.

In the case of Dr. Shepard, he cultivated a number of partnerships among community entities and leaders that helped to propel NCCU into a well-regarded, state-supported institution. One of his strongest allies was C. C. Spaulding, president of NC Mutual Life Insurance. Charles Spaulding, a prominent figure in Durham's Black and White communities, wrote a letter in the local newspaper advocating for more monetary support for NCCU (Seay, *A History of the North Carolina College for Negroes*, 1941, North Carolina Central University Archives, Durham, NC).

In his letter, he charged other Black and White community members of Durham and the entire state of North Carolina to support this "Negro institution" (Seay, *A History of the North Carolina College for Negroes*, 1941, North Carolina Central University Archives, Durham, NC). With the support of Spaulding and other respected community members, Shepard was able to maintain NCCU's finances, which, in turn, created a number of institutional opportunities such as an increase in the number of newly erected buildings and new course offerings (*Annual Catalogue of the North Carolina College for Negroes*. North Carolina Central University Archives, Durham, NC).

While Spaulding's advocacy on behalf of NCCU was needed, it also fair to say the way he negotiated the support of the institution could be called into question by those who did not have the full context of his meaning. In Spaulding's letter, he spoke about the main accomplishment made by NCCU as an institution, which was developing students, who would build and preserve the Black community. However, Spaulding also expressed how this "Negro institution" would decrease delinquency, laziness, and violence (Seay, *A History of the North Carolina College for Negroes*, 1941, North Carolina Central University Archives, Durham, NC).

In reviewing Spaulding's words, he implies the primary reason for providing financial support for NCCU was to maintain a sense of community decorum and order, and the way to control for aforementioned socially unaccepted African-American behavior was through education. The authors of this chapter posit that Spaulding, in congruence with Shepard's institutional vision, understood the language and disposition needed during this period in race history that most effectively encouraged Whites to support the education of the Negro.

To be sure, Black institutions during these times had to strategically manage their brand messaging in an effort to offset dissention and garner support. Spaulding's linguistic maneuverings parallel those of early missionaries and White philanthropists. While many of these individuals helped to create Black normal schools, which later became HBCUs, they also used these institutions to extend their own agenda, which was "Christianizing" African-Americans and training a workforce (Gasman & Drezner, 2008).

Shepard, understanding that many Whites still held these same viewpoints, was able to use these enduring views to his advantage and create a legacy for educating Blacks in the city of Durham and state of North Carolina. The effects of the collaborations highlight Shepard's visionary collaborative leadership style, as it yielded transformative outcomes for the institution.

The pathway to achieving innovation, as part of social change, must consist of a leader committed to creating an institution in which there remains a focus on providing an optimal learning environment for students, obtaining world-class faculty, and increasing course offerings, co-curricular engagement, and state-of-the-art facilities. Ferdinand Bluford's vision, which was the cornerstone for the development and growth of NC A&T State University is an example of how these objectives can be successfully envisioned and met.

Before Bluford's presidency, NC A&T State University was a very small institution with relatively few options other than industrial and agricultural courses. Bluford's vision helped propel NC A&T State University into an institution of vast curricular and co-curricular opportunities for students and a specialized academic focus around the Engineering field.

In 1925, when his tenure began as president of NC A&T State University, the institution had a limited enrollment of 350 students, a campus covering of 25 acres worth two million dollars, and a rating of "C." By the time Bluford retired, the institution had grown extensively, with more than three thousand students enrolled, the physical area of the campus grew to 35 buildings worth 12 million dollars, which extended across 110 acres and 600 acres of farmland, and an academic rating of "A." It had grown into one of the largest Black institutions in the nation (Kelley, 1964, p. 39).

Dr. Bluford's vision not only resulted in the physical growth of the NC A&T State University campus, but it also led to the development of a number of academic programs. The graduate school was introduced, as well as the nursing school, and more courses were offered in the college of arts and sciences (N.C. A&T State University Bulletin, vol. 45, no. 2).

Not only did this extension transform the curriculum, but student clubs and organizations such as honor societies, literary clubs, student government, the glee club, the drama club, and the French clubs were all introduced as co-curricular activities (A&T State University Bulletin, vol. 30, no. 1). With these programs set in place, students were exposed to diverse worldviews through language, music, and the arts.

An increased focus on the curricular and co-curricular not only assisted in laying the foundation for student persistence and graduation, but also provided students with a mechanism to interpret the value and importance of life skills as well as evaluate the state of society. According to Kelley (1964), "Before Bluford formulated a philosophy for the college, in his mind were three prerequisites: first, his deep rooted conviction, and his cherished faith in the ultimate victory of education; second, his conception that for a people to develop their latent potentials individually and collectively- education is necessary. Finally, for people in a democracy to occupy their rightful places and to live wisely under such a system—education is necessary" (p. 33). Bluford's collaborative leadership and commitment to expansion and change catapulted NC A&T into one of the nation's most respected HBCUs (Kelley, 1964).

Bluford's vision led him to establish a liberal arts curriculum. However, in doing so, he came under fire with the Board of Trustees (Kelley, 1964). His critics cited that NC A&T State University was established under the Second Morrill Act of 1890, which meant there was a focus on vocational training. They also argued there was no need to offer a liberal arts curriculum when it was being offered at NCCU, a neighboring institution (Kelley, 1964).

Despite the opposition, Bluford was not deterred and responded to the criticisms via his May 1939 *Annual Report*, in which he stated the objectives of the institution had not changed, but instead the quality of education at agriculture and technical college would be enhanced by a liberal arts curriculum. To support his claim, Bluford used several studies that focused on the educational practices at NC A&T State University, which were published by important educational officials including: Dr. Arthur J. Cline, Chief of the Division of Higher Education, United States Department of Education; and Dr. W.C. Bagley, School of Education, Columbia University (Kelley, 1964).

Bluford continued to work, collaborate, and engage his internal and external community in order to articulate his vision for a curricular modification in an effort to provide NC A&T State University students with a world-class education, preparing them to become active and involved agents of change within their respective communities. Thus, Bluford was able to develop NC A&T State University into an institution that has transformed beyond simply the "grounds for vocational training" (Kelley, 1964).

Collaborative leadership was employed during the presidency of Shepard and Bluford and was well-situated within the educational, political, and societal challenges they faced.

Shepard and Bluford's use of the Seven C's of social transformation leadership was critical to the growth and maintenance of the Black colleges in the South. Specifically they understood how collaborations, even those that may have been considered controversial within the Black community, were important in propelling their respective universities to national recognition and prominence. Consequently, without the vision of the president and his/her constituencies, the necessary resources and alliances to effectively realize a strategic plan of action for institutional sustainability is unattainable.

COURSE BULLETINS AND CURRICULUM DESIGN

Examining the curriculum of NCCU, NC A&T State University, and Bennett College, it can be determined that while they have noticeable differences, these institutions curriculum fostered necessary skills that would not only benefit students, but benefit the community as well. These skills all combine to develop a critical consciousness. The universities discussed were imperative in developing a working force of Black teachers, accountants, and farmers, who would help sustain the African American community.

In reviewing course catalogues that correlated with the presidencies of Dr. James E. Shepard, NCCU; Dr. Ferdinand D. Bluford, NC A&T State University; and Dr. David Dallas Jones, Bennett College, the authors will review the course offerings and co-curricular activities available to students that align with the principles of civic engagement. Unlike Bennett College and NCCU, which were established as liberal arts colleges, NC A&T State University originated as a mechanical and technical college.

Though the focus was industrial education, the administration saw the efficacy of a liberal arts curriculum interwoven into the existing technical education. To be sure, The Negro Agricultural and Technical College Bulletin published during the years 1925–1927 acknowledges this ideal by declaring the following,

> Recognizing that a college course ought to include not only intellectual training and the knowledge and skill requisite for breadwinning, but also preparation for citizenship, and for moral and social life, the Agricultural and Mechanical Colleges have intertwined their vocational work and study with this department. The subjects offered in the Academic Department are those that most directly make for culture and efficiency. (1925, pp. 67–71)

To this end, the efficiency of the liberal arts curriculum helped to transform the academic purpose of the agricultural and technical degree in very distinct ways that enhanced student engagement and made meaning of social activism. Conversely, NCCU and Bennett College shared an inception around the liberal arts curriculum, alone.

While all three institutions adopted a liberal arts curriculum, Bennett College was the only campus requiring students to take a Negro History course. NCCU and NC A&T State University; however, offered this course as well as others related to the experiences of Black Americans as an option for those who wished to do so.

For example, a sociology course offered at NCCU titled, *The Negro in American Life*, "studied the conflict, situations, and progress of the Negro. Soundness of various political, economic, religious, and psychological techniques for the Negro and minority groups will be discussed." (*Annual Catalogue of the N.C. College for Negroes*, p. 90, 1937, North Carolina Central University Archives, Durham, N.C.). A&T offered a similar sociology course titled, *Minority Groups in the U.S.* This course surveyed the status of minority groups in the United States as well as policies and trends that affected them (*A&T State University Bulletin*, vol. 42, no. 2, 1950–1951).

A fundamental part of critical consciousness is developing a sense of identity or self, which primarily includes racial identity (Freire, 1973). Understanding this idea, there are plausible reasons for the failure on the administration's part to require these courses including the notion that administrators were confident students would register for courses on their own.

Upon review of a course catalogue at NCCU, the description of the class, *History of the Negro Race*, suggests, "There has been a steady demand by students in Negro schools for a broader knowledge of the past of their own people and now that adequate historical material has been made available, it is felt that such a course will meet a long felt need." (*Annual Catalogue North Carolina College for Negroes*, p. 28, 1927–1928. North Carolina Central University Archives, Durham, NC).

One could also argue NC A&T State University and NCCU are state-supported institutions and may have been apprehensive of the perception among Whites, as racial uplift and race pride among Blacks was not a priority for non-Blacks. While *History of the Negro Race* was not a required course, all three of the institutions mandated all students, regardless of their major, take several years of English.

The courses consisted of grammar, composition, literature, and public speaking (*Annual Catalogue North Carolina College for Negroes*, vol. 17, 1942–1943. North Carolina Central University, Durham, NC; *A&T State University Bulletin*, vol. 30, no. 1, 1939–1940; & *Bennett College for Women Bulletin*, vol. 11, no. 2, 1936–1937). The incorporation of a multi-year English curriculum developed and enhanced student oral and written skills, so they could best negotiate and articulate their reactions to the ever-present occurrence of racism and discrimination.

Religious indoctrination was also a prevalent theme throughout the catalogues. Bennett and NCCU required students to attend chapel as well as Vesper or an evening prayer, service, or hymn. Of the three study sites, NCCU was most pronounced in their religious indoctrination, as the charter states, "The idea of the National Religious Training School is that real religion is the foundation on which the State, Educational, and Community life should stand. Religion awakens...energies of the individuals and turns them into channels of usefulness and service. It builds up better citizenship...." (*Annual Catalogue of the National Training School*, 1917. North Carolina Central University Archives, Durham, NC).

While the National Religious Training School and Chautauqua for the Colored Race was the original name of what is now NCCU, the institution's mission transformed to usher in a liberal arts curriculum and the name changed to North Carolina College for Negroes (N.C. College for Negroes) in 1925. At the same time, institutional leaders continued to instill this particular ideology, as illustrated in the Annual Catalogue of the N.C. College for Negroes during 1929 and 1930,

The N.C. College, although non-sectarian, feels that no institution which fails to emphasize religion is fulfilling its mission to humanity. Unless one has spiritual discernment and moral appreciation, one is not prepared for social responsibility. (p.19)

Religious ideology was also ever-present within the administration at the Agricultural and Technical College (NC A&T State University). When President Bluford began his term as president, he had a specific philosophy that would direct his administration. Part of this philosophy included combining religious ideology to inform the necessity of civic engagement was employed not only to establish the importance of being a moral citizen, but also to stay true to African-American Christian ideology around community.

To this end, a review of co-curricular activities revealed many clubs and organizations were faith-based community service organizations. The young women at Bennett College could participate in organizations such as the Queen Ester Circle, created for students interested in foreign and home mission work, or the World Fellowship Committee that provided a scholarship for a Liberian student (*Bulletin of Bennett College for Women*, 1927–1928).

The faith-based organizations were not the only entities that yielded a sense of civic engagement within students. For instance the YMCA, which had chapters at NC A&T State University as well as NCCU were orchestrated for "the development of student leadership" (YMCA History, 2011, para. 2).

Other clubs and organizations such as the lyceum, academic clubs, and debate teams (*Annual Catalogue North Carolina College for Negroes*, 1927–1928, North Carolina Central University Archives, Durham, NC & *A&T State University Bulletin*, vol. 36, no. 4, 1944–1945) were also elements that developed a sense of civic engagement within students, as they provided useful skill sets for advocacy on behalf of their communities.

For example, students involved in the debate team were able to cohesively piece together an argument that made their viewpoint legitimate. This was an important skill in the development of race leaders as they fought against social ills and injustices. Aside from students actively participating in a variety of clubs and organizations, all three of the institutions hosted guest speakers and held monthly lectures during which speakers impressed upon students the importance of civic engagement and social activism.

Respected Black leaders, prominent ministers, and public officials in their respective college towns and cities, called for students to become leaders within their community by charging them with the necessity of social activism, civic engagement, and mobilization. Aside from lectures presented from influential people outside of the university community, faculty also played a major role in identifying to students important life values and purpose.

For instance, at North Carolina Central University, students were mandated to attend orientation lectures including, "The Progress of Man, Significant Steps in World Progress," and "The Negro in Business" (*Annual Catalogue North Carolina College for Negroes*, 1927–1928, North Carolina Central University, Durham, NC). These orientation lectures engaged students in a number of topics that allowed them to critically think about globalism and their positions in the world as citizens. These lectures also provided students with a strong understanding of civic engagement and social activism; we can reference this by looking at one of the times for an orientation lecture presented during the school year of 1927–1928, which was entitled, "The Development of Social Consciousness."

With a liberal arts curriculum spearheading the educational practices of these institutions and co-curricular activities that engaged students in tenets associated with a liberal arts education, these things done in conjunction yielded an ideology of critical consciousness and civic engagement within these campus environments.

As Black college presidents discussed in this chapter employed social transformation leadership, they each helped develop critical consciousness and civic engagement in students. Using the purpose and mission of the HBCU to inform how a liberal arts curriculum aligns with principles of critical consciousness and civic engagement, facilitates the development of the HBCU brand around social activism and change among its student populace.

STUDENT PROTEST: CIVIC ENGAGEMENT IN ACTION

As mentioned earlier in the chapter, two themes emerged upon a review of archival documents: student activism for Civil Rights and student protest against university administration's stringent rules and policies, which excluded them from having personal freedoms as young adults (Morrison, 1960; Robinson, 2011). Specifically, rules that stated females were not being allowed to ride in cars with boys, a curfew to return to campus, and the attendance of chaperones at social events was a mandate (*Bulletin of A&T College*, vol. 28, no. 1, 1937).

During the 1930s and 1940s students began to voice concerns with administration in small and tactful ways; however, tensions grew and by the 1960s and 1970s students had become annoyed, agitated, and aggravated with administration and began to become more organized in voicing their concerns. Like many institutions, HBCUs had adopted the philosophy of "in loco parentis," a Latin term which means "in place of a parent."

Colleges and universities enlisted this tactic by being, "...considerably more stringent than parents..." (Cohen, 1998, p. 66). The limitation of perceived rights and freedom caused many students to resist and the student newspaper was used as a platform to express concerns to institutional leaders and senior administrators. To be sure, students used the campus newspaper to advocate for more rights as well as to simply give voice to their grievances.

While some students maintained a cordial response to existing campus rules and expected codes of conduct, others would angrily attack administration and often times show hostility. The hostility was demonstrated verbally via the student newspaper to articulate students' distrust of administration.

Though concerned with changing the dynamics of stringent school policy and rules that would grant personal freedoms and allow students to become more independent of administration on campus, they also were compelled to change forms of oppression and discrimination occurring outside of their respective campus walls. With the onset of the Civil Rights Movement, one could argue students at HBCUs would be at the forefront and participate in the Movement at an unparalleled level than their counterparts attending other institution types. Scott's (2000) interpretation of HBCU student engagement during the Civil Rights Movement maintains,

> During the 1960s, students from historically Black colleges and universities exercised the highest and most intensive form of 'civic engagement' when they led the movement to engage the entire country in the pursuit of social justice, the first such student engagement in the history of the republic. This action exemplifies the dual mission of HBCUs both to produce and educated populace and to prepare the students for civic engagement. (p. 265)

The A&T Four were chronicled throughout campus and local city newspapers. The four young men: David L. Richmond, Ezell Blair, Jr. (Jibreel Khazan), Franklin E. McCain, and Joseph A. McNeil became heralded as the catalyst to what would become known as sit-ins. Unlike the agitated or demonstrative reactions to campus administration policies, student activism during the Civil Rights Movement was non-violent and methodical.

Accordingly, students attending NC A&T wrote an open letter to the Attorney General of N.C., Malcolm Seawell, accusing him of advocating a "no trespass law" to hinder students from sitting-in at the lunch counters (*A&T Students Rap Seawell in Letter: Official Accused of Advocating 'No Trespass' Law in Sitdown, para. 2, Greensboro Daily News*, 1968. NC A&T State University Archives, Greensboro, N.C.). Students also wrote a letter to the Woolworth's headquarters asking they eliminate their racial biases. In the letter, students eloquently expressed their dismay and disapproval of the company to allow racial discrimination to continue even though they had a number of Black patrons.

By using elements of their liberal arts curriculum and their critical consciousness, students responded to Woolworth's racial discrimination by stating, "How can a nation who professes to be a great bulwark of Christianity and democracy be so hypocritical on a matter of such gross discrimination as denying rights of an American citizen while giving the same rights to other Americans?" (*We Ask Your Company to Eliminate Bias, A&T College Students Request Woolworth Stores*, para. 3, *Carolina Times*, 1968. NC A&T State University Archives, Greensboro, NC)

Students' utilization of their religious ideals as well as civic understanding of government allowed them to engage in a thoughtful critique of what was occurring at the Woolworth's counter. Student use of non-violence and political tactics such as boycotts, sit-ins, and calling for government officials to remedy a social order that encouraged racism illustrates how critical consciousness ignited a sense of urgency among students to act on behalf of their race.

To this end, the liberal arts curriculum and the mission of HBCUs provided students with a toolbox to counter racism and oppression successfully through non-violent doctrine. This commitment to their race and community would persist upon graduation and entry into graduate school, or the workforce.

RETENTION AND INSTITUTIONAL EFFECTIVENESS IN NORTH CAROLINA

After the *Brown v. Topeka Board of Education* decision in (1954), desegregation of secondary schools was enacted. Once the decision was passed to desegregate elementary and secondary schools, many Black college presidents were fearful this same fate would occur for HBCUs. If the courts decided to desegregate higher education, Black colleges and universities might be targeted for elimination due to an influx of Black students racing to predominately White institutions (Avery, 2009).

While student enrollment persisted at HBCUs, Black college presidents had legitimate reasons for their concerns, as an exodus to PWIs did occur. As the federal government passed certain legislature that helped to increase the enrollment of African-Americans at PWIs, enrollments of Black students at HBCUs declined dramatically (Avery, 2009). Aside from the decline in enrollment at HBCUs, they were also faced with issues related to the types of students attending their schools.

Gasman and Drezner (2008) explore some of the issues stating, "Black colleges were faced with raising scholarship money for low income students as well as funds for remedial programs for under prepared students" (p. 84). With an influx of many affluent and academically prepared Black students deciding to attend majority schools, Black colleges faced tough decisions on how to provide financial support for their specialized student populations. To this end, the 1960s and 1970s were difficult times for HBCUs.

Despite the decline in enrollment during the 1960s and 1970s, the 1990s reveals an influx of Black students choosing to attend HBCUs (Fryer & Greenstone, 2010). Noting the increased enrollment of Black students at HBCUs, we will use data sets from 1993 to 2008 to review retention and persistence rates at public HBCUs in the state of North Carolina.

When reviewing this data, it shows persistence rates at public HBCUs were on par with PWIs within the UNC System. These public HBCUs include: Elizabeth City State University, Fayetteville State University, North Carolina A&T State University, North Carolina Central University, and Winston Salem State University.

While student retention after Year One remained consistently within the 70th percentile for all years viewed, retention after Years Two, Three, and Four declined significantly (see Table 6.1). Although retention rates decreased at HBCUs from 1996 to 1999 and 2003 to 2005, they were still on par with peer institutions that comprise the UNC System.

In response to the shift in focus for recruitment to retention within the UNC System as of 2004, HBCUs can position themselves competitively, so student outcomes around critical consciousness and civic engagement can be used as methods to retain and graduate students. The University of North Carolina Report on Retention and Graduation, June 2008 found graduation and retention rates had become an area of concern, and in 2004 a conference was held for targeted institutions. Due to the results of the conference, the chief operating officer felt the need for all UNC System institutions to actively participate in the conference that addressed graduation rates and retention.

Within this report, a focus on specific issues around retention and ways in which to counter its adverse effects were discussed. While retention and graduation has become a focal point for UNC System institutions, these issues are not only problematic within the state of North Carolina, but are also an issue for all institutions within the spectrum of American higher education.

In a study conducted by the *Journal of Blacks in Higher Education* (JBHE) during the 2007–2008 academic cycle, graduation trends of HBCUs were examined. The study revealed graduation of Black college students at all institutional types currently stand at 44% (The Journal of Blacks in Higher Education, Winter 2007/2008).

In his report, *Contemporary HBCUs: Considering Institutional Capacity and State Properties,* Minor (2008) identifies disparities in enrollment and graduation attainment for over a dozen southern states, which is where the majority of African-Americans and HBCUs reside. In developing a deeper understanding of the implications the stated data has on HBCU sustainability, it is important to note how this particular institution type can compete in the higher education market around Black student persistence and graduation outcomes.

TABLE 6.1 Retention, Graduation, and Persistence of First Time, Full-Time Freshmen at Historically Black Universities (HBCU) in the UNC System—Group: Black Students

Year of Entry	Number in Class	After Year 1	After Year 2	After Year 3	After Year 4	After Year 5	After Year 6
Retention							
2000	3,580	77.7	65.7	59.3	33.2	10.8	4.9
2001	3,942	77.7	66.8	60.7	34.5	12.5	5.0
2002	4,349	75.8	64.2	58.8	32.6	12.1	5.1
2003	4,982	76.2	63.8	56.0	33.2	12.3	5.1
2004	5,142	75.1	60.7	53.6	32.6	13.0	N/A
2005	5,409	71.6	59.3	53.3	33.6	N/A	N/A
2006	4,852	74.0	62.1	55.9	N/A	N/A	N/A
2007	4,728	74.0	60.9	N/A	N/A	N/A	N/A
2008	4,667	77.8	N/A	N/A	N/A	N/A	N/A
Graduation							
2000	3,580	0	0	0.2	20.8	38.7	43.1
2001	3,942	0	0	0.2	20.8	37.5	43.9
2002	4,349	0	0	0.3	18.5	35.4	41.2
2003	4,982	0	0	0.3	17.1	33.3	39.1
2004	5,142	0	0	0.3	15.6	31.7	N/A
2005	5,409	0	0	0.2	15.2	N/A	N/A
2006	4,852	0	0	0.2	N/A	N/A	N/A
2007	4,728	0	0	N/A	N/A	N/A	N/A
2008	4,667	0	N/A	N/A	N/A	N/A	N/A
Persistence							
2000	3,580	77.7	65.7	59.6	54.0	49.5	48.0
2001	3,942	77.7	66.8	60.9	55.3	50.0	48.9
2002	4,349	75.8	64.2	59.1	51.0	47.6	46.3
2003	4,982	76.2	63.8	56.3	50.3	45.6	44.2
2004	5,142	75.1	60.7	53.9	48.2	44.6	N/A
2005	5,409	71.6	59.3	53.4	48.8	N/A	N/A
2006	4,852	74.0	62.2	56.2	N/A	N/A	N/A
2007	4,728	74.0	60.9	N/A	N/A	N/A	N/A
2008	4,667	77.8	N/A	N/A	N/A	N/A	N/A

Note: Table 6.1 is descriptive of the grad., retention, and persistence rate of Black students at HBCUs between 2000-2008. Adapted from "Retention, Graduation, & Persistent Rates," by Institutional Research & Analysis. http://www.northcarolina.edu/ira/ir/analytics/retgrper.htm. Copyright 2011 by the University of North Carolina: A Multicampus System

Minor's (2008) study reveals that HBCUs, "...are doing proportionately better than most of their PWI counterparts at enrolling, retaining, and graduating African-American students in today's high need industries such as health professions, the sciences, technology, engineering, physics, and teacher education (p. 4). Minor not only acknowledges how HBCUs are graduating a disproportionate number of African-Americans in specific fields, but also identifies these institutions that are doing an exceptionally better job at graduating African-American males.

In her Foreword to the HBCU Project, Bakersville notes, "HBCUs are doing an especially laudable job recapturing lost and fallen youth, especially disproportionate numbers of African American males at a time when 60% of them do not graduate from high school with their cohorts" (Minor, 2008, p. 4).

HBCUs are working to increase the numbers of the Black male population through the intentionality of programs focused on the African-American male initiative. The authors realize and conclude emphasis should be placed on effective pedagogical and practitioner practices at HBCUs around the liberal arts curriculum and student retention and success. While student engagement outcomes are necessary for persistence, the inextricable role of collaborative leadership can also emerge or re-emerge as part of the institutional mission, purpose, and effectiveness of Black colleges. Specifically, HBCU leaders within the state of North Carolina can situate themselves as models for student success in retention and persistence to graduation rates.

In this way, institutional leaders must possess a clear vision and work to ensure the aims of the institution are being met for such student populations as first generation, low income, and under-represented. Historically, HBCUs have served as, and continue to remain centers of resistance and influence for mass access to Black education and the development of critically conscious, civically engaged citizens and leaders.

Aside from institutional leaders and specific colleges and universities placing a special emphasis on student engagement, organizations such as NSSE can also be a helpful instrument in dictating what effective student engagement is. While NSSE has had over 1400 universities participate in their survey since their inception (Quick Facts, 2011), few of these institutions have been HBCUs.

Ultimately, it is an institutional imperative that a focus be placed on how HBCUs and other minority-serving institutions (MSIs) foster elements of student engagement to retain and graduate students, as there is an increase in minority students attending college (Minor, 2008). Initiatives such as the now defunct Building Engagement and Attainment of Minority Students (BEAMs), was a multi-year project, which worked exclusively with minority-serving institutions.

The BEAMs project report focused on ways HBCUs and other minority-serving institutions could use this data to implement effective ways to enhance student success (Bridges, Cambridge, Kuh, & Leegwater, 2005). Though no longer in existence, projects such as BEAMs work to enhance data collection at HBCUs and MSIs on student engagement and success, and can be used as a tool to construct conversations around the necessity of HBCUs as part of the college and university continuum.

CONCLUSIONS AND IMPLICATIONS

As society becomes more global, it is increasingly important to ensure students are socially engaged and culturally competent. HBCUs have seemingly made great strides to ensure their matriculates are intentionally prepared for this charge. Sullivan (2000) maintains, "In the absence of an updated version of its founding conception of itself as a participant in the life of civil society, as a citizen of American democracy, much of higher education has come to operate on a sort of default program on instrumental individualism" (p. 21).

With institutions of higher education struggling to find innovative, yet practical ways to instill within students the necessity of social activism and civic engagement, non-HBCUs could reference historically Black colleges and universities as a model for how to create a curricular and co-curricular campus culture around this particular student outcome. The current chancellor of NCCU, Charlie Nelms, affirms, "HBCUs provide a culturally affirming, psychologically supportive environment.

Students don't have to prove they belong here. NCCU provides its students intentional, intrusive, focused academic assistance" (Goode, 2011, para. 2). It is this intentionality around the academic success and personal validation that develops efficacy for HBCU matriculates.

HBCUs continuously seek to galvanize their student populace and other campus community members around the significance of community service. To this end, many institutions have incorporated community service graduation requirements.

An example of this is the 1995 implementation at North Carolina Central University in which an Academic Community Service Learning Program requiring 124 hours of community service for graduation (Hall, 2010). Additionally, in 2006 the university established the Institute for Civic Engagement and Social Change whose mission is to, "increase the level and quality of civic engagement on the campus and in the community" (Hall, 2010, p. 44).

There is a distinctive way in which HBCUs engage their students in civic engagement in comparison to their White institutional counterparts. Ward and Wolf-Wendell (2000) recognize service learning at predominately White institutions, "emphasize service that is centered on the campus, that is, service that is focused on doing for the community" (p. 768). This is very different than the service practiced at HBCUs, which is service focused on doing *with*, rather than for, the community (Ward & Wolf-Wendell, 2000).

Variations in the way community service is executed at HBCUs versus PWIs create a very different dynamic in how these services are perceived, approached, and assessed. Ward and Wolf-Wendell (2000) further maintain, "Relying upon Morton's paradigms of service learning, service that is focused on doing *for* is more aligned with charity than social change" (2000, p. 768). Thus, PWIs create a paradigm in which the individuals of the community are not able to fully engage in their own advocacy and, thereby, limits their participation in social justice.

Specifically, because PWIs feel they know what is best for recipients of assistance within the community, social activism and civic engagement can be rendered inauthentic, generic, and purposed only to satisfy the objectives of those offering assistance rather than maintaining a focus on the objectives of community members. Conversely, service learning at HBCUs allows members of the community to organize, galvanize, and obtain goals and objectives they set for themselves. In this way, they become their own best advocates.

The authors argue that because HBCUs are marginalized institutions, they have an innate competency around the education and development of marginalized groups and individuals. In this way, Black colleges have the capacity to situate their purpose and mission so they can compete in the higher education marketplace. The authors further argue the HBCU approach to student development around liberal arts and critical consciousness cultivates identity formation and knowing of oneself as well as an understanding of positions of privilege within a complex social system.

Ultimately, intended student outcomes cannot successfully exist absent of the foundational practice of collaborative leadership, as it becomes the method through which curriculum and holistic student development intersect. To be sure, institutional leadership must envision an institutional purpose and culture that effectively enhances the stated mission.

Through the use of collaborative leadership, there can be changes made in philosophy and policy. The ability of HBCUs to develop an intrinsic sense of social activism and civic engagement has been recognized as resulting in positive student outcomes (Fryer & Greenstone, 2010). Studies show Black students who attend HBCUs are more civically engaged than their Black and White counterparts who attend predominately White institutions (PWIs).

In recognizing the ability to facilitate this set of competencies within students, institutional leaders and others within the higher education community can glean a deeper understanding of the potential effects of this particular pedagogical and professional practice on student retention and civic engagement.

REFERENCES

Agricultural and Technical College. (1933). *Bulletin of A&T College, 25*(2). North Carolina A&T State University Archives, Greensboro, NC.

Allen, W. (1992). The color of success: African American college student outcomes at predominately White and historically Black public college and universities. *Harvard Educational Review, 62*(1), 26–44.

American Council of Learned Societies. (2005). *Liberal arts Colleges in American higher education: Challenges and opportunities* (59). New York, NY: American Council of Learned Societies.

Avery, S. (2009). Taking the pulse of historically Black colleges. *Academic Questions, 22*(3), 327–339. doi:10.1007/s12129-009-9116-8

Bennett College for Women. (1927–1928). *Bulletin of Bennett College for Women, 1*(3). Bennett College Archives, Greensboro, NC.

Bennett College for Women. (1936–1937). *Bennett College for Women bulletin, 11*(2). Bennett College Archives, Greensboro, NC.

Bridges, B., Cambridge, B., Kuh, G., & Leegwater, L. (2005). Student engagement at minority serving institutions: Emerging lessons from the BEAM project. In G. H. Gaither (Ed.), *What works: Achieving success in minority retention. New Directions for Institutional Research, no. 125*. San Francisco: Jossey-Bass. Retrieved from: http://nsse.iub.edu/html/pubs.cfm

Carolina Times (1960, February 2). We ask your company to eliminate bias, A&T college students request Woolworth Store. F. D. Bluford Library Archives, North Carolina Agricultural and Technical State University.

Cohen, A. (1998). *The shaping of American higher education: Emergence and growth of the contemporary system.* San Francisco: Jossey-Bass.

Dane, F. (1990). *Research methods.* California: Brooks/Cole Publishing Company.

Freire, P. (1973). *Education for critical consciousness* (1st ed.). New York, NY: Seabury Press.

Fryer, R., & Greenstone, M. (2010). The changing consequences of attending historically Black colleges and universities. *American Economic Journal: Applied Economics, 2*(1), 116–148. Retrieved from http://dspace.mit.edu/handle/1721.1/64654

Gasman, M., & Drezner, N. (2008). White corporate philanthropy and its support of private Black colleges in the 1960s and 1970s. *International Journal of Educational Advancement, 8*(2), 79–92. Retrieved from http://www.education.umd.edu/EDHI/about/faculty_pages/ndrezner/GasmandandDrezner%202008%20White%20Corporate%20Philanthropy.pdf

Goode, R. (2011, February 15). The HBCU Debate: Are Black colleges & universities still needed? *Black Enterprise.* Retrieved from http://www.blackenterprise.com/2011/02/15/are-hbcus-still-relevant/

Hall, J. (2010). The campus, the community, and voter mobilization. *National Civic Review, 99*(2), 43–47.

Hilliard, A. (2001). "Race," identity, hegemony, and education: What do we need to know now? In W. Watkins, J. Lewis, & V. Chou (Eds.), *Race and education: The roles of history and society in educating African American students* (pp. 7–33). Needham Heights, MA: Allyn & Bacon.

JBHE Foundation. (2007/2008, Winter). Here is good news on Black student college graduation rates but a huge racial gap persists. *The Journal of Blacks in Higher Education, 58,* 46–56. Retrieved from http://www.jstor.org/stable/25073827

Jean-Marie, G. (2006). Welcoming the unwelcomed: A social justice imperative of African-American female leaders at historically Black colleges anduniversities. *Educational Foundations, 20*(1–2), 85–104. Retrieved from http://www.eric.ed.gov/PDFS/EJ751762.pdf

Jencks, C. & Riesman, D. (1967). The American Negro college. *Harvard Educational Review, 37*(1), 3–60. Retrieved from http://www.metapress.com.proxy.lib.iastate.edu/content/121179/?Copyright=1967&sortorder=asc&v=condensed&o=10

Kelderman, E. (2010, June 27). Historically Black colleges see a need to improve their image. *The Chronicle of Higher Education.* Retrieved from http://chronicle.com/article/Historically-Black-Colleges/66045/

Kelley, C. H. (1964). *Profiles of five administrators: The agricultural and technical college history digest.* Greensboro: Agricultural and Technical College of North Carolina.

Krippendorff, K. (2004).*Content analysis: An introduction to its methodology* (2nd ed.). Thousand Oaks, CA: Sage Publications.

Kuh, G. D. (2007). Built to engage: Liberal arts colleges and effective educational practice. In F. Oakley (Ed.) *Liberal arts colleges in American higher education (ACLS Occasional Paper)* (pp. 122–150). New York, NY: American Council of Learned Societies.

Kuh, G. D., Kinzie, J., Schuch, J. H., & Whitt, E. J. (2005). *Student success in college: Creating conditions that matter.* San Francisco, CA: Jossey-Bass Publishers.

Mbajekwe, C. (Ed.). (2006). *The future of historically Black colleges and universities: Ten presidents speak out.* Jefferson, NC: McFarland & Company, Inc.

Morrison, J. (1960, March 31). A&T students rap Seawell in Letter: Official accused of advocating 'no trespass' law in sitdown, *Greensboro Daily News.* F. D. Bluford Library Archives, North Carolina Agricultural Technical State University.

Minor, J. T. (2008). *Contemporary HBCUs: Considering institutional capacity and state priorities.* Michigan State University, College of Education, Department of Educational Administration, East Lansing, MI.

National Training School. (1917). *Annual catalogue of the National Training School.* North Carolina Central University Archives, Records and History Center, Durham, NC.

North Carolina College for Negroes. (1927–1928). *Annual catalogue North Carolina College for Negroes.* North Carolina Central University Archives, Records and History Center, Durham, NC.

North Carolina College for Negroes. (1929–1930). *Annual catalogue North Carolina College for Negroes.* North Carolina Central University Archives, Records and History Center, Durham, NC.

North Carolina College for Negroes. (1937). *Annual catalogue of the North Carolina College for Negroes.* North Carolina Central University Archives, Records and History Center, Durham, NC.

Price, G., Spriggs, W., & Swinton, O. (2011). The relative returns to graduating from a historically Black college/university: Propensity score matching estimates from the national survey of Black Americans. *The Review of Black Political Economy, 38,* 103–130. Retrieved from http://hbcuconnect.com/images/forums/uploads/21/206.pdf

Robinson, B. A. (2011). *Student power: A history of student unrest and protest at North Carolina Central University, 1933–1974* (Master Thesis, North Carolina Central University). James E. Shepard Memorial Library Archives, Durham, NC.

Scott, G. (2000). A historically Black college perspective. In Ehrlich, T. (Ed.), *Civic responsibility and higher education* (pp. 263–278). Westport, CT: The American Council on Education.

Seay, I. (1941). *A history of the North Carolina College for Negroes* (Master thesis, North Carolina Central University). North Carolina Central University Archives, Durham, NC.

Sherman, R. R., & Webb, R. B. (1988). *Qualitative research in education: focus and methods.* London: Falmer Press.

Singleton, R. (1988). *Approaches to social research.* New York: Oxford University Press.

Span, C. (2004). I must learn now or not at all: Social and cultural capital in the educational initiatives of formerly enslaved African Americans in Mississippi, 1862–1869. In V. Franklin & C. J. Savage (Eds.), *Cultural capital and Black education: African American communities and the funding of Black schooling, 1865 to the present* (pp. 1–14). Charlotte, NC: Information Age.

Strayhorn, T. L., & Hirt, J. B. (2008). Social justice at historically Black and Hispanic-serving institutions: Mission statements and administrative voices. In M. Gasman, B. Baez, & C. S. V. Turner (Eds.), *Understanding minority-serving institutions* (pp. 203–217). Albany: State University of New York Press.

Sullivan, W. (2000). Institutional identity and social responsibility in higher education. In T. Ehrlich (Ed.), *Civic responsibility and higher education* (pp. 19–36). Wesport, CT: The American Council on Education & The Oryx Press.

University of North Carolina. (n.d.). *University of North Carolina.* from http://www.northcarolina.edu/

The University of North Carolina General Administration. (2008). *The University of North Carolina Report on Retention and Graduation.* Retrieved from: www.northcarolina.edu/reports/index.php?page=download&id=104

Ward, K., & Wolf-Wendel, L. (2000). Community-centered service learning: Moving from doing for to doing with. *American Behavioral Scientist, 43*(5), 767–780. doi: 10.1177/00027640021955586

CONCLUSION

Vickie L. Suggs

One of the fundamental factors in the sustainability of the Black college is the idea HBCUs must be relevant within the American higher education system before we can expect them to be considered as part of the American educational imperative. It is troubling that institutions which have educated virtually all African-Americans during the 20th century and have histories dating back to the early 19th century are, in many cases, reduced to a sub-theme in the study of post-secondary education in the United States. Thus, this omission leaves Black colleges as an outside, disconnected factor in the many themes guiding higher education policy. Educating the American citizenry about this institution type and their distinct mission will give context to their founding, history, purpose, mission, and educational aims. This knowledge will provide future scholars with the inquiry tools needed to conduct a scope of research which accounts for all points of access existing within the American higher education landscape and how each access point has very specific implications on the education of this nation's citizens and the ways in which each citizen will contribute to the larger society once educated.

Social transformation leadership has persisted as a leadership competency among Black college presidents since inception. In order to operationalize this style, one must have the fortitude to commit to the values of the Seven C's (consciousness of self; congruence; commitment; collaboration;

common purpose; controversy with civility; and citizenship, HERI, 1996, p. 21). Selfless leadership for the Black race in America was a prerequisite in accomplishing even the slightest measure of success in the quest for societal change around education, economics, and politics. HBCUs not only had to define its purpose and mission, but also its spirit statement to complement the purpose and mission of the institution.

This ideal is evidenced in the motto or spirit statement of the institutions examined: Morehouse College, "*Et Facta Est Lux*" or "*Truth is Light*," Bethune Cookman University, "*Sustaining a Legacy of Faith Scholarship and Service*," North Carolina Central University, "*Truth and Service*," and Philander Smith College, "*Think Justice*." Morehouse College, for example, uses the loose translation from Latin of the spirit statement: *"Truth is Light."* More directly translated, it means, *"Light was Made."* A reference to this particular translation is captured by Robert M. Franklin, Jr. in his Inaugural Address titled, "Let Us Make Man...Morehouse Man," delivered February 15, 2008. The Morehouse alum and former president explains:

> In my opening Convocation address, I focused on our College seal and its Latin motto inspired by the creation narrative of Genesis, *et facta est lux* (and then, there was light or "light was made"). Out of the chaos and darkness of a cataclysmic Civil War, our ancestors made light by founding Morehouse in Augusta, GA. The Genesis creation narrative continues beyond the making of light to making the rest of the natural environment and then to making humans. After the Creator gives shape to creation, the Creator looks around and discerned that something was missing. God confers with the gathered hosts and declares, "Let us make man." In order to complete creation, God declares, "Let us make something new and special." (Franklin, 2008, para. 30–31)

Upon review of the spirit statements mentioned above, it is not surprising they each suggest the recognition of the HBCU as a persistent arena of activism and social transformation. Ideals linked to HBCU spirit statements serve as a point of reference from which current and future leaders might bring into focus the enduring effectiveness of social transformation leadership. In this way, Black college traditions inspire its future.

In the same spirit of maintaining traditions of Black culture, Howard University professor, Kelly Miller, argued in 1936 for "the use of 'race-specific' strategies [as] a program African Americans needed to consider in their quest for empowerment" (Mbajekwe, 2006, p. 13). Miller posits,

> This educational segregation should be recognized, not merely as a fact imposed upon the Negro by the prejudice of the White race, but should be utilized as an agency for developing the best powers and possibilities of Negro youth, partly under their own auspices. The Catholics operate catholic institutions for the development of the peculiar type of character and qualities

demanded by the Catholic Church. If Jews support and operate their own institutions to cultivate their own geniuses and perpetuate their own tradition, if Baptists, Methodists, and Presbyterians undertake the extra expense of operating purely denominational schools purely for the sake of developing peculiar tenets of these several sects, why should not the Negro even without the compulsion of segregation favor and foster institutions of higher learning that cater to the talent and genius of the race? (1936, p. 491)

Miller concludes the disenfranchisement of Blacks should serve as agency for collective advancement and racial uplift. Miller goes on to note, "The educational policy of the Negro will be constantly adjusted and readjusted to suit the mood of the Nordic mind which is the dominant factor of his educational and general life.... The education of the Negro will be adjusted as a resultant of the White man's conclusion of what he can safely accord to the Negro without jeopardizing his race arrogance and pride and in a lesser degree what the Negro thinks and feels about his own educational policies and programs. The reorganization and readjustment of the education of the Negro—primary, intermediate, and higher—will be the common product of these two racial factors operating separately and cooperating conjointly. The White race furnishes the wherewithal." (pp. 487–488). It is conceivable Miller understood the seemingly unending fight for survival HBCUs would experience beyond his own life and times. This foreshadowing of the many readjustments and challenges to the uses of the Black college becomes instructive to current and future leaders.

In American colleges and universities, changes in leadership are inevitable. In the early years of higher education, the terms and tenures of presidents often lasted decades and resulted in a more intentional, methodological upbuilding of an institution. The longevity in leadership also led to social change and now informs the Social Change Model of leadership. Though changes in executive leadership occur more frequently in today's Academy, this does not preclude proactive management of the change process. Rather, contemporary leaders may benefit from the implementation of the Seven C's as essential competencies to develop and perpetuate.

Brown and Davis (2001) describe Walter Allen's 1992 identification of "six specific goals endemic to [HBCUs]" (p. 32) in the *Harvard Educational Review*. These goals include:

1. The maintenance of the Black historical and cultural tradition (and cultural influences emanating from the Black community)
2. The provision of key leadership for the Black community given the important social role of college administrators, scholars, and students in community affairs (i.e., the HBCU functions as a paragon of social organization)

3. The provision of an economic function in the Black community (e.g., HBCUs often have the largest institutional budget within the Black community)
4. The provision of Black role models to interpret the way in which social, political, and economic dynamics impact Black people
5. The provision of college graduates with a unique competence to address the issues between the minority and majority population groups
6. The production of Black agents for specialized research, institutional training, and information dissemination in dealing with the life environment of Black and other minority communities. (p. 32)

The subjects of the research substantiate many of the stated goals and make clear the uniqueness of HBCUs and purpose they serve for underrepresented populations.

Rather than debate or defend the value of HBCUs, this book seeks to examine a specific leadership typology and how its implementation might affect Black college sustainability. Accordingly, the framework of social transformation leadership adds value to the entire spectrum of American higher education and its contemporary purpose to provide access to education for all citizens.

The ideal to (re)purpose the old university so that it more effectively meets the needs of contemporary challenges speaks to a renewed social role for the American higher education system as responsive, intentional, and solution-oriented entity. Regrettably, mainstream institutional mission and vision statements are not entirely equipped to successfully meet current and future considerations of underrepresented student populations, thus any form of oversight for the needs and abilities of all matriculates directly impacts college access, choice, financial aid, retention, and graduation rates. As previously mentioned, the mission statements of distinct mission institutions are unified; however, the vast majority of predominantly White institutions have varied mission statements that do not always live up to their stated rhetoric with regard to access, inclusion, and social justice. In this way, Enarson's (1989) call for the Academy to more deeply examine the ecology of changing and emerging student demography is connected to usable knowledge production.

As HBCU leaders look to the future and contemplate how matriculates might continue to reap the benefits of the seeds early college presidents initially sowed, the vision of current and future leaders can continue to sow seeds of regeneration by investing not only in privileged matriculates who expect to attend college, but also those for whom college attendance is not a viable option.

The author challenges HBCU leaders to revisit their institutional DNA and reconstitute past practices of social transformation leadership. The merits of this leadership model have been exampled by the subjects of and issues around student outcomes included in the text. It is the assertion of the author that if *all* of American higher education considers the implementation and continuation of social transformation leadership, the mission statement of any institution will become a living, breathing document that moves beyond mere words on paper. In this way, the mission can become instructive and inform strategies employed by chief academic officers to address complex internal and external institutional challenges. Throughout this book, the author has highlighted past, current, and contemporary leadership responses to educational, political, economic, and social conditions unfavorable to Blacks. The findings illustrate how visionary leadership and a progressive disposition of each leader enhance partnerships instrumental in building, (re)building, and sustaining HBCUs. To this end, the leaders examined personify and operationalize a social transformation and competency around difference that many PWIs are striving to adopt in an effort to better prepare for emerging student populations and, thus, changing institutional needs. Even more profound than the years leading up to now are the years to come. The encouraging news is that HBCUs have a blueprint upon which to continue the practice of social transformation, engaged participation, and shared power at individual and institutional levels.

It is the author's assertion that institutional leaders who embrace a culture of social transformation leadership will more effectively articulate the purpose and mission of the Black college by returning to its origins (i.e., charter, mission, purpose) for direction and inspiration. To this end, the research promises knowledge production for not only those who champion HBCUs, but also those who critique their institutional effectiveness and student outcomes. By examining and discussing identifiable characteristics and the practical effects of social transformation leadership and the Seven C's that have been at work at Black colleges since 1837, this institution type can situate itself at the center of a contemporary best practices intended to (re)vision, (re)define and (re)purpose tomorrow's college and university.

REFERENCES

Brown, M. C., & Davis, J. E. (2001). The historically Black college as a social contract, social capital, and social equalizer. *Peabody Journal of Education, 76,* 31–49.

Enarson, H. L. (1989, August). *Revitalizing the land-grant mission.* Paper presentation. Blacksburg, VA: Virginia Polytechnic Institute and State University.

Franklin, R. M. (2008). *Let us make man... Morehouse man.* Atlanta, Georgia. 10th Inaugural Address of Morehouse College. Retrieved at https://www.morehouse.edu/inauguration/cer_address.html

HERI. (1996). *A social change model of leadership development.* Los Angeles: Higher Education Research Institute, UCLA. Retrieved at http://www.heri.ucla.edu/PDFs/pubs/ASocialChangeModelofLeadershipDevelopment.pdf

Mbajekwe, C. (Ed.). (2006). *The future of historically Black colleges and universities: Ten presidents speak out.* Jefferson, NC: McFarland & Company, Inc.

Miller, K. (July, 1936). The reorganization of the higher education of the Negro in light of changing conditions. *Journal of Negro Education, 5,* 484–494.

APPENDIX

List of Historically Black Colleges and Universities (HBCUs)

Alabama

Four-Year Public
  Alabama A&M University
  Alabama State University

Four-Year Private
  Concordia College Selma
  Miles College
  Oakwood University
  Selma University
  Stillman College
  Talladega College
  Tuskegee University

Two-Year Public
  Bishop State Community College
  Shelton State Community College, C.A. Fredd Campus
  Gadsden State Community College, Valley Street
  J.F. Drake State Technical College
  Lawson State Community College
  Trenholm State Technical College

Arkansas

Four-Year Public
University of Arkansas at Pine Bluff

Four-Year Private
Arkansas Baptist College
Philander Smith College

Two-Year Private
Shorter College

Delaware

Four-Year Public
Delaware State University

District of Columbia

Four-Year Public
University of the District of Columbia

Four-Year Private
Howard University

Florida

Four-Year Public
Florida A&M University

Four-Year Private
Bethune-Cookman College
Edward Waters College
Florida Memorial University

Georgia

Four-Year Public
Albany State University
Fort Valley State University
Savannah State University

Four-Year Private
Clark Atlanta University
Interdenominational Theological Center

Morehouse College
Morehouse School of Medicine
Morris Brown College
Paine College
Spelman College

Kentucky

Four-Year Public
Kentucky State University

Louisiana

Four-Year Public
Grambling State University
Southern University A&M College
Southern University at New Orleans

Four-Year Private
Dillard University of Louisiana
Xavier University

Two-Year Public
Southern University at Shreveport

Maryland

Four-Year Public
Bowie State University
Coppin State College
Morgan State University
University of Maryland Eastern Shore

Michigan

Two-Year Private
Lewis College of Business

Mississippi

Four-Year Public
Alcorn State University

Jackson State University
Mississippi Valley State University

Four-Year Private
Rust College
Tougaloo College

Two-Year Public
Coahoma Community College
Hinds Community College, Utica

Missouri

Four-Year Public
Harris-Stowe State University
Lincoln University

North Carolina

Four-Year Public
Elizabeth City State University
Fayetteville State University
North Carolina A&T State University
North Carolina Central University
Winston-Salem State University

Four-Year Private
Barber-Scotia College
Bennett College
Johnson C. Smith University
Livingstone College
Shaw University
St. Augustine's College

Ohio

Four-Year Public
Central State University

Four-Year Private
Wilberforce University

Oklahoma

Four-Year Public
  Langston University

Pennsylvania

Four-Year Public
  Cheyney University of Pennsylvania
  Lincoln University

South Carolina

Four-Year Public
  South Carolina State University

Four-Year Private
  Allen University
  Benedict College
  Claflin University
  Morris College
  Voorhees College

Two-Year Public
  Denmark Technical College

Two-Year Private
  Clinton Junior College

Tennessee

Four-Year Public
  Tennessee State University

Four-Year Private
  Fisk University
  Knoxville College
  Lane College
  Lemoyne-Owen College
  Meharry Medical College

Texas

Four-Year Public
  Prairie View A&M University
  Texas Southern University

Four-Year Private
  Huston-Tillotson University
  Jarvis Christian College
  Paul Quinn College
  Southwestern Christian College
  Texas College
  Wiley College

Two-Year Public
  St. Philip's College

Virginia

Four-Year Public
  Norfolk State University
  Virginia State University

Four-Year Private
  Hampton University
  Saint Paul's College
  Virginia Union University
  Virginia University of Lynchburg

West Virginia

Four-Year Public
  Bluefield State College
  West Virginia State University

U.S. Virgin Islands

Four-Year Public
  University of the Virgin Islands

Source: U.S. Department of Education, White House Initiative on Historically Black Colleges and Universities, September 9, 2013. http://www.ed.gov/edblogs/whhbcu/one-hundred-and-five-historically-black-colleges-and-universities/

ABOUT THE CONTRIBUTORS

Vickie L. Suggs, PhD—Suggs is former Assistant Professor of Higher Education at the University of North Carolina at Greensboro. A student affairs and academic affairs administrator for over 14 years, her research agenda focuses on historically Black college leadership and examines this institution type through the lens of rhetorical action, liberal arts education, and college choice. In 2011, she co-authored, with Shayla Mitchell, "The Emergence of Women's Centers at HBCUs: Centers of Influence and the Confluence of Black Feminist Epistemology and Liberal Education," in C. R. Chambers (Ed.), *Support Systems and Services for Diverse Populations: Considering the Intersection of Race, Gender, and the Needs of Black Female Undergraduates*. In 2012, Suggs co-edited a special issue on HBCUs for *The Urban Review* with Silvia Bettez.

Shayla Mitchell, PhD—Mitchell is an Associate Professor and Field Experience Coordinator in the Department of Teacher Education at Clayton State University. A former high school social studies teacher, her research agenda includes educational policy and history of American Education. In 2010, she co-authored, with Suggs, "The Emergence of Women's Centers at HBCUs: Centers of Influence and the Confluence of Black Feminist Epistemology and Liberal Education," in C. R. Chambers (Ed.), *Support Systems and Services for Diverse Populations: Considering the Intersection of Race, Gender, and the Needs of Black Female Undergraduates*.

Jennifer Tomon Stephens, MS, LPC, NCC—Stephens is Director of the Teaching Fellows Program at the University of North Carolina at Greensboro, where she is also a doctoral candidate in the Educational Leadership and Cultural Foundations (ELC) program. A former K–12 educator and college advising counselor, she has published and presented her research and will continue to pursue research related to P–20 collaborations and cultural studies within the field of education.

Torry Reynolds, MEd—Reynolds is Lead Success Coach/Title III Activity Director at Central Carolina Community College and a doctoral candidate in the Higher Education program at the University of North Carolina at Greensboro. She holds a Masters of Education in Student Affairs from Kutztown University and a Bachelor of Arts in Afro-American Studies from the University of Pennsylvania. Her research interest includes academic support programs, developmental education, and student advocacy.

Malika Butler, MEd—Butler is a graduate of the University of North Carolina at Chapel Hill, where she majored and received her teacher's license in elementary education. Butler also received her Masters of Education in Higher Education and Student Affairs at Indiana University Bloomington where she was a Graduate Research Assistant for the Vice President for Diversity, Equity, and Multicultural Affairs. Butler is a third year doctoral student in the Higher Education program at Iowa State University with research interests in HBCU faculty issues and HBCU graduation rates of STEM students.

* * *

I would like to thank the following for their participation in, and commitment to, the successful completion of this project: contributing authors, Shayla, Jen, Torry, and Malika; Andre D. Vann, University Archives, Records and History Center, James E. Shepard Memorial Library, North Carolina Central University; Gloria Pitts, University Archives, F. D. Bluford Library, North Carolina Agricultural and Technical State University; Marcellaus A. Joiner, University Archives, Thomas F. Holgate Library, Bennett College for Women, archivists at NCCU, NC A&T, Bennett College; Marybeth Gasman; Vanessa Suggs Wallace; Mrs. Samuel Du Bois Cook; Ernie Suggs; Pia Forbes; and my invaluable support system of family and friends.

I would like to extend a very special note of gratitude to Dr. Samuel Du Bois Cook for his generosity and support of the project by agreeing to write the "Foreword." It is in the spirit of collaborative social transformation, I realize I could not have accomplished this important undertaking absent the commitment, encouragement, and contributions of all who participated.

—Vickie L. Suggs

CPSIA information can be obtained at www.ICGtesting.com
Printed in the USA
BVOW11s2118050914

365722BV00004B/24/P

9 781623 964573